THE TALKING CURE

Also by Colin MacCabe

JAMES JOYCE AND THE
REVOLUTION OF THE WORD

THE TALKING CURE

Essays in Psychoanalysis
and Language

Edited by Colin MacCabe

St. Martin's Press New York

Library of Congress Cataloging in Publication Data

Main entry under title:

The Talking cure.

Bibliography: p.
Includes index.
1. Psycholinguistics—Therapeutic aspects.
2. Psychoanalysis. 3. Lacan, Jacques, 1901–
I. MacCabe, Colin. [DNLM: 1. Language—Essays.
2. Psychoanalysis—Essays. WM460.5.L2 T146]
RC489.P73T34 1980 150.19'5 79-28551
ISBN 0-312-78474-0

Contents

References and Abbreviations

All references in the text, except for the majority of those to Freud and Lacan, refer to the consolidated bibliography. Where there is a reference to a text written in a foreign language and an English translation exists, I have given both references thus: (Laplanche and Leclaire 1961:112/1972:160). When a contributor has given a reference to an English translation I have not reconstituted the original context.

All references to Freud's *Standard Edition* are contained in the text thus (*SE* xix: 236) and similar abbreviations are used for the *Gesammelte Werke* and the *Collected Papers*. References to Lacan's *Ecrits* and the volumes of *Le Séminaire* are also contained in the text. The existing English translations of Lacan have been followed, when available, unless it was felt that they were erroneous.

Notes on the Contributors

Tony Cutler lectures in Sociology at Middlesex Polytechnic. He is the co-author with Barry Hindess, Paul Hirst and Athar Hussain of *Marx's 'Capital' and Capitalism Today*.

John Forrester is a research fellow in the history and philosophy of science at King's College, Cambridge. He is the author of *Language and the Origins of Psychoanalysis*.

Paul Henry holds a research post at the Centre National de la Recherche Scientifique in Paris. He has written a book on language entitled *Le Mauvais Outil* and is shortly to publish a study on the history of psychology.

Charles Larmore is Assistant Professor of Philosophy at Columbia University.

Colin MacCabe lectures in English language and literature at Cambridge University, where he is a Fellow of King's College, Cambridge.

Jacqueline Rose is a lecturer in English at Sussex University.

Moustapha Safouan is a psychoanalyst and a member of the Ecole Freudienne de Paris. He has written several books on psycho-analytic theory, two of which, *On Structure in Psychoanalysis* and *Pleasure and Being* are shortly to appear in English. He has translated into Arabic Freud's *Interpretation of Dreams* and Hegel's *Phenomenology of Spirit*.

Martin Thom is a writer and translator.

Preface

This collection has its origin in a seminar on psychoanalysis and language which was held in King's College, Cambridge throughout the academic year 1976–7. The papers by John Forrester, Paul Henry, Moustapha Safouan, Tony Cutler, Charles Larmore and Jacqueline Rose were all delivered in some form to that seminar or its successor in the Easter term of 1978. The opening paper by Martin Thom and the closing paper by myself formed part of the original context of the seminar but then underwent extensive revision when I edited the papers in Paris in January and February of 1979. A happy coincidence meant that Martin Thom was in Paris at that time and the extensive reworking of his first paper resulted in him finally contributing two pieces to the collection.

The purpose of the original seminar was to provide a site for discussion of psychoanalysis, a discussion which, in the universities at least, had found renewed vigour and edge since the dissemination of Lacan's texts outside the institutions of psychoanalysis—a dissemination that commenced in 1966 with the publication in France of the *Ecrits* and which was experienced in England as a series of translations and commentaries, which culminated in 1977 with the appearance of the English version of the *Ecrits* and *Le Séminaire* xi. If Lacan's texts demanded a renewed interest in the whole psychoanalytic tradition and literature, it was an interest inflected by his constant stress on the primacy of language in psychoanalytic theory and practice, and it was this inflection which was captured by organising the seminar around the theme of psychoanalysis and language. This emphasis did not mean that there was a pious intention to unveil the Lacanian truth—the papers in this collection bear witness to a variety of positions critical of Lacan—but it did mean that it was generally recognised that Lacan's work marks a crucial moment in the history of psychoanalysis, a moment which will perhaps prove as significant as Freud's original discovery of the unconscious.

Not the least significant fact of Lacan's readings and elaborations of Freud is his insistence on the major revaluation of cultural and social reality that· the discovery of the unconscious entails, a revaluation which affects the very conditions of knowledge and its divisions. It was the force of this general revaluation which drew to the seminar representatives from every arts and some science faculties. What united the participants in their interest was as much political questions of the production and transmission of knowledge as particular academic questions that Lacan raised in their 'professional' fields. The open-mindedness of King's College Council and of King's College Research Centre, who funded the seminar, offered an unusual opportunity to cut across such 'professional' divisions and to engage with a set of questions which pose the problem of the condition of knowledge and which are, for that very reason, all the more heartily detested by those who claim to speak from the place of knowledge without reckoning the imaginary investments that are necessary to assume that voice.

In its original conception the seminar purported to do no more than offer a site for discussion but in the transformation of the spoken into the written word, this collection gained a more substantial unity. This was achieved partly by the very processes of editing and rewriting and partly by the failure of some of the contributions to achieve written form.

If this collection then has a structure which is not deducible from its origins, it may be considered appropriate to indicate briefly its major divisions. It falls neatly into three sections, each comprising three papers. The first three papers deal directly with Lacan's claims about language, attempting to understand their relation to contemporary linguistic conceptions of language as well as the more traditional philological concerns that formed the theoretical context to Freud's own reflections on language. The second series of three papers, those by Safouan, Cutler and Larmore, investigate the claims made by psychoanalysis about language in relation to philosophical discourse. The final three essays all undertake the specific analyses of concepts, of a varying degree of generality; which operate within the discourse of Lacanian psychoanalysis. In each case the analysis is concerned to locate the moments at which a concept that could be considered internal to the specific discourse of psychoanalysis produces in its operations a set of problems that open out onto a wider area of cultural and political analysis.

I have already mentioned the generosity of King's College which made the seminar possible but one must also thank Yves Mabin, the cultural attaché at the French Embassy who was most helpful in facilitating the arrival of French speakers, and the British Academy whose grant allowed me, amongst other things, to complete the editing in Paris. I would also like to thank the librarian of the Ecole Freudienne, Nicole Sels, for her valuable help. Finally I would like to thank Terry Counihan for the contribution he made to this collection through his participation at the original seminars.

London
July 1979

COLIN MacCABE

1 The Unconscious Structured as a Language

MARTIN THOM

I

This paper is concerned with Jacques Lacan's statement 'the unconscious is structured like a language'. It is a reading of Freud through Lacanian spectacles, a reading that refers to those aspects of the work of de Saussure and Jakobson that informed Lacan's original concept of the unconscious chain. It is an inadequate account in so far as it reduces the complexity of Lacanian theory in favour of a clarity that can only mislead. This simplification derives in large part from this article's reliance on a paper by Jean Laplanche and Serge Leclaire, entitled 'L'Inconscient: une étude psychanalytique' (1961/1972).

At the time at which the first versions of this paper were written [1] the Laplanche/Leclaire article was considered, both by myself and by others, an accurate representation of Lacanian psychoanalysis. In Part II of the present paper I present a criticism of the misreading of Lacan that was in evidence both in the Laplanche/Leclaire paper and in my reading of it. The two parts of this paper are closely linked, in that I try, in the second part, to put right certain misconceptions that mar the first.

THE TALKING CURE

Anna O. (Bertha von Pappenheim) dubbed Freud's therapeutic method 'the talking cure', and it is there—from the mouth of one who is to be cured—that psychoanalysis founds its own discourse.

Yet, in the third and fourth decades of the century, there were all too many analysts who acquiesced in the repression of this aspect of psychoanalysis. In contrast to this, Lacan's *Discours de Rome* of 1953 is concerned above all with the patient's word: 'Whether it sees itself as an instrument of healing, of formation, or of exploration in depth, psychoanalysis has only a single medium, the patient's speech' (*E* 247/40). But the talking cure is characterised not by bringing the symptom to consciousness: it is made word. It is the insistence of the letter that causes the symptom to stand out 'in relief' against the subject's body, and it is because psychoanalysis has a structure adequate to this discourse that it succeeds in eliminating the symptom. Yet this success is not attributable to the good faith or love of the analyst. The analyst does not direct the consciousness of the patient, for the patient's ego is not synthetic or totalising. Caught up in language and in the imaginary captures that language takes for its own, the analyst directs a cure, and in the analytic situation his own being (through the transference and counter-transference) is also put into question (*E* 586–7/227–8).

This article is therefore concerned with the capture of the human animal within 'the nets of the signifier', so that it is then an animal gifted with speech, gifted even in that despotic sense that Marcel Mauss elicits. Once within the clutches of a Symbolic order whose existence precedes that subject's birth, it has no choice but to be as torn as the sign itself is. Broken in two, as the Greek etymology for Symbol (συμβολον) indicates (cf. *E* 380), the subject is condemned to search for a totality whose essence (since it inheres only in relations) can only elude it. But where in Freud is there a discussion of signifier and signified, of the linguistic aspects of the unconscious? This question is uneasily answered, for one can either answer everywhere or nowhere. It is everywhere, in that there is hardly a page of Freud's writing that does not make reference to language and to symbol. It is nowhere, in the sense that the structural linguistics that Lacan refers to is not yet born when Freud produces his major texts on the unconscious formations (on the dream, the lapsus, the joke). There is instead a reference to nineteenth century philology and to linguistic science that fits hardly at all with structural linguistics. Yet, reference to language and to its operations there is in plenty, and if Freud used linguistic concepts that are now of no use to us, his actual practice as analyst of unconscious formations was modern. Thus, even as early as *Studies on Hysteria*, the clinical study that Freud wrote with Breuer, there are definite linguistic insights as regards the working of the psychic apparatus.

However, it is in *The Interpretation of Dreams* that we find a way forward to a linguistic formulation of the nature of the unconscious. Freud there makes a clear division between the manifest dream-text and the latent dream-thoughts. The manifest dream-text is the text of the dream that the subject assembles on waking, whereas the latent dream-thoughts comprise the more complete dream underlying the former: 'The dream-thoughts and the dream-content are presented to us like two versions of the same subject matter in two different languages' (*SE* IV:277). The unconscious is presented here as a different language underlying the manifest language. The dream-content is described as a 'transcript' of the dream-thoughts 'into another mode of expression' and we are asked to 'compare the original and the translation'.

CONDENSATION AND DISPLACEMENT

To make Freud's thought clear, we should concentrate, as he does, on the operations that link the manifest content of the dream to the latent dream-thoughts. The two key operations are those of condensation and displacement.

I will consider condensation first. If we compare the manifest content of the dream as we assemble it upon waking, or again as it is told to the analyst, with the latent dream-thoughts that are teased out of the words and silences in the analysis itself, we find that the latent dream-thoughts are far more extensive than the manifest content. To put it simply, the manifest dream is laconic. It has been condensed, and radically so. Many of the examples given in *The Interpretation of Dreams* are approximately four or five lines long, whereas the dream-thought that Freud draws out of them, like the endless stream of silk scarves tied to each other that a magician draws from his hat, are often four or five pages long. Condensation is immense, in fact so immense that interpretation is never final. If we take any one element in the manifest dream we find that it is condensed, it is 'over-determined'. When we say that it is over-determined we mean that it has multiple connections with other elements in the latent dream-thoughts. Freud notes in his analysis of the dream of the 'botanical monograph' (*SE* IV: 169–76), that the word 'botanical' led 'by numerous connecting paths, deeper and deeper into the tangle of dream-thoughts'. Because the word is so heavily over-determined, it is described as 'a regular nodal point in the dream'. Elsewhere Freud uses the term 'switchword' to describe the same idea, and in this metaphor the idea of a 'points' system is evoked, where the word is seen as a kind of switch located at the intersection of several different tracks or pathways.

Displacement, the second key operation in the formation of dreams, refers to the fact that 'the dream is, as it were, differently centred from the dream-thoughts' (*SE* IV: 305). Elements which are central to the manifest content may be peripheral to the latent dream-thoughts. In the same way, elements which are crucial to the latent dream-thoughts may be completely absent from the manifest text. It is the work done by the patient in his free association that allows us to retrace the connections between the two systems. Displacement is therefore a form of 'distortion', a distortion made necessary by the existence of 'censorship' between the different systems of the psyche.

METAPHOR AND METONYMY

According to de Saussure (1972/1974), any linguistic sign involved two modes of arrangement, combination and selection. Combination refers to the fact that each sign is made up of constituent parts and can only occur with other signs. De Saussure stressed the linear nature of the signifying chain (1972: 102; 1974: 70)[2]—in fact it is the second property he singles out for emphasis after the arbitrariness of the linguistic sign. It is combination that unites the links of the signifying chain, one to each other, and once they have been combined they are in a relation of contiguity to each other.

The axis of combination is concerned with the message. It is diachronic and can best be represented horizontally. It represents in Saussurean terms, speech rather than language, event rather than structure.

The other mode of arrangement of a linguistic sign is known as selection and it refers to the selection of signs from a set. Any selection from a set implies the possibility that another sign might be substituted in its place. It is naturally assumed that selection and substitution are both aspects of the same operation.

The axis of substitution is concerned with the code, and can best be represented as vertical. It represents language (*langue*) rather than speech (*parole*), structure rather than event. It is essential to note that, in normal speech, the two axes operate in conjunction. It is only in language disorders that we can clearly perceive the separate nature of the two modes of arrangement. Thus, it was through his study of the different kinds of aphasia that Jakobson was able to distinguish one from the other (Jakobson 1971).

From his study Jakobson concluded that there are basically two poles of language, the metaphoric and the metonymic, and that these two poles are linked to the two modes of arrangement of the linguistic sign. Depending on the type of aphasia (contiguity disorder; aphasia disorder) the sufferer would tend to produce a kind of language centred either on the metaphoric or the metonymic poles.[3]

The concepts of metaphor and metonymy developed by Jakobson are used in a slightly altered form by Lacan to account for the mechanisms by which the unconscious is ordered. It is therefore asserted that the Freudian concepts of condensation and displacement are directly homologous with the Jakobsonian definitions of metaphor and metonymy (*E* 495/148). To explain how this homology works I want now to consider the dream that is analysed by Laplanche and Leclaire in their 1961 paper.

Philippe's Dream
The dream given in this article (it is in fact one of two) is taken from a session that an obsessional patient spent with Serge Leclaire. The text is as follows:

> La place déserte d'une petite ville; c'est insolite, je cherche quelque chose. Apparaît, pieds nus, Liliane—que je ne connais pas—qui me dit: il y a longtemps que j'ai vu un sable aussi fin. Nous sommes en forêt et les arbres paraissent curieusement colorés, de teintes vives et simples. Je pense qu'il y a beaucoup d'animaux dans cette forêt, et comme je m'apprête à le dire, une licorne croise notre chemin; nous marchons tous les trois vers une clairière que l'on devine en contrebas.

The English translation (an English translation) is as follows:

> The deserted square of a small town; it is unfamiliar, I am looking for something. Liliane appears, barefoot—I don't know her—she says to me: it's been a long time since I've seen such fine sand. We are in a forest and the trees seem curiously coloured with bright

and simple colours. I think to myself that there must be plenty of animals in this forest and just as I am about to say it, a unicorn crosses our path; all three of us walk towards a clearing that one can just make out down below. (1972: 136)

This dream-text on its own tells us almost nothing. Without the free association of the dreamer it is worthless. It has its fragile beauty and nothing more. This fact cannot be stressed too much. In the text, the significance of the words present in it is not given to us, but is discovered in the process of analysis. The precise formation of the dream derives from several sources: (1) events of the previous day, which, in the context of the dream are described by Freud as 'daytime residues'; (2) stimuli originating from within the body, in this case the need to drink (the subject having eaten salted herrings the previous evening); and (3) events from the past, and, in particular, memories stretching far back into childhood. Freud describes dreams as 'hypermnemic', and insists on the permanence of the memory-trace within the psychic apparatus. As early as 1895, in *The Project for a Scientific Psychology*, he had stressed that no psychology worthy of the name would lack a theory of memory, that such a theory would in fact be the very foundation of an adequate psychology. This assertion is fully borne out by the subsequent development of Freud's theory of the psychic apparatus, and by the accounts of the mechanisms of repression that he gives. These problems are discussed in greater depth in my second paper. Here I proceed with the analysis of Philippe's dream.

Events of the Previous Day

These were present in the dream in two forms: (1) daytime residues; and (2) internal somatic excitations.

There were various daytime residues, in the form of memory traces of what Philippe had done the previous day, that contributed to the formation of the dream. Philippe had in fact taken a walk the previous day in the forest with his niece Anne. They had noticed, at the bottom of the valley where the stream ran, traces of deer and roe-deer where they came to drink. On this walk, Philippe remarked that it was a long time since he had seen (*il y a longtemps que j'ai vu*) heather of such a rich flaming colour. These daytime residues play a significant part in the dream, as can be ascertained by glancing back at the original text.

As far as somatic excitations are concerned, we notice that

Philippe had eaten some herrings that evening and therefore had a *need* to drink. Dreams, it will be remembered, are described by Freud as the guardians of sleep. In this case, the dream guards Philippe's sleep against the organic fact of his thirst, against his physiological need to drink. The dream guards his sleep by fulfilling a (repressed) wish. It cannot fulfil his need to drink: only liquid can do that. The dream fulfils a (repressed) wish or desire to drink (a desire that is inscribed on one of the subject's memory systems) and subsumes the (temporary) organic need of the subject's body within its own (timeless) trajectory.

Childhood Memories

The first memory was of a summer holiday when he was three years old. He tried to drink the water which was flowing in a fountain. He cupped his hands together and drank out of the hollow that his cupped hands formed. The fountain was in the square (*place*) of a small town and had a unicorn (*licorne*) engraved in the stone.

The second memory was of a walk in the mountains when he was three years old. The walk was tied to the memory of imitating an older child cupping his hands and blowing through them, imitating the sound of a siren. This memory was also associated with the phrase *il y a longtemps que j'ai vu.*

The third childhood memory was of an Atlantic beach (*plage*) and again the phrase *il y a longtemps que j'ai vu un sable aussi fin*. This was associated with Liliane—a barefoot woman in the dream who said precisely that.

In the course of the analysis Philippe took apart the name Liliane and separated it into the two components, Lili and Anne. Anne, as we already know, was his niece, and Lili, his mother's cousin. Lili had actually been with him on that Atlantic beach when he was three years old, at the beginning of those same summer holidays when he had been taken to the town with the fountain and the unicorn engraved on it. It is important to bear the French not the English words in mind, and to note the various 'homophones' (between *Lili* and *licorne*, *place* and *plage*, etc.). These linguistic connections will be shown to be more and more significant as the work of interpretation advances.

We have already seen that, if, as Freud has said, all dreams are the fulfilment of a repressed wish, then this dream, from all angles, finds its centre, its unity, in the need or desire to drink. On that hot July day, when he was three, Philippe had said again and again, and with great insistence, '*J'ai soif*' or '*choif*', Lili, his mother's cousin, used to tease him, and say '*Alors, Philippe, j'ai soif?*', and it became a kind of formula, and the sign of a joking relationship between them: '*Philippe–j'ai–soif*'.

At this point, this nodal point, we remark that Philippe's thirst is (at the least) doubly determined. It derives organically from his *need* to drink that night when he dreamt the dream, but it also derives psychically from the *desire* to drink which the *demand* emanating from the Symbolic has caused to be inscribed in him, in the waxen surface of his memory. Since dreams are 'hypermnemic' (Freud), since they permit a privileged regression to that point at which childhood memory appears to constitute its unthinkable origins, we are concerned with the 'primal' (and therefore mythically constituted) formation of *desire*. We are concerned with the point of entrance of the drive into psychical life. Dreams, and indeed lapses, are a privileged path, a royal road back to that mythical moment at which 'difference' is established and the global calibration of signifier to signified almost obscures the continuing effect of the death drive, of 'affect', as it operates with redoubled fury in the very heart of representations.

As I have said, need has no place in psychical life. Only the 'representatives' or 'delegates' of need may enter the agencies of the mind. If we consider Philippe's dream, we can identify the ideational representative of the oral drive, which is 'the first to be distinguished in post-natal development' (Laplanche and Leclaire 1961: 104; 1972: 140). At the level of need, Philippe was easy to feed and easily satisfied, but we are not concerned with need but with the fixation of drives to their ideational representatives. We are concerned with both death and sexuality, although the representative of the death drive is most clearly discernible in the dream left unanalysed here. We find two representatives of the oral drive in the dream. One is a gesture, the other a formula. They are not present in the manifest content of the dream but can only be identified after free association.

The gesture 'registered' or 'inscribed' as an image is that of cupping the hands together in a conch shape to produce a siren call. We learn from the analysand that this gesture is tied to the cupping together of the hands at the fountain of the unicorn and thus signifies 'quenched thirst'. The second representative of the oral drive is the formula *J'ai soif*. It is a kind of representative in this boiling hot summer of Philippe's ego. The formula is also associated with Lili, as we saw in the narration of the third childhood memory (of the Atlantic beach), elicited in the course of the analystic session. Since we are concerned with the oral drive, we are by definition concerned with the problem of thirst, and in this context it is important to note that the acoustic chain 'Li' is common to both *Licorne* and Lili, the woman who listens to his cry of thirst and is in a position, it seems, to receive his word. It seemed like that to Philippe because Lili was seen by him to have an 'ideal' marriage, and she thus represented the idea of a harmony and satisfaction not present in Philippe's mother's marriage. A harmony and satisfaction doubly associated with the acoustic chain 'Li' in French: for 'Li' can be metonymically connected with *lit* (bed), and Lili with *lolo*, which signifies 'milk' or 'breast' in French baby talk.

THE UNCONSCIOUS STRUCTURED LIKE A LANGUAGE

When Lacan claimed that the unconscious was structured like a language, he seems to have meant exactly what he said:

> The analysable symptom, whether it be normal or pathological, is distinguished not only from the diagnostic index but also from any imaginable form of pure expressivity in that it is supported by a structure which is identical to the structure of language. And by that I do not mean a structure to be situated in some sort of so-called generalised semiology drawn from the limbo of its periphery, but the structure of language as it manifests itself in the languages which I might call positive, those which are actually spoken by the mass of human beings. (*E* 444)

When Lacan asserts that the symptom is upheld by a structure that is identical to the structure of language, one has to try to measure the weight of the term 'identical'. There are certain objections to this term implicit in Freud's writings and I want to consider these objections before continuing the argument.

Freud wrote of language as operant in the preconscious, and in the secondary process (which is at work in the preconscious), but the processes he considered to be operant in the unconscious were of a very different sort. The fact of there being no negation, no logic, no syntax, and no time in the unconscious makes it hard for us to accord any process there the status of a language as spoken by 'the mass of human beings'.

There was a language in the primary process, Freud stressed, but it was the language of psychosis, and of dreams in their regression to the form of images:

> in schizophrenia *words* are subjected to the same process as that which makes the dream-images out of latent dream-thoughts—to what we have called the primary psychical process. They undergo condensation, and by means of displacement transfer their cathexes to one another in their entirety. The process may go so far that a single word, if it is specially suitable on account of its numerous connections, takes over the representation of a whole train of thought. (*SE* xiv: 199)

Here, in the 1915 paper on 'The Unconscious' we clearly have some kind of conception of an unconscious structured like a language. As Ricœur points out (1970: 400), 'the problem is to assign an appropriate meaning to the word "like" '. Is language a privileged model that we compare with the structure of the unconscious? Or does the term 'a language' merely mean that the unconscious is structured with reference to language as it is in operation in the preconscious and conscious?

THING-PRESENTATIONS AND WORD-PRESENTATIONS

In his analysis of the relations between the different agencies of the psychic apparatus Freud introduced a new terminology in 1914/15 (in the Papers on Metapsychology). He distinguished sharply between what he called 'thing-presentation' (*Sachvorstellung*) and 'word-presentation' (*Wortvorstellung*). It is significant that the nuances of these terms were often lost in early translations, which would render *Vorstellung* as 'idea' and not as 'presentation'.[4]

Thing-presentations are essentially visual, they are perceptual entities, images or memory-traces. Freud's account of them in *The Ego and the Id* as 'optical memory residues' shows in fact how little conflict there is between this new terminology and the terminology of inscription that runs constantly through Freud's writing from 1895 onwards, whereas in 1915 he had been quite adamant that the new terminology rendered the old one redundant. Word-presentations are essentially 'auditory'—'In essence a word is after all the mnemic residue of a word that has been heard' (*SE* xix:

21)—and in this sense may be aligned with the acoustic chain as analysed by de Saussure.

Freud expressed the relation between the thing-presentation and the word-presentation, and their participation in the different agencies in this way: 'The conscious presentation comprises the presentation of the thing plus the presentation of the word belonging to it, while the unconscious presentation is the presentation of the thing alone' (*SE* XIV: 201). The unconscious presentation is stated here to be 'the presentation of the thing alone'. In what sense can this kind of presentation be said to be linguistic? The linguistic sign has two basic components, the concept and the acoustic image.[5] How may the thing-presentation be aligned with this conception? It should be clear by now that Freud, working with another linguistics altogether, was uncertain, and that not all of his statements are consistent with each other. He was at least clear in his own mind that the thing-presentation could not attain consciousness without being 'bound' to a word-presentation and the thing-presentation would seem to be simply the Saussurean concept, as in the formula:

$$\frac{\text{concept}}{\text{acoustic image}} \qquad \frac{\text{signified}}{\text{signifier}}$$

initially set out by de Saussure in his *Cours* (1972). However, it is clear from Freud's own writing that he would not have been happy with a two-tiered formula and would have wished to suggest that there is some sort of signifying chain in action in the unconscious too. This paper is largely concerned with the different attempts that have been made to formulate clearly Freud's often fleeting perceptions as to the relation between the unconscious and language.

The original formula of de Saussure places the signified above the signifier, thus:

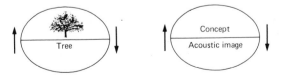

Lacan, for reasons related to the nature of repression and the unconscious, reverses this formula:

Tree

Acoustic image
————————
Concept

Using the symbols 'S' and 's' to represent signifier and signified, Lacan then writes the formula in this way:

$$\frac{\text{S (signifier)}}{\text{s (signified)}}$$

The formula is inverted because Lacan holds that the signifier has priority over the signified, and that sense is therefore constituted through the relation between signifiers (*E* 498/150). Like Lévi-Strauss (1950), Lacan would argue that meaning is created by a chain of signifiers that, in its globality, created meaning *d'un seul coup* (in one go). When the two global registers (S/s) were created in that cruci-formation to which myths and dreams bear witness, Lévi-Strauss argues that a 'supplementary ration' was necessary to support symbolic thought in its operations (1950: xlix). For, given that the two registers are created simultaneously 'as two comp-lementary blocks',[6] human thought could only appropriate other-ness through 'a surplus of signification'. This excess represents the margin beyond language that makes of language something more than 'a name-giving system or a list of words, each corresponding to the thing it names' (de Saussure 1972: 97/1974: 65). For, such a theory of 'labelling' would imply that the signified was a thing in itself rather than a concept, and that implication would be anathema to Lacan as to de Saussure.

Lacan is, however, actually concerned to modify the de Saussure of the *Cours*. He rejects the Saussurean illustration of the relation existing between signifier and signified because it suggests to us that 'the signifier answers to the function of representing the signified'. Lacan would hold, rather, that meaning springs from (metonymic and metaphoric) relations between signifiers. Rather than being a 'representation', meaning in Lacanian psychoanalysis is a question of production. Lacan justified his emphasis on the Saussurean conception of the signifier by referring to de Saussure's stress on 'the incessant sliding of the signified under the signifier' (*E* 502/154). For Lacan, the signified becomes less and less important simply because it eludes us, it slips away from us. The intrusion of the signifier into the domain considered to be that of the subject thinking itself is a necessary effect of the subversion of the subject that Lacanian theory demands. Just as it is impossible to admit that the subject bathes in the radiance of its own thought, so also is it mistaken to construct the two distinct entities 'language' and 'thought' in order to fuse them later as if they were in the service of some perfectly calibrated celestial machine. For Lacan is concerned with the prior existence of the signifying order and with the effects of that priority on consciousness. He is concerned with the (metonymic) movements of language and the progressive–regressive movement of desire that insists there, with the (metaphorical) blossoming as the chain is momentarily suspended and that which is suspended from it intrudes.

In the section of the *Cours* that treats the mutability of the linguistic sign (1972: 104–13/1974: 71–8), de Saussure writes of a loosening of the bond between the acoustic image and the concept, of a shift in the relation between the two. His examples are of changes in Old German and Modern German, or between classical Latin and French (viz. the Latin *necare* (to kill), becomes the French *noyer* (to drown)). These are clearly changes that take place over long periods of time, indeed whole centuries. The inference, however as far as Lacan is concerned, is quite clear: 'Language is radically powerless to defend itself against the forces which *from one moment to the next* are shifting the relationship between the signified and the signifier' (italics added) (de Saussure 1972: 110/1974: 75). It is the change 'from one moment to the next' in the relation between signifier and signified that allows Lacan to superimpose Saussurean linguistics on to the Freudian dream-text. The dream-text is a finely spun web of linguistic interconnections, yet analysis cannot exhaust it. Analysis of a dream is indeed interminable. Yet, at certain points, the work is halted. It runs up against 'nodal points' which are, in Freud's words, 'unplumbable'. For Lacan, these nodal points are points at which the two registers (S/s) are anchored to each other: he describes them as *points de capiton* (as raised buttons on a mattress or an armchair). These *points de capiton* are the points at which need is represented in psychical life, and in anchoring the two 'chains' to each other 'they bring to a halt the otherwise indefinite sliding of meaning' (*E* 805/303). Lacan compares the analyst to a fisherman who 'is fishing in the flow of the pre-text', but who cannot hope to catch the actual movement of the fish. The signified is here marked with a bar ($\math{s}$) because it is always receding, disappearing.

As I have said, the bar in Lacan's formulae represents the repression of the signified, and therefore the maintenance of the signifier and the signified as two radically separate orders. In de Saussure's *Cours* the bar does not have a value of this sort but is simply the line that separates the two chains. For Freud, the preconscious and the unconscious are both separated and linked; there is a 'censorship' separating them and yet derivatives of a repressed element do cross the bar. Indeed, if we are to avoid the 'psycho-physical parallelism' against which Freud warned, this crossing has to occur. If certain passages (following the image of the Russian censorship) are blacked out, there are aspects (derivatives) of the original text that can still be deciphered in spite of the obliterations on either side. Thus, the pure linearity of the signifying chain, as de Saussure described it in the *Cours*, has to be modified so as to include the intrusions of another chain that lies beneath it and insists that it be read: 'There is in effect no signifying chain which does not have, as if attached to the punctuation of each of its units, a whole articulation of relevant contexts suspended vertically, as it were, from the point' (*E* 503/154). This 'other' chain that lies beneath, and is suspended vertically from particular points, is composed of signifiers that have fallen to the rank of signifieds. To understand what is meant by this it is necessary to consider the connection between metaphor and repression.

METAPHOR AND REPRESSION

In metaphor, as Lacan sees it, a new signifier replaces the original one. The original signifier then falls to the rank of the signified (*E* 708). If we represent the new signifier as S', we can illustrate the process diagrammatically:

STAGE I: STAGE II:
$\underline{S}$ (original signifier) $\underline{S}'$ (new signifier)
s (original signified)   S (original signifier fallen to the rank of the signified)

To understand these diagrammatic representations, it is vital to remember that we are here concerned not just with the structure of language, as it is analysed by linguists, but with repression. In a language without repression, things would be just as the linguist describes them, but since Freud we have learnt that intrusions (of slips, jokes, etc.) into the text of daily life make stage 1 S/s a purely hypothetical case: 'In a language without metaphors, there would indeed be relations of signifier to signified which may be symbolised by S/s; but there would be no equivocation, nor any unconscious to decipher' (Ricœur 1970: 401). Lacan describes repression as a snag or rip or rent in the tissue of speech and such snags make it difficult to sustain a structural linguistics as pertinent to psychoanalysis if such a linguistics is constructed solely on the basis of a bar separating an acoustic chain from a conceptual one. The general Freudian category of 'distortion' demands some recognition, for it was Freud's achievement in the monographs on dreams, jokes and parapraxes to show that there was a locus of language to which the conscious subject was, in Lacan's word, 'excentric'.

Repression, for Lacan, 'is' metaphor. The snag in the tissue marks the place where the original signifier is, as it were, vertically suspended. It has been 'displaced' and has fallen to the rank of the signified. Once it has fallen (and the topographic idiom is, I think, faithful to this process) it persists as a repressed signifier itself. This persistence and insistence of a repressed chain is precisely what gives poetry the quality of saying what it says as much by what is not there as by what is. Thus, in 'The Agency of the Letter in the Unconscious', Lacan asserts de Saussure's interest in poetry some years before his writing on the uses of the anagram in Greek or Latin poetry was first published: 'But one has only to listen to poetry, which Saussure was no doubt in the habit of doing, for a polyphony to be heard, for it to become clear that all discourse is aligned along the several staves of a score' (*E* 503/154). There is, however, a slight problem involved in equating metaphor and repression. It is this: if metaphor is seen as corresponding to repression, the existence of a repressed chain suggests that, from the paradigmatic axis, only two elements are involved (the new signifier, S', and the original signifier fallen to the rank of the signified, S). Thus, whereas the paradigmatic axis is defined by the possible substitution of all its elements, one from another, the concept of repression would seem to endow certain signifiers with a more privileged position than that of others along the paradigmatic axis. But just as there is no language without metaphor so also—if one excludes the form of aphasia that Jakobson terms contiguity disorder—there is no language without metonymy. Since metonymy affects both the message and the code, it is the metonymic movement of language that connects the repressed chain of signification with the rest of the elements in the code. In Lacanian terms, this movement is the movement of desire, and it is the restlessness of this desire that psychoanalysis sees as intruding on language. Lacan's position therefore represents a subversion of the science of language and those linguists who criticise his work from the point of 'normal' language are really missing the point (*E* 467).

Another approach to the problem of the fixity that the metaphor/repression equation seems to ascribe to the workings of language is that developed by Laplanche and Leclaire in their analysis of Philippe's dream. They argue that the persistence and insistence of a repressed chain demands representation in terms of four levels instead of the two that are shown to us by de Saussure.

These four levels divide up into what Laplanche and Leclaire call the Preconscious and the Unconscious Chains:

$$\frac{S'}{s} \quad \text{The Preconscious Chain}$$

$$\frac{S}{S} \quad \text{The Unconscious Chain}$$

This formula represents the relation between the preconscious and the unconscious in a way that allows one to make a close correlation between metaphor and repression. Yet this diagram's meaning cannot be grasped without reference to Freud's own writings on the nature of repression. I will also have to consider the problem of the origins of the unconscious and the relation of this origin to language. Until these problems are tackled the meaning of the lower half of the diagram, where there is a signified that is apparently its own signifier, can only elude us.

REPRESSION

If the formulation of the concept of the unconscious was the crucial event in the history of Freudian psychoanalysis, repression too was a concept indispensable to its development. It is worth noting that Stekel abandoned the concept of the unconscious and repression too—'the cornerstone on which the whole structure of psychoanalysis rests' (*SE* xiv: 16). In discussing this cornerstone my key points of reference are to the two papers of 1915, on the unconscious and on repression, respectively.

In considering repression one is necessarily led to consider the relations between the systems of the psyche as Freud defined them, the relations between the unconscious and the preconscious, and between the preconscious and the conscious. I have already looked at these relations in terms of presentations, in terms of 'word-presentations' and 'thing-presentations', and have shown how persuasively the terminology of structural linguistics has been used to describe these concepts.

The fact is that repression, although described by Freud at one point as 'a failure in translation', demands some kind of use of energetic terms. The initial definition in the 1915 paper—that *'the essence of repression lies simply in turning something away, and keeping it at a distance from the conscious'* (*SE* xiv: 147)—is quite a mild expression of the force with which a censorship must be invested.

Freud divides repression into two phases, primal repression, and after-repression or repression proper.

Repression Proper

In repression proper, the presentation which is repressed is affected by two different 'forces'. It is, first of all, repulsed by the preconscious system, and cathexis is withdrawn. Secondly it is attracted by a chain already existing in the unconscious (the repressed chain of signification, i.e. S/S in the diagram above), a repressed chain to which it is attracted. Some explanation then has to be made for primal repression. To understand the relation between repression proper and primal repression it has to be accepted that our reconstruction of it is necessarily a fictional one.

Primal Repression

Freud was intensely preoccupied with the problem of origins, a preoccupation that on occasion overrides his more Saussurean concerns. In the case of primal repression, since it is so closely concerned with the entrance of the drive into psychical life, it is of especial interest to Freud. If this primal repression happens—at least as a mythical event—then we have to postulate a kind of mythical state apprehended not through experimental psychology, nor through psycholinguistics, but through the archaeology of the subject that psychoanalysis represents.

Briefly, what happens in the primal repression is this. The ideational element is refused entrance to consciousness but is (as representative of the drive) inscribed in the unconscious. A *fixation* is then established —'the representative in question persists unaltered from then onwards, and the instinct (drive) remains attached to it' (*SE* xiv: 148). With this fixation, the instinct (drive) accedes to the order of the signifier. The idea of fixation expressed here, since it so explicitly suggests an immutability, can be compared to Freud's model of the psyche as a 'writing-machine' on to whose mnemic systems traces are inscribed. It is the ideational representatives of death and sexuality that are fixed in primal repression and Ernest Jones's claim that there is a limited range of symbolic reference in the unconscious (life, death, one's kinsfolk, one's body) can only be understood in terms of this meeting between the body and the signifier.[7]

In the case of Philippe, whose dream we have been considering, the formula (*J'ai*) *soif* becomes the representative of his need—it represents the oral drive, such that his need to drink is from then on inextricably entangled with his desire. With the primal repression, the unconscious is mythically constituted. It is the unconscious chain created at this point that underlies and supports language. The psychoanalytic evidence suggests that this unconscious chain is constituted through the agency of certain 'key-signifiers'. These key-signifiers, operating as hinges between the universe of rules and that of blind need structure human language. Here is how Laplanche and Leclaire conceive of key-signifiers:

> In the formula for metaphor, it is necessary here to concede of the existence of certain '*key-signifiers*' placed in a metaphorizing position, and to which is assigned, because of their special weight, the property of ordering the whole system of human language. (1961: 116/1972: 160)

The key-signifier here, (*J'ai*) *soif* (*choif*) is then the one that because of its 'particular weight' organises Philippe's insertion into the symbolic order, the order of language. The myth can be reconstructed.

Prior to his entrance into the symbolic order—and we can note in passing the presence of the *je* in the formula, which, in grammatical terms, is a shifter, and through its duplex structure, its duplicity, organises the relations between message and code in human language—(Jakobson 1963: 176–97) we can imagine Philippe as a child who simply existed within the non-signifying world of his own need. In this (mythical) time, to have thirst is simply to be engulfed in a blind need which is then satisfied by taking in the wanted thing. Suddenly, with Lili's joking remark, *Philippe–j'ai–soif*, the world is rendered significant, and what had been a blind instinctual impulse is caught 'in the nets of the signifier'. This is illustrated diagrammatically as follows:

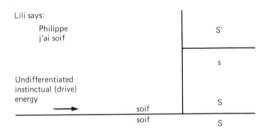

Thus (*J'ai*) *soif* is one of the kernels of Philippe's unconscious. The work of analysis, in its untiring elimination of the outer husk, will always come up against this 'knot of signification'. It is a 'point of umbilication' (Lacan) because it is so radically over-determined. Thus, it should be noted that Philippe's memory is of Lili saying '*J'ai soif*'. His insertion into the symbolic order occurs then, through the mediation of another whose name (Lili/*lolo*: 'breast', 'milk' in French baby talk) invokes his dual relation with his mother. However, it is also significant that the name 'Lili' was not Philippe's aunt's name at all, but merely the affectionate nickname by which she was known by her husband, and by her husband alone. Thus, the desire to drink, around which Philippe's dream is organised, is multiply over-determined. Besides the desire to drink, there is in play Philippe's desire for Lili, Lili's own desire to drink and Lili's desire for her own husband. Since Philippe was one of those children who said *moi-je* (i.e., he had not mastered the use of 'shifters') the formula *J'ai soif* signified the dizzy moment in which he was to move from a narcissism, where Lili/*lolo* was merely an extension of his being, to a symbolic order that placed the other under the hegemony of the Other. If it was Lili who had been the mediating element in this transformation that would have been because the spell of the dual relation with the mother would have to give before an order organised in terms of an Oedipal structure of three separate persons. In such a structure, being is not narcissistic closure (i.e. *moi-je*), but a locus of subjectivity in language that cannot be appropriated. However, regression from the symbolic to the imaginary is always possible. For, as need is transformed into desire through demand, the radical lack of being of the child whose organism has been altered (from a calyx of bright, only partially centralised slivers of light, into the fused silver of a total mirror-recognition) is re-inscribed at the level of the signifier, whose movement itself invokes the flaw it labours to conceal.

Indeed, if the formula (*J'ai*) *soif* is able to act as the kernel of the dream, if it is so heavily over-determined, it is because the derivatives of the repressed representative of the drive do still find their way into language. If there is sufficient 'distortion' of the derivatives to overcome the censorship then they have free access to the preconscious and conscious, and in the process of free association Freud notes that the analysand goes on spinning associative threads 'till he is brought up against some thought, the relation of which to what is repressed becomes so obvious that he is compelled to repeat his attempt at repression' (*SE* XVI: 149–50).

In Philippe's dream it is possible to identify some of the derivatives of the instinctual representative (*J'ai*) *soif*. In the manifest text of Philippe's dream the word *place* appears. Here is how this particular signifier can be related diagrammatically to what is suspended vertically from it:

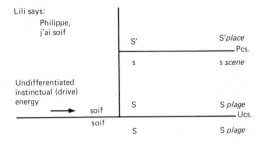

This diagram again gives the four-tiered formula and represents metaphor (repression) as the superimposition of signifiers. The new signifier (*place*) is superimposed on to the original signifier *plage*, which has fallen to the rank of signified. The signified is the scene (*scène*) where the action takes place and here it is of course confused with the original signifier *plage*. Our problem is one of conceptualising a four-tiered system in terms of a two-tiered signifier/signified system. As I have already noted, since all language involves metaphor (repression), there will be no language that is not underpinned by a repressed chain of signification. The radical condensation of the dream-work is in fact the result of the crossing of the Saussurean bar between the language of conscious and preconscious and that operating in the repressed chain. Condensation operates, as it were, vertically, between a signifier and another signifier that has fallen to the rank of the signified. Condensation is then a feature of language that is never completely there, but exists somewhere between the work of distortion and the work of interpretation, the latter in its guile simply reversing the former:

> The creative spark of the metaphor does not spring from the bringing together of two images, that is, of two signifiers equally actualised. It flashes between two signifiers one of which has taken the place of the other in the signifying chain, the occulted signifier remaining present through its (metonymic) connection with the rest of the chain. (*E* 507/157)

The operations of metaphor and metonymy are therefore, as I had emphasised in the discussion on Jakobson, mutually interdependent. If metaphor creates a superimposition of signifiers, metonymy effects a continual sliding of signifiers: ' . . . the one side (*versant*) of the effective field constituted by the signifier, so that meaning can emerge there' (*E* 506/156). The point is that metonymy, for Lacan, concerns only the relations between signifiers, it does not concern the signified at all, for the signified is continually slipping away underneath.

The nature of metonymy can be better understood by returning to the diagrammatic representation of Philippe's dream. I have already attempted a description of the fiction of primal repression. I have also shown how it is that a signifier such as *place* exists by virtue of a signifier that it has displaced—*plage*. Or to put it another way, we have seen how the original signifier *plage* is in a metaphorizing position with regard to the signifying chain 'above' it. Since we are concerned with what Freud calls the 'derivatives' of the repressed instinctual (drive) representative, we need to trace the connections between the right and left-hand side of the diagram.

Freud's initial point in separating out the two different kinds of repression was quite simply a logical one. If it was argued that, for repression to occur, the 'presentation' had not only to be repulsed by the preconscious but also to be attracted by a chain already existing in the unconscious, then a primal repression had to be postulated. The associative chains connect the already existing chain in the unconscious to the (distorted) derivatives of the repressed instinctual representative around which the unconscious chain is organised

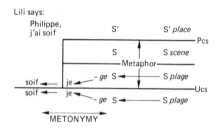

Thus, when the work of distortion is undone, we find the original signifier/signified relation *plage/scène*. The final syllable *ge* is phonetically linked to the *je* in the *J'ai soif* of the unconscious chain, and we can therefore postulate a metonymic sliding to the left of the diagram, from *plage/plage* to *-ge/-ge* to *je/je* and so to (*J'ai*) *soif*.

II

In the original version of this paper I concluded with a summary of my doubts as to the nature of the unconscious chain. These doubts (and confusions) were, for the most part, to do with the use of the term 'signifier'. What exactly was the link between its usage in linguistics and its usage in psychoanalytic theory? In relying overmuch on the Laplanche/Leclaire paper I was led to answer this question in too reductive a manner. Instead of preserving the tension between the forms of knowledge that linguistics and psychoanalysis each produce, I tended to suppress it—the signifying chain was reduced to an elementary signifying unit, and, since I was working with Freud's papers on metapsychology from volume xiv of the *Standard Edition*, I was led to think of it in terms of the distinction between a word-presentation and a thing-presentation.

It is clear, however, that Lacan always writes very explicitly of the signifying *chain* and firmly rejects the quest for an elementary signifying unit. Both the discussion of the Saussurean relation between signifier and signified, in 'The Agency of the Letter in the Unconscious', and the 'elementary cell' (*E* 805/303), posited in 'The Subversion of the Subject and the Dialectic of Desire', are good evidence for this assertion. If you look carefully at the 'graphs' that Lacan uses to illustrate this 'elementary cell' it is quite clear that they do not imply an anchored relation between one signifier and one signified. They concern, rather the retroactive effect of the code on the message and the syntactic disturbances that then ensue.

The search for an elementary signifying unit implies the search for a sign, and it is in emphasising the distinction between sign and signifier that Lacan repudiates this search. An imaginary narrative will explain this distinction best. Suppose a car with blacked-out windows and a driver who is a trained musician. In this total darkness he will have to play for his life. For there is a code, a 'score', and if he follows it, note for note, the machine that encases him will not come to grief. The 'score' is therefore, according to Peirce's definition, a *sign* (or a series of signs) for it represents something (the road) to someone (the driver). Notice how, in this fable, the sign permits control and conscious manipulation. Notice too that fidelity to the score is all that is required. It is not a question of style, of *duende*; the road is a red carpet unrolled by the divinity for any perfect sight-reader. Yet Lacan deliberately avoids this usage of the term *sign* and opts for the term *signifier*—'the signifier represents the subject for another signifier'. In this formulation, the subject is displaced with respect to the signifying chain, which exists ever ahead of it and subverts its claim to represent either itself or an object in language. At the risk of constructing a kind of palimpsest I want to consider this question once more, and to comment again on the original Laplanche/Leclaire article in order to show how it is that a too great reliance on its formulations tends to obscure certain crucial aspects of Lacan's interpretation of Freud.

If this endless recasting should seem a tedious exercise it is worth bearing in mind that it has been a common mistake, and not mine alone, to regard the Laplanche/Leclaire article as an adequate representation of Lacan's work. It was central to the 1960 Congress of Bonneval and was subsequently translated into English and Spanish. Its influence did doubtless stem from the clarity of its exposition, and one would therefore have thought that, given hindsight, criticism would be a simple matter. But the task is actually more complicated than one would at first suspect. In her book, *Jacques Lacan* (1970/1977), Anika Lemaire analyses the article at some length, and I had at first thought that it would be enough to summarise, in this second part—as Lemaire does—the aspects of the article that represent a divergence from Lacan's own teaching. But it is as if one pupil had fallen (Laplanche) and the other one had been saved (Leclaire); the logic of that grace, withheld or granted, is not analysed. Lacan himself has on several occasions disowned the article, and in so doing he has tended to imply the same clear-cut division between the two, a division that would coincide with an ' institution's edict (Lemaire 1970: 9–20/1977: vii–xv).

My initial and most obvious concern is to understand Lacan's thought by reference to that of certain of his pupils, but my wish to interpret the relation that links a teacher's work to that of his followers will necessarily run up against certain obstacles. I do not know exactly how the different psychoanalytic institutions reproduce themselves through training analyses, and am therefore stranded between an anecdotal history of factional dispute and fission— which I distrust—and an adequate theory of the symbolic conditions ordering that history. This theory exists only in an inchoate form, and there is, beyond this difficulty, another one. For, in any theoretical argument in psychoanalysis, I feel constrained—at one moment or another—to be silent in the face of a clinical practice of which I know so little. When the argument touches, as this one does, on the nature of psychosis, it is a little awkward to imagine oneself assuming the caution and reticence of a science in the same manner as one had assumed its confidence and garrulousness. Yet one is still permitted, outside of all reference to clinical practice, to consider a series of theoretical statements and to try and construct a logic of the discrepancies that arise there. This permission is more particularly granted in those periods in which psychoanalysis enjoys a rapid and triumphant advance. For the dislocations between the work of this or that pupil are also, in such periods, enormously instructive; their stumblings will tend to mirror the ones that we would for ourselves, in the face of a difficult teaching, imagine. Between 1957 and 1960 Lacan wrote a series of major texts and these, together with the seminars whose basic formulations they condense, laid the ground-work for what people now call Lacanian psychoanalysis. Laplanche and Leclaire's article is, for this reason, of especial interest. This interest lies both in its claim to represent Lacan's theory at that date and also in the fact that Lacan has disowned certain aspects of it.

His statements on this article have been predominantly con-cerned to correct an error of Laplanche's that derived from his transposition, in too literal and frozen a form, of a formula that had been used by Lacan to account for the structure of psychotic speech. These statements are elaborated by Lemaire in her book, and, as I have suggested, there is a sense in which the orthodoxy of one pupil and the heresy of another are taken to be self-evident facts.

In this second part I have also given a fairly comprehensive criticism of Laplanche's contribution to the original 1961 paper. One effect of Laplanche's formulations was to drive a wedge between the structure of neurosis and psychosis as they are understood in Freud's writing, and my criticisms of Laplanche here therefore demand a discussion of the technical vocabulary used first by Freud and then by Lacan, in the analysis of psychosis. It is clear that Freud had sought to define a mechanism peculiar to psychosis and it is also clear that Lacan's 'On a Question Preliminary to any Possible Treatment of Psychosis' (*E* 531–83/179–225) is meant as a return to this. But the existence of a mechanism peculiar to psychosis does not in itself cast the psychotic back into a realm beyond understanding and beyond therapeutic intervention. Whilst Lacan's preliminary questioning hinged on the possibility of understanding what it was that was being said, Laplanche's formulations make it quite impossible to grasp the logic of paranoiac psychosis and, in terms of linguistic structure, the production by Schreber of a *Grundsprache*, a basic language (*SE* XII: 23). In this second part I try to demonstrate this and also to avoid attributing a kind of substance to the unconscious. Linguistics will not be given the privileged status that an excessively structuralist interpretation of Lacan had led me to impute to it in the first part of the article.

PRIMAL REPRESSION

At a critical moment, then, in 'L'Inconscient: une étude psychana-lytique', Laplanche argues for the division of the primal repression into two separate stages, as if the unconscious required two different levels of symbolisation in order to come into being (1961: 117–18/ 1972: 161–62). In the first of these stages there is a net of signifying oppositions thrown over the subject's universe but there is no anchorage of signifier to signified. Laplanche defines this stage as a mythical one but accepts that the kind of language that is in evidence in paranoiac psychosis represents it well enough. In that use of language there is, he writes 'an uncontrollable oscillation of a pair of differential elements' (1961: 118/1972: 162). It is the second level of symbolisation to which Laplanche accords the description of primal repression (Freud) or metaphor and it is that creates the ballast that is lacking in a psychotic's world:

> It is that which really creates the unconscious, by introducing that ballast which will always be missing in a unilinear language, and which is lacking—to a greater or a lesser extent—in the symbolic world of the schizophrenic. The signified is from then on caught in specific meshes, at certain privileged points: the indefinite oscillation of + and −, O and A, 'good' and 'bad', right and left, comes to a halt. (1961: 118; 1972: 162)

According to Laplanche, this anchorage is manifested in the existence of 'key-signifiers' (eg. *soif* in the Philippe case-study in Part 1) or of an unconscious chain and it is these that enable the neurotic to speak rather than being spoken, because the unconscious provides the ballast for language to work. Thus, for Laplanche, the unconscious is the condition necessary for language. However, for Lacan, it is quite clearly language that is the condition for the unconscious.[8] To account for the confusion that has occurred here, I want to look in more detail at Laplanche's division of the process of primal repression into two stages, a division that corresponds to the four-tiered formulation as presented in Part 1.

By dividing the process of the primal repression into two stages Laplanche is able to obscure the question of the fixation of the drive to the signifier, and therefore the function of the death drive in the human unconscious. In addition, this division misrepresents Lacan's work on psychosis in that it tends to drive the psychotic back into an unplumbable domain irretrievably separate from neurosis.[9] But Laplanche's most critical misconceptions derive from the excessively rigid schematisation that he gives of formulae that were originally presented as being 'good to think with': one can, I believe, compare Lacan's use of graphs, schemae and formulae in the 1950s with Freud's own use of a schema in Chapter VII of *The Interpretation of Dreams* to represent the psychic apparatus. It is only in this chapter that some of Freud's boldest speculations as to the structure of the psychic apparatus are first *publicly* stated. The first properly topographic conceptualisation of the psyche occurs here and in presenting it Freud is careful to contrast the speculative nature of this chapter with the more solid ground of the previous ones. But in presenting a graphic representation of the psychic apparatus he warns that one should not mistake the scaffolding for the building.[10] This warning as to the usage of such devices would seem to me to apply to Lacan's work also: his schemae, his graphs, his formulae are all intended (if one transposes the terms used) 'to make the complications of mental functioning intelligible by dissecting the function and assigning its different constituents to different component parts of the apparatus'. In the 1961 article of Laplanche and Leclaire there is a confusion of just the sort that Freud had anticipated. The concept of the *points de capiton* and the *formula of the metaphor* are both taken too far from the contexts in which they were originally developed and they are thus irremediably altered.[11] The point is, of course, that diagrams have the power to fascinate the person who looks at them, but the bizarre complexity of the different 'graphs' militates against that kind of imaginary capture. For, by the time one has thought one's way through to a term-by-term transposition of the Freudian and (nascent) Lacanian terminology on to the vectors of the graph, the graph will have served its purpose and one will be able to *say* what it *does*. The vectors are then cords to the frame of a Lazarus: he may have looked death in the face but his body will only at the gift of the word arise. The concept of the *points de capiton* has therefore to be considered in relation to the diagrammatic representations that first nurtured it. Once it is properly understood—as an attempt to grasp the mechanisms whereby discourse is synchronically and diachronically punctuated—it could as easily as not be jettisoned. It is clear that Laplanche attributes an excessive concreteness to the concept and that this concreteness in its turn implies a too absolute division between neurosis and psychosis (where one is anchored and the other not).[12]

For what Laplanche has called a lack of anchorage and has therefore reduced to the non-pinning of a particular signifier to a particular signified should more properly be understood as a fault in discourse that affects the speaking subject's relation to the two orders (signifier, signified) in their entirety. In the highly dense pages of the 1961 Laplanche/Leclaire article in which the concept of the *points de capiton* is first cited, Laplanche slips a little too quickly between the various writings from which these different formulations were abstracted. His first citation of the S/s formula derives from Lacan's 'The Agency of the Letter in the Unconscious or Reason since Freud', but having asserted, with Lacan, the radical distinction between signifier and signified that the Saussurean bar establishes, a distinction that implies the endless shifting of one order beneath another, he then proceeds to modify that distinction by reference to the concept of the *points de capiton*. In the endless sliding of one order beneath another, the order of the signifier, since it is not anchored to the signified, can only refer to itself: each signifier therefore *is* by reference to its differential relation to every other, and it is only as a totality that the order of the signifier enters into relation with the order of the signified. But Laplanche, since he divides the process of primal repression into two stages, fails to see that what he terms a fiction (the myth of language in a reduced state) is fictional only in the sense that it is constructed backwards at the moment of fixation of the death drive to the signifier, or, more exactly, at the moment of the 'abolition' of the paternal signifier. The imprisonment of the schizophrenic within a symbolic universe that is divided into left and right, good and bad, light and dark, derives from the pre-existence of the Symbolic order and of the subject's relation to it. Fiction it is not, when winged creatures beat out your name in 'the courts of the sun'. It is rather the failure to assume one's name by sacrificing the most narcissistically invested (if imaginary) part of one's body that leads hallucinatory figures to return in the real, flooding through the unstopped. For not assuming one's name and therefore one's thirdness (for the signifier is handed down by another) one is condemned to repeat a chant with two terms, oneself and a God (Leclaire 1958: 397–8). There is no need though, to posit a prior and fictional stage: if the psychotic is 'spoken' and can no longer assume his own messages (they return to him in an inverted form—they begin as a declaration of love, 'I love him', and return as 'he hates me') it is because of a disordered relation to the 'treasury of signifiers'. This fault in primal repression can be illustrated by the acts of naming to which another of Leclaire's patients, Pierre, was forced to submit. On coming to a particular session he announced that he had called his mackintosh 'Beaujolais'. He explained that he called it this because his wife had said how pretty (*joli*) it was when he had purchased it, but once he had heard this he was assailed by doubts. Why had she not commented at the same time on *his* pleasing appearance, and if she had not done so was it not because the compliment about the mackintosh was really addressed to a lover of his wife's youth, called 'Jo'? In order therefore, to eliminate the hazards connected with the fact that the mac had been called *joli*, Pierre called it 'Beaujolais'—in order to signify that he, Pierre, was *beau* and Jo was *laid*. His delusions of jealousy therefore took the form of an act of magical naming. But the naming is a troubled one, the signifier will not hold. For the container of flesh and blood that he seeks to label is his own body, and he is forced to be ever mediating (as Jo/*Je*) the rival claims of beauty and of ugliness. A fault in the order of the signifier allows any metonymy at the level of phonetic resemblance to flood the body, and he is therefore condemned to be ever vacillating between his own supreme claim to beauty and the troublesome fact that lesser mortals are needed to acknowledge it. It is therefore a particular tilt to the ratio that links the discourse of those already installed in the world to the paternal metaphor that gives the signifier the opportunity to draw in (as by breath) the container/contained dialectic peculiar to the narcissistic ego.

And so Pierre continues to elaborate on the name of the mac: he dubbed it 'Apolloche'. This represented his desire to be *beau comme Apollo* but at the same time he had to call it 'Apolloche', for Apolloche, like Beaujolais, contained the name of another rival, 'Polo'—if Pierre was as Apollo, Polo was then *moche*, 'ugly'. It is thus by essentially magical means that he wards off the dangers that the signifier, in making contact with another, invariably brings. For want of a resolution to dual structures of narcissism, Pierre is condemned to wear a name instead of bearing it. But Laplanche's 'fiction of a language in a reduced state' says nothing about the mechanisms that are at the origin of the linguistic structures peculiar to psychosis. It simply divides a mechanism's two aspects into two temporal stages, and this temporal division is a critical misrepresentation of what primal repression is. Most crucially, it divides the body from the signifier, whereas Lacan's concept of the paternal metaphor (inseparable from the formula of the metaphor) is intended as an account of the shock delivered the narcissistic ego by the Symbolic order. Consider, in addition, Laplanche's brief citation of the *Fort Da* game. Laplanche cites it in the context of his 'fiction of a language in a reduced state' and separates it from the metapsychological commentary in which it was originally embedded. Since Leclaire's divergence from Laplanche in the original 1961 paper is expressed in terms of the differing interpretations one might give of the fixation of the death drive to the signifier I want here to approach the *Fort Da* game in terms of that metapsychological account. By means of this preliminary discussion of the problem of the death drive I hope to clarify the subsequent account that I will give of Laplanche's use of the concept of the *points de capiton* and of the formula of the metaphor.

THE DEATH DRIVE

In *Beyond the Pleasure Principle* Freud isolated, more explicitly than thitherto, a phenomenon that he called *Wiederholungszwang* (the compulsion to repeat) (*SE* XVII: 1–67). His previous references to repetition had been explicitly concerned with the phenomena that emerged in the course of an analytic treatment (repetition and remembering occurred in inverse ratio to each other) and treated repetition as an effect of the transference: with *Beyond the Pleasure Principle* Freud elevated the compulsion to repeat to the status of the *daimonic*. The examples that Freud produces are interpreted as evidence for the operations of a death drive that works in direct contravention to the tendency towards ideal homeostasis characteristic of the pleasure principle. In repeating experiences that did not offer a yield of pleasure neurotic subjects were therefore under the sway of something *beyond* the pleasure principle, and in trying to grasp the nature of this *beyond*, Freud, at least in the 1920s, made the most extraordinary theoretical detours (via both speculative biology and a new formulation of the basic dualism of the drives). Many psychoanalysts have taken the thoroughly speculative nature of much of Freud's rumination on the death drive as being good reason for jettisoning what seems to them a purely mythological construction. But such an aversion to myth is mistaken and to strike out a concept that Freud adhered to so stubbornly one would have to prove that the repetition compulsion was in some way separable from the death drive. Another possible line of reasoning would involve adducing a scientific basis for the residue of nineteenth century psycho-physics that permeates Freud's theoretical work on the nature of the libido: thus Laplanche, with Pontalis, in the *The Language of Psychoanalysis*, asserts that much of the difficulty and confusion surrounding the question would be resolved 'by a preliminary discussion of the ambiguity surrounding terms such as "pleasure principle", "principle of constancy" and "binding"' (1973: 80).

I would not deny that there is need for clarification with respect to Freud's account of the primary process and of the dependence of that account on concepts derived from Fechner. But if one considers the whole range of writings in which reference to the compulsion to repeat is made, it would seem a little forced to suppose that understanding of it would be gained simply by isolating a purely economic factor that the compulsion contravenes. I would put it, rather, that it is neither purely a question of the signifier nor of the economic, but that it is a question of the logic of the signifier in so far as it has an economy irreducible to a formal linguistics. By formulating it thus it is possible to reconcile the fact that in a technical paper like "Remembering, Repeating and Working-Through" (*SE* XIX: 157–70) the compulsion to repeat is interpreted in terms of the transference (though the order is also inverted: 'the transference is itself only a piece of repetition') whereas in *Beyond the Pleasure Principle* it is given a highly elaborate biological infrastructure.

To settle for the second account alone would be to settle for a vulgar materialist account of the human psyche, and 'energy' would become palpable, quantifiable, as it is in Reich's later work. But to settle for the first alone would be to leave the problem unsolved. Both of these positions represent a kind of fascination (or aversion, which is equivalent) with the concept of the death drive. Lacan has, from the very beginning of his work, refused a too simple acceptance of libido theory, and he has therefore tended to argue against purely 'energetic' notions of the death drive and against 'primordial masochism' as a concept. For him, if the order of human desire was implicated in the contravention of the tendency towards an ideal homeostasis, this order should then be identified with the structure of a signifying chain rather than with a death drive of a purely 'biological' kind (*Le Séminaire* II: 79–85). The margin beyond the pleasure principle is therefore the Symbolic order inasmuch as it is organised around a barred signifier that is insistent in its pulsating effect. This latter proviso is critical, for without it the Symbolic order is conceived simply as a structuralist combinatory and what Laplanche and Leclaire call the 'capture' of the drive 'in the nets of the signifier' would thereby lose its fatal sting. There is in fact a 'dissymmetry' between the two loci represented in Lacan's 'elementary cell' (designated locus of the Message and locus of the Code in Schema 1 cf. below) and this dissymmetry is indicative of something less than the total capture of the death drive. This can be more clearly appreciated by discussing the *Fort Da* game, for there Freud witnesses a child compelled to repeat an unpleasurable experience, and this compulsion is clearly tied to the child's assumption of symbolicity.

THE *FORT DA* GAME

In *Beyond the Pleasure Principle* Freud gives an account of a game that he had watched his grandson playing. The game involved the flinging of small objects into the corner of the room and uttering the German word *fort* (gone)—articulated as 'o' but recognised by the adult entourage as the complete word. Among the many different things that he threw away there was a wooden reel with a piece of string attached to it and by means of the string the child could make the reel appear and disappear: its reappearance would be greeted by a joyful *da* (here). What did this game represent?

Freud begins by asserting that it represents 'the child's greatest cultural achievement—the instinctual renunciation (that is, the renunciation of instinctual satisfaction) which he made in allowing his mother to go away without protesting' (*SE* XVIII: 15). But why does the child repeat an achievement that was so distressing—given that the aspect of reappearance was an fortuitous aspect of the game caused by the presence of the reel among the child's toys?[13] Does the child tirelessly repeat the game (and the *fort* part of the game too, all on its own) because it is, as Freud stresses, a *cultural* achievement? In such an interpretation the child uses a signifier to represent presence and absence and therefore, through the use of this signifier, enters the Symbolic domain. This way of interpreting the *Fort Da* game is correct in so far as the phonemic opposition 'o–a' represents the combinatory of differential elements that is the Symbolic order and it is precisely this order into which the child moves. Lacan's supplementation of Freud's account would therefore seem to involve nothing more than pointing out that the vocalisation accompanying the game does indeed correspond to a phonemic opposition. But the critical aspect of the process concerns the manner in which the child, by these Symbolic manipulations, has an altered structure of desire. Many Lacanian interpretations have simply seen the cotton reel as achieving presence through absence, and the game—as is the case with Laplanche's whole approach—would then be divided into two separate stages. Or to put it more exactly, the symbolic operations involved in the game would be preceded by a stage in which a wounded consciousness had taken cognisance of the fact of the absence of the mother and had then—by means of the game—acted to assume a novel form of mastery:

> It was probably in relation to his mother's words that the child was attempting to situate himself. The real mother disappeared and he put to the test the magic power of the word (the mother disappeared but the word remained) . . . What was apparent from the 'gone–here' relationship was that the Symbolic dimension had entered into the mother-child relationship. It is owing to the existence of this dimension that mastery can be acquired, the child acting out on himself the abandonment and rejection in a context of childish omnipotence; it is he who is abandoned and who rejects, retaining within himself a sufficiently secure mother figure so as not to have to die at her departure in reality. (Mannoni 1970: 17)

This account of the transformation of a dual Imaginary relationship into a mediated Symbolic one by means of repetitive play would seem to smuggle in too literal a reference to the actual mother and to the child as one who takes it upon himself to represent a person's absence by means of a thrown toy and a word. The child is therefore able to think 'absence' prior to his entrance into the signifying order, which would in fact be the sole means available to him of thinking it. It is moreover assumed that the second part of the game is an integral part of it, whereas (as a recent commentary by Safouan (1979: 76) clearly shows) the presence of the cotton reel among the other toys was quite fortuitous. The child's mastery—as expressed in the above quotation—is not of that order, and the magic of the word cannot be reduced to that instrumental symbolicity so beloved of Malinowski in his discussions of 'primitive' magic . . . a little abreaction and a little symbolic control!

In fact the *Fort* game (and one should perhaps resolve to call it this) represents more than a response to privation and does not have as its aim the reappearance of the mother. If it is the moment of the child's entrance into the signifying order, it is not the assumption of some cloak that—emblazoned with a combinatory—would fall around the shoulders. It is rather the 'drive' outwards that makes it possible for the drive itself to be represented, by means of the symbol of negation, in the psychic apparatus. The moment of the throwing out of the toy has a double structure: it affirms the presence that it constructs at the moment of constructing it, but this affirmation is itself denegated, such that the affirmation 'it is she' or 'it is my mother' nestless within the denegation 'it isn't she', 'it isn't my mother'. It is the catastrophic moment of entrance into an universal order (that therefore elicits the singularity of a presence, a *face*, against the suddenly unfolded backdrop of absence) that Laplanche's account modifies. The point is that the child's cultural achievement entails the installation of a repetition compulsion in the unconscious (the symbolic debt that the murder of the father in the mythical account in *Totem and Taboo* constructs, a debt that prohibits incest but opens the cycles of exchange and therefore offers promise of an ideal *jouissance* in a future time) (*SE* XIII: 141–43). Much of the difficulty of this moment in the analysis stems from the need to embark on an analysis of Freud's 'Negation' paper (*Die Verneinung*), but even without the new approaches that such an analysis would here open up, one can still locate the basic errors in Laplanche's argument. For, whilst Laplanche accepts that presence and absence are themselves constructed by the signifying action itself—as in the myth, earth and sky are in the same instant separated and named—he still tends to conceive of the two phonemes o–a as representing the child's symbolic *mastery* of the mother's presence and absence (1961: 110–11/1972: 153). This mythological reference which accords with Lévi-Strauss's own remarks as to the suddenness with which universality of signification is constructed (from nothing meaning anything, everything comes to mean something) does however obscure the Freudian account of primal repression and the specific mechanism that allows for the fixation of drive to signifier (Lévi-Strauss 1950). It is therefore at this point that Laplanche cites the Lacanian *points de capiton*, starts to discuss the formula of the metaphor and it is also at this point—and quite logically—that Leclaire announces his theoretical divergence from Laplanche. It is no coincidence that Laplanche's account so closely echoes Lévi-Strauss's own myth as to the signifier's birth and to the subsequent relation between the order of the signifier and the order of the signified. For in his account of that myth Lévi-Strauss rules out psychosis as being of the order of the *idiolect*, and this fact confirms my persistent insinuation that a too 'structuralist' interpretation of Lacanian psychoanalysis renders an explanation of psychosis impossible.

THE POINTS DE CAPITON AND THE FORMULA OF THE METAPHOR

The *points de capiton* represent, in Lacan's theory, points of intersection between the order of the signifier and the order of the signified. Introduced in relation to Graph 1 in 'The Subversion of the Subject and the Dialectic of Desire', the concept is intended to take account of the way in which 'the signifier halts the otherwise indefinite sliding (*glissement*) of signification' (*E* 805/303). But there is a massive and critical distance between the account that Lacan gives of it in the ensuing paragraphs, and the account that Laplanche gives in the 1961 paper. For Laplanche, perhaps a little dazzled by the diagrammatic representations, gives the impression of considering the points of intersection between the vector SS′ and the vector $A as being points of anchorage at which, once and for all, a signifier and a signified are bound together. This impression is confirmed in the subsequent moments of his argument, in which the four-tiered formula gives the unconscious chain S/S as *ballast* for language. However, in the very passage from Lacan that Laplanche himself cites, it is asserted that the '*points de capiton*' are mythical and that they do not finally pin down anything (1961: 112/1972: 155). When Lacan uses the concept of the *points de capiton* in an (unpublished) 1959 seminar, entitled 'Le Désir et son interprétation', it is quite apparent that the three different schemae (that reappear in 1960 as Graphs I, II, III) are not chronologically ordered—such a chronology suggesting the kind of temporal division into two stages that Laplanche seeks to establish—but logically ordered (Lacan 1959–60: 264–5). Thus the Schema 1 (comparable to the Graph 1) is defined as introducing 'the topology of the relation of the subject to the signifier, reduced to what is observable in the linguistic fact'. But this 'reduction' is later corrected by the addition of the further elements: thus the specular ego is written in at the bottom of Schema 3 (whereas, if the sequence was a chronological one, it would have been already in place in Schema 1). Laplanche's 'fiction of language in a reduced state' is therefore a misinterpretation of what is at stake in these formulations, for it drives a wedge between the linguistic fact and narcissistic desire, and this separation allows a too conscious and too masterly infant to be considered as engaged in utilitarian play.

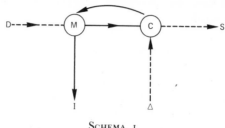

SCHEMA I

In this diagram the vector DS (cf. the vector SS′ in Graph I of 'The Subversion of the Subject and the Dialectic of Desire' (*E* 805/ 303)) represents 'an oriented succession of discrete elements' (ie., the signifying chain). But this signifying chain is punctuated by the vector Δ I. This retroactive effect (retroactive in the sense that the vector Δ I runs against the diachronic succession of the signifying chain) means that signification is completed ahead of itself, in the sense that signifiers have a retroactive effect on those that preceded them in the signifying chain. The vector Δ I therefore passes through the locus of the code (C) before it passes through the locus of the message (M), and this primacy of the one locus over the other— which is a necessary effect of the pre-existence of the Symbolic order—is in evidence in any human speech, psychotic or otherwise. Laplanche's 'fiction of language in a reduced state', fiction or no, abstracts the vector Δ I from the short-circuit C.M. M.S. (which is the 'uncontrollable shifting between a couple of differential elements') and therefore splits the narcissistic ego from the Symbolic order, whereas the flaw in the first is intimately connected to the metonymic displacement integral to the second. If one overhears a bloodcurdling drama as narrated on a bus, and if the last words are left unspoken, or are spoken elsewhere, the 'and then he . . . ' with which the alerted listener is left is already completed (' . . . cut her up into tiny little pieces'), and not because the 'scene' had a witness, but because the phantasy of the fragmented body has, by means of primal repression, passed like night into language. But herein lies the difference between phantasy and an hallucination, for when Schreber leaves his sentences unfinished they are completed for him by voices in auditory hallucination. A broken chain therefore entails the existence of its complement ahead of it itself in all human speech, and when, in paranoiac psychosis, a special language is constructed for 'voices' to speak—as is the case with Schreber's basic language, his *Grundsprache*—it represents the Code in its unpunctuated, retroactive effect on the Message. Lacan notes that Schreber's amputated messages break off just at the point at which the index-terms (e.g. shifters) end, and from then on one has to do with 'the properly lexical part of the sentence, in other words that which comprises the words that the code defines by their use, whether the common code or the delusional code is involved' (*E* 540/186).

Yet the difference between the 'common' and the 'delusional' code is not exhausted by reference to the Manichean aspect of Schreber's cosmology or to the use of euphemisms that turn a word into its opposite (reward for punishment; poison for food). For one has, first of all, to accept that these hallucinatory impositions of code on to message cleave to what linguists call 'autonyms', and that the retroactive effect of the code on the message is therefore common to all human speech. A brief reference to Martinet's discussion of the concept of the 'moneme', in *Eléments de linguistique générale* (1970), should help to illuminate this. What are monemes, and how does one analyse a statement into its constituent monemes? In Chapter IV, 'Les Unités significatives', Martinet tries to formulate a theory of the moneme as the elementary signifying unit: in choosing one signifier rather than another, the speaker determines the value to be given to the message (1970: 101–44). Monemes are therefore, in theory, substitutable one for another, and this substitution determines the subject of the enunciation. To identify a moneme, though, it is necessary to correlate a minimal phonetic difference with a minimal semantic difference: thus, whilst in French /ilkur/ (*il court*) and /nukuriõ/ (*nous courions*) share the segment /kur/ and also the notion of 'running', there is still a massive difference between the two as to both signifier and signified. Whereas, in the case of /nukuriõ/ (*nous courions*), /vukurie/ (*vous couriez*), and nukurõ/ (*nous courons*), /vukure/*vous courez* there is a minimal difference (/i/) for the signifiers and a minimal difference for the signifieds (where the presence or absence of the /i/ denotes *imperfect* or not). This argument is, as Martinet admits, complicated by the fact that, in another context, the signifier /i/ may represent the subjunctive or that in the third person (/ilkurè/ (*il courait*)) it is the signifier/è/ that denotes the imperfect tense, but his basic point is that there are elementary units of signification and that the subject chooses one rather than another in placing himself within an utterance as the subject of the enunciation.

There are, however, a whole range of linguistic facts that resist this concept of the moneme, and in taking account of them Martinet is forced to modify the concept by introducing sub-categories (grammatical monemes, lexical monemes, etc.). He therefore admits that monemes are often linked into 'autonomous syntagms', and these may be compared with what Lacan, in the essay on Judge Schreber and psychosis, calls 'code phenomena'. For Lacan emphasises that the treasury of the signifier depends not on an univocal correspondence of sign to concept but on syntactical imperatives that work backwards. For the simultaneous installation of the repetition compulsion in the human unconscious and the setting in place of the function of negation in human language means that the locus of the Code is necessarily always already the locus of the Other. These two linked moments ensure that the retroactive efficacy of Code on Message assumes the form of autonomous syntagms rather than, say, holophrases. A syntagm is, in Martinet's terms, a combination of monemes, and an autonomous syntagm is one whose elements may not be divided one from another (as is not the case with the syntagm 'with pleasure', since it may, with great pleasure, and sometimes with very great pleasure, be extended). There is usually, Martinet notes, a 'functional' moneme (as *en* in *en voiture*) and this prohibits the choice, the pure substitution which is the guiding principle of Martinet's original concept. These 'functional' monemes are one of the sorts that can be described, within an autonomous syntagm, as 'grammatical monemes', and their operation, in psychosis, shows that the linguistic disruptions are disruptions of a syntax that pre-exists the subject. This pre-existence (which can be a zero-choice, as with the autonomous syntagm *au fur et à mesure* which, for every French speaker, already exists in a completed form once *au fur et* is uttered) simply assumes a different form in psychosis. The completion of the phrase which might ordinarily be uttered—for it is a fact of human speech that we hear ourselves speaking when we speak—is then attributed to another. What of the *point de capiton?* The *point de capiton*, in its diachronic aspect, is what I have been trying to explain here in the last few pages. Here is how Lacan writes of it:

> The diachronic function of this anchoring point [*point de capiton*] is to be found in the sentence, in so far as the sentence completes its signification only with its last term, each term being anticipated

in the construction of the others, and, inversely, sealing their meaning by its retroactive effect. (*E* 805/303)

Thus, the *points de capiton* are the points at which the signifying chain and the vector **Δ** I (which in Schema 1 represents the subject in an unformed state and in relation to an Ideal) intersect, both diachronically and synchronically. But what is the synchronic aspect of the *points de capiton*?

Once again, the *points de capiton* would seem to be nearer to an 'uncoupling' or an 'unpinning' than to a pinning down, for the synchronic aspect is metaphor. Lacan cites the example (taken from a French children's song) of the dog that goes 'miaow' and the cat that goes 'woof'—for the child, 'by disconnecting the animal from its cry, suddenly [*d'un seul coup*] raises the sign to the function of the signifier and reality to the sophistics of signification' (*E* 805/303–4). This citation of a child's game should bring to mind the *Fort* game already discussed, and indeed should help to make it clear once again how it is that Laplanche excludes the critical question of the repetition compulsion from formulation. For Laplanche the *Fort Da* would be in some way chronologically separate from the primal repression, yet for Lacan they are linked—and the separation suggested by the different diagrams is meant only to aid comprehension. Once the animal is separated from its cry the child is in the order of representation, but—and this is what Laplanche's formulations obscure—the lost animal still intrudes in the play of the signifier. The totemism that returns in childhood is violent beyond the forms of a totemic classification and is better represented by the North West Coast masks with shutters than by the 'totemic operator' (Lévi-Strauss 1969 and 1972). For the moment of revelation—at which the masks fly open—offers beyond the first figure another that may bring catastrophe with its sudden glance. Yet if the blow is a glancing one it is not less decipherable in the disturbances in the signifying order that result from the return of repressed material. Laplanche's concept of *ballast* disregards the duplicity of primal repression, for *dénégation* allows repressed material to return, whereas, in Laplanche's formulation, the notion of a ballast in the unconscious chain would prohibit this return.

Once Laplanche, in the 1961 paper, has cited the S/s relation and the concept of the *point de capiton*, he turns to Lacan's 'formula of the metaphor' as cited in 'On a Question Preliminary to any Possible

Treatment of Psychosis'. But Lacan's presentation of the formula is situated in a very specific context and given a very exact gloss—in abstracting it from this context Laplanche makes of it a quite general formula for linguistic symbolisation rather than one primarily concerned with primal repression. The formula actually makes no sense at all if one does not refer it to the concept of the 'Name of the Father', but by oscillating rather too quickly between 'On a Question Preliminary to any Possible Treatment of Psychosis' and 'The Agency of the Letter in the Unconscious' Laplanche obscures the significance of this crucial reference. For Lacan's citation of the paternal metaphor is closely linked to his elaboration of the function of the death of the symbolic father as formative of the law, and this elaboration is pivotal to his conception of what primal repression is. Earlier sections of this second part had been concerned with Laplanche's interpretations of the death drive and the *Fort Da* and my criticisms there are clearly linked to my criticisms of the use of the formula of the metaphor. Laplanche presents this formula simply as an algebraic one, representing linguistic symbolisation in general:

$$\frac{S'}{S} \times \frac{S}{s} \to S' \times \frac{I}{s}$$

The formula is then re-written by Laplanche, using the following transformation:

$$\frac{A}{B} \times \frac{C}{D} = \frac{\dfrac{A}{D}}{\dfrac{B}{C}}$$

to give:

$$\frac{S'}{S} \times \frac{S}{s} \quad \frac{\dfrac{S'}{s}}{\dfrac{S}{S}}.$$

But this re-writing, which presents us with the unconscious chain S/S, actually achieves the opposite of what Laplanche must have intended. For if he had meant to show how it is that the signifier S that has fallen to the rank of the signified continues to have 'effects', his insistence that the unconscious chain is what provides ballast for conscious language runs quite counter to this. Laplanche's presentation of the formula of the metaphor is a formalist one and he therefore separates it from the very terms that would lend it any real meaning. The two concepts of metaphor and of the Name of the Father are inseparable in Lacan, yet Laplanche, having cited the formula of the metaphor, considers the paternal metaphor only as an after-thought (as one of a series of 'key-signifiers'). Anyone who turns back to the original presentation of the formula of the metaphor, and the densely written passages that follow it, will be able to see for themselves what a startling misrepresentation of Lacan's position this is. Lacan's original version of the equation in the psychosis paper was as follows:

$$\frac{S}{S'} \cdot \frac{\not{S}'}{x} \to S\left(\frac{1}{s}\right)$$

and he has subsequently pointed out that it was never a question of mathematical formulae here (Lemaire 1970: 16–17/1977: xii). The bar represents not a fraction but the Lacanian modification of the Saussurean bar between signifier and signified. But this misrepresentation, that anyone could in all good faith have made, might have been avoided if more attention had been paid to the manner in which Lacan comments on the formula: 'The capital Ss are signifiers, *x* the unknown signification and *s* the signified induced by the metaphor, which consists in the substitution in the signifying chain of S for S'. The elision of S', represented here by the bar through it, is the condition of the success of the metaphor' (*E* 557/ 200). The success of the metaphor therefore demands the elision of S' (the desire of the mother) which, prior to the action of the metaphor, is signified to the Name of the Father (in that the mother's desire is already constructed as the desire that it be the phallus to her) and signifier to the unknown signified *x* (which represents the child as not yet caught up in the constituent effects of the signifying chain). Thus, in the psychosis article, the formula is written out as follows:

$$\frac{\text{Name of the Father}}{\text{Desire of the Mother}} \cdot \frac{\text{Desire of the Mother}}{\text{Signified to the subject}} \to \left(\frac{\text{O}}{\text{Phallus}}\right)$$

$$\frac{}{\text{Name of the Father}}$$

As I understand this formulation, the child's capture in the imaginary order, as one who has a specular ego, is inseparable from the action of a primal repression that places him or her within a Symbolic order. It is this interdependence that Laplanche's formulations, both here and in relation to the *points de capiton*, erase, for Laplanche attributes a leaden quality (he calls it *ballast*) to what persists in the unconscious and will not be quieted. For Lacan, everything happens at once. The double bar in the formula represents the catastrophic action of the metaphor insofar as it separates mother from child and child from mother, and also—in other terms—the double movement of affirmation (*Bejahung*) and denegation (*Verneinung*) by means of which the child's ego is split in relation to the threat of castration and the ideal possibility of assuming a place in the Symbolic order is offered.[14] There is, however, no possibility of understanding these processes simply by reference to such devices as the formula of the metaphor. They are mnemonic instruments whose purpose is didactic. They do not contain a complete account of the processes that they represent, and taken literally they encourage a too simple understanding of what it is that the child's prior subordination to the Symbolic entails. They also favour a kind of collapse between the Real, Symbolic and Imaginary dimensions of the adults already installed there and later split several ways and invested with a 'wealth' of kingly and priestly powers. In spite of Lacan's express warnings (*E* 578/218) this reduction will cause people to look for a psychoticising mother or father, when there is invariably a multiplicity of factors that work together at different points to construct an impossibility whose violence touches more on the impossibility of formulating the thing in a language than of being or having it in some more literal sense. Rather than attributing blame to an adult for failing to impart his or her sense of the libidinal to the child—as Leclaire does in *Psychanalyser*—one should attend to the ratios that link the different dimensions. How are they torn apart, one from another, and how are they stitched together? It is to these further questions that my second article in this collection (pp. 162–187) is addressed.

NOTES

1. The original versions of this paper were published in *Journal of the Anthropology Society of Oxford* vol. 6, no. 2 (1975) and in *Economy and Society* 5: 434–69.

The Laplanche/Leclaire article on which the paper relies so heavily had been translated into English (*Yale French Studies* 48: 118–76) and it was all too easy, given the structuralist framework in which Lacan's work was translated and presented to make the kinds of error that were so rife in the earlier version (and in its concluding passages in particular). This version is shortened and the conclusion is omitted but the major criticisms are reserved for Part II.

2. But cf. also his analysis of anagrams used in Greek and Latin poetry—MSS. assembled by Jean Starobinski, *Les Mots sous les mots* (1971).

3. It is worth stressing that aphasia represents language in a state of disintegration and that in most human speech the two poles operate in conjunction. Jakobson, and, after him, Barthes (1967: 21), thus reserve the term *idiolect* primarily to describe the language of the aphasic (see Part II of this essay for a warning as to the dangers implicit in the opposition between a normal 'social' use of language and an incommunicable idiolect).

4. Cf. Joan Rivière's translation of *Die Verneinung* (*CP* IV: 181–5).

5. But cf. E. Benveniste, 'The Nature of the Linguistic Sign'. (1966: 49–55/ 1971: 43–48).

6. The phrase is from Lévi-Strauss (1950: xlix) but Lacan also refers to the S/s relation as being that of two registers. The word register meaning here two articulations taken in their globality (*E* 444). He insists that there is no bi-univocal (i.e. term to term) relation involved, but only that of register to register.

7. E. Jones in *Psycho-analysis* (1935). Lacan, in his essay 'Sur la théorie du symbolisme d'Ernest Jones', comments as follows: 'These primary ideas indicate the points where the subject disappears under the being of the signifier: whether it is a question, in effect, to be oneself, to be a father, to be born, to be loved or to be dead, how can one not see that subject, insofar as it is a subject who speaks, only supports itself from discourse' (*E* 709).

8. This is particularly apparent in the commentary that Lacan gives to a paper of Melanie Klein, in *Le Séminaire* I: 81–83; 95–103.

9. It has been argued that Lacan's theory of the structure of psychosis has this effect too, and that the concept of *Verwerfung*, in the interpretation that Lacan gives it, casts the psychotic back into the darkness in which Kraepelin had left him or her (cf. Mannoni 1979). This interpretation surely disregards the fact that Lacan's original work on these problems is presented as a preliminary clearing of the ground and was not itself intended as a direct contribution to therapeutic practice. Leclaire's 'A la recherche des principes d'une psychothérapie des psychoses' (1958) is written in the wake of Lacan's original article, and although its therapeutic suggestions are startlingly modest and tentative, there is no question there of abandoning the psychotic to a destiny so flawed as to be beyond redemption.

10. Freud writes as follows:

I see no necessity to apologise for the imperfections of this or of any similar imagery. Analogies of this kind are only intended to assist us in our attempt to make the complications of mental functioning intelligible by dissecting the function and assigning its different constituents to different component parts of the apparatus. So far as I know, the experiment has not hitherto been made of using this method of dissection in order to investigate the way in which the mental instrument is put together, and I can see no harm in it. We are justified, in my view, in giving free rein to our speculations so long as we retain the coolness of our judgement and do not mistake the scaffolding for the building. (*SE* v: 536)

Cf. also his warning as to the use of Figure 2 in 'On Transformations of Instinct as Exemplified in Anal Erotism' (*SE* xvii: 132).

11. The original statement of the formula of the metaphor is to be found in 'On a Question Preliminary to any Possible Treatment of Psychosis' (*E* 531–83/179–225). The crucial passage on the *points de capiton* is to be found in 'The Subversion of the Subject and the Dialectic of Desire' (*E* 793–827/292–325).

12. In 'A la recherche des principes d'une psychothérapie des psychoses' (1958) Leclaire cites the example of a patient for whom the use of the word *vert* (green) is complicated by the fact that the signifier *ver* also entails a reference to *ver de terre* (earthworm), the letter V, and also to other words within which it may nestle (e.g. *ver/seau*; *ver/tèbre*; and most critically, in the aphorism *l'intro/ver/sion c'est le ver solitaire*). In Section vii of Freud's paper 'The Unconscious' (*SE* xiv: 200–5) there is a long discussion as to the different linguistic structures in evidence in the transference neuroses and in psychosis, and Freud concludes that (in schizophrenia) word-presentations have absolute autonomy with regard to thing-presentations, and that sometimes one word (e.g. *vert/ver* for Pierre) will monopolise a whole range of different associations. Yet this treatment of a signifier as a thing in itself—separate from the signified—is not in itself indicative of psychosis, for verbal play is all too often based on this fascination with the inner 'colouring' of phonemic clusters, which, loving language, seem to us the very heart of the word. There is a whole poetic tradition (Baudelaire, Rimbaud, Leiris) that works to attribute colour values to vowels and consonants, and this attribution is simply dependent on the priority of the signifier over the signified. It is not merely that the concept of 'greenness' is found wherever the signifier 'green' decrees it ('They called it Greenland to encourage settlement', as the poem has it). For beyond such symbolic effects, primal repression installs a metonymy in relation to the lost object of desire, a verbal play not dissimilar to the form that Pierre's speech takes. It is not therefore a pinning of the one signifier to the one signified that defines neurosis as distinct from psychosis, it is rather the resolution of the meeting between the body and the signifier that is critical for the form that the intellectual functions will subsequently take.

13. Chapter v of M. Safouan's *L'échec du principe du plaisir* (1979) is, for the most part, devoted to an exegesis of the *Fort Da* game, and in this chapter Safouan clearly shows how it is that in Freud's account the *Da* is an accidental and secondary aspect of the game.

14. The references are to Freud's paper 'Negation' (*Die Verneinung*; *SE* xix: 233–39) and to its crucial importance for the debates hinted at here.

2 Philology and the Phallus

JOHN FORRESTER

Indeed, in an age when no prejudices of artificial decency existed, what more just and natural image could men find, by which to express their idea of the beneficent power of the great Creator than that organ which endowed them with the power of procreation, and made them partakers not only of the felicity of the Deity, but of his peculiar attribute, that of multiplying his own image? (Sir William Hamilton, *The worship of Priapus. An account of the Fete of St. Cosmo and Damiens . . . at Isernia in 1780 . . . To which is added some account of the phallic worship, principally derived from A discourse on the worship of Priapus, by R. P. Knight.* (London, 1883) (100 copies).)

It is not as if psychoanalysts have ever stopped reading Freud. Indeed, when compared with the social habits of practitioners of the natural sciences, and even those of the human sciences such as anthropology, psychoanalysts have always behaved in a peculiar manner towards that shelf of books cryptically known in English as the *Standard Edition*. One might more profitably criticise psychoanalysts for their slavish scanning of the Master's texts than accuse them of an attenuated repression of them. But, of course, or perhaps, this misses the point of Lacan's advocacy of a return to Freud, which is articulated upon the thesis that psychoanalysts have systematically misread his works. Firstly, they start chronologically at the wrong end: they read the *Ego and the Id* (1923) (*SE* xix: 12–66) before *The Interpretation of Dreams* (1900) (*SE* iv, v), *Inhibitions, Symptoms and Anxiety* (1926) (*SE* xx: 87–174) before *Studies on Hysteria* (1895) (*SE* ii). And, with much vitriolic insinuation, Lacan accuses his fellow analysts of neglecting the other two 'royal roads' to the unconscious, signposted by *The Psychopathology of Everyday Life* (1901) (*SE* vi) and *Jokes in Their Relation to the Unconscious* (1905) (*SE* viii).

Lacan wishes to cast doubt upon the value of ego psychology, itself based upon the second topography of Freud, in which the ego became both the focus of therapeutic activity and of theoretical

45

interest. 'Back to 1900' is the chronological imperative Lacan utters. Understand the ego via the concept of narcissism (1914), not by *The Ego and the Id*. Understand that the theory of interpretation in *The Interpretation of Dreams* is the alpha and omega of the practice of analysis.

Curiously, then, for a structuralist, as he is known to some, Lacan's pedagogy advocates a return to origins. If we can get close enough to the original inception of the concept (before it became corrupted), he seems to argue, we will clarify its function and its meaning. Lacan utilises historical arguments in order to bolster a particular reading of the concepts of psychoanalysis. For example, Lacan thinks it is necessary to read the 'technical writings' of Freud as part of the development from the formalism of his practice found in the period 1904–9 to the metapsychological and structural writings of 1914–20 (*Le Séminaire* I: 15). Or, to support his theory of the formation of the ego via an oscillation between what stands seeing in front of a mirror and the images seen in that mirror, he connects what is read in 'On Narcissism' (*SE* XIV: 73–102) with a selective reading of *The Ego and the Id*, in which he highlights Freud's concept of the formation of the ego through a series of identifications (*Le Séminaire* I: 194).

Hence we can establish that Lacan reads Freud forwards—he reads from 1900 to 1923 and not vice versa (with the exception of the key point in Lacan's system, to which we shall return). Secondly, the earlier works are, in themselves, more important—it is not just a matter of reading *The Ego and the Id* and the papers on identification and narcissism together. He gives conceptual priority to the earlier works. So the 'return to Freud' is truly a chronologically reversed movement—not just back to Freud but an attack on reading Freud backwards. We are to take seriously Freud's description of *The Interpretation of Dreams*: '. . . insight such as this falls to one's lot but once in a lifetime' (*SE* IV: xxxii). Lacan turns our attention to the work of interpretation that, for him, forms the essence of psycho-analysis on the one hand, the interpretations of texts (dream-texts, absences in texts and jokes), on the other hand, the fruits of the method of interpretation as practised by the psychoanalysts: the case-histories. Understand these works of Freud, Lacan seems to say, and the rest will follow. Words before penises, meanings before libido, interpretation before explanation.

Lacan states in his 'The Agency of the Letter in the Unconscious':

In the complete works of Freud, one out of every three pages is devoted to philological references, one out of every two pages to logical inferences, everywhere a dialectical apprehension of experience, the proportion of analysis of language increasing to the extent that the unconscious is directly concerned. (*E*: 509/ 159)

Right here, in this absolutely accurate characterisation of the character of Freud's writings, we have the seeds of a sliding of meaning, namely, from philology to language. Philology is not a term that comes easily to modern analysts. Yet the writings of Freud are rife with philological references and models. The metaphors of translation, the reconstruction of texts, the dialects of the body, the insistence of meaning from lost languages—all these are the bread and butter of Freud's thought. But they are not 'just' metaphors, not just way-stations of thought.

Freud looked to the *Geisteswissenschaften* for the documentation and methods of his new science. In the late nineteenth century, the discipline of philology was the queen of these sciences. Through the construction of a non-individual concept of the space in which the units of philology played—the *Volksgeist*—the nineteenth-century philologists, mythologists and linguists[1] established the foundation for the elucidation of meanings hidden in a set of texts. What we would call sociology and anthropology were established by the philological method.[2] With respect to the activities of the members of a homogeneous social unit (itself defined through the evidence of language),[3] the *Volksgeist* took up the same place that the concept of the unconscious took up with respect to the linguistic productions of the individual. The parallel between *Volk* and individual was guaranteed by a series of recapitulation laws: the history of the individual recapitulates the history of the *Volk*, thus ensuring that communal connotations can be transferred to the individual *without him knowing it*.[4] We note the more extreme version of the recapitulation doctrine in some of Freud's biological speculation (*Beyond the Pleasure Principle*) (*SE* XVIII: 7–64) and in Ferenczi's *Thalassa* (1923/4), a work which attempted to show that the history of the species is recapitulated by the individual, so that the symbols interpreted by the analyst are a distant echo of the aqueous history of mammals, itself reconstructed from the interpretation of symbols.

So with the work of philologists and mythologists in the late nineteenth century a concept was generated—the *Volksgeist*—that carried some of the essential characteristics of the unconscious. One of the primary characteristics of the individual utterance's relation to the unconscious—the expression of knowledge without knowing that one knows it—was taken for granted and gave rise to a great freedom of interpretation, especially in comparative studies of symbolism. But the major source for the study of 'key words' was etymology. Historical word-chains, trans-linguistic homologies, and the homogenisation of the field of the sign generated a 'polyglot *Geist*'.[5]

Freud's method of analysis took over this etymological pre-eminence and grafted on to it one crucial additional feature. Words with similar structures pointed backwards to an historical identity (*SE* II: 180ff.), but Freud's method utilised both individual etymologies and socially constructed ones. Putting it in this fashion obscures the essential fusion of individual and collective that Freud always maintained (*SE* XXIII: 132). The etymological method provided a foundation and a conclusion for the process of analysis, by securing connections between words and by ensuring that these chains of connections would come to an end at a point determined as much by the level of language attained as by the chance vicissitudes of the subject's relation to that language. To see the manner in which this functioned in practice, one only has to take a dream at random from *The Interpretation of Dreams* to find that 'individual' and 'social' elements mutually absorb one another in the elucidation of the dream: a reference to Hebrew, a quotation from Goethe, a piece of gossip from the cafés of Vienna, a word whispered over the cradle and a play on words criss-crossing between the six or so languages that were common currency to Freud and maybe even to his patients.

Now, is it to this support of psychoanalytic theory and practice that Lacan is appealing? It would seem not, if we read his theoretical arguments derived from de Saussure, in which a synchronic set of homophonies would seem to define the interpretative nodes through which is uncovered the determination of the history of the subject. Now, Lacan's work is as full of plays on words and etymologies as Freud's. For both, it is the function of free association to supply the relations between a manifest piece of nonsense and a system that supplies meaning. But, sad for the psychoanalyst to say, the connections are often lacking. At this point, Freud would resort to a number of methods, one of which was that of the philologist, etymology. A previous meaning constitutes a later meaning, even if this constitution must be made retroactively.[6] Such a recourse to the full play of meanings made available by the recondite researches of mythologists and philologists into arcane literature and forgotten languages, chiefly of the Aryan 'peoples',[7] was the working version of the theory that Freud clung to to the end of his days, namely, his belief in the inheritance of acquired mental characters. What is at issue there is the presence of a connection between two historical events, each represented by a 'signifier'.

But, it might be argued, we are not dealing with a simple sense of 'history' here, one in which a signifier is inexorably tied to the chronologically dated and fixed event. Nor is it as if the signifier is trying to make its escape from a historical cul-de-sac, trying to make its weight fall in the scales of the present. The signifiers are both found related in the here and now: their historical reference is retrospective and is contingent upon the possibilities offered by the system of signification. But this synchronic approach, suitable possibly for the analysis of myth, is not sufficient for the purposes of psychoanalysis. As has been argued by Green (1967), what is at stake in the work of interpretation of psychoanalysis is the charge that is given to the signifier in so far as it is barred, hidden, repressed from the play of signifiers available to the conscious subject. And the task is to reveal such signifiers. Without a concept guaranteeing a form of historical necessity, what method is open to the analyst, if not that offered by the analysand, namely, free association (Major 1977: 167ff.)?

But the sliding of the signifier, whomsoever it belongs to, must stop somewhere. Freud introduced the concept of the primal in order to accomplish this. Now, it is most significant that the primal signals the 'mythical' dimension of psychoanalysis, as Laplanche and Leclaire demonstrated with respect to primal repression (Laplanche and Leclaire 1961/1972), but obvious enough when we come to the anthropology of *Totem and Taboo*, with its primal father and primal horde, primal murder and primal meal. The concept of primal that Freud introduced entailed a set of events standing outside of an order of causality conceived of as a succession through time, and thus legitimated the concept of regression, not as the sliding back along a chronologically fixed developmental sequence, but as the insertion of an additional cause into an already constituted sequence of events, thus realigning what has already been laid down.[8] We will return to the problem of the primal, but for the moment we should return to the language of analysis.

The explicit emphasis in Lacan's work is less upon the philological reconstruction of a forgotten text than upon the rhetorical meanderings of a legal subject. When Freud referred to the 'internal' rules for the reconstruction of meanings—the interplay of terms within a text, the etymological chains that connect a given textual element with those significant terms that are not explicitly found in the text—Lacan shifts the emphasis on to the relation between the 'subject' of the text and the other ('reader'), on to the relation between the text and the Other. We can read his Schema L in this fashion, by substituting 'text' for 'ego' (*moi*) (*E* 548/193). Lacan points his prospective disciples towards the medieval *trivium* (grammar, rhetoric, dialectics) and, beyond those, to Quintilian (*E* 288/76), rather than to the etymologists and philologists of the nineteenth century, those, like Lazarus, Steinthal and Kleinpaul, who supplied the linguistic evidence for so many of the conclusions arrived at by Freud's disciples.

What does this difference in linguistic approach amount to? Essentially Lacan has shifted the ground of psychoanalysis from analysis to dialectics. Rhetoric is the natural language of the neurotic and the object of the analyst's free-floating attention. In contrast, in Freud's discussion of the structure of neurosis, we are confronted with a grammatical analysis rather than the rhetorical play the subject makes for the other, rather than the rhetorical ploy with which the subject fools the other. For example, the analysis of Schreber's memoirs centres around the sentence 'I love him' and its simple grammatical transformations. We find similar arguments in the paper ' "A child is being beaten" ' and in a set of examples I have discussed in Chapter IV of Forrester (1980), under the rubric of 'primal sentences'. With Freud, grammatical and syntactical complexity is an index of the functioning of the defences. True, when it is a question of what is *said* in analysis, Freud repairs to what we might call rhetoric, but the latter, significantly enough, is often described as a process of translation. The flight *into* language, so important a defence in many Freudian texts, confirms this: we have only to think of the bizarre spectre of Anna O., translating her neurosis into English hymns, or the 'foreign' word behind which the Wolf-man hides when the screen memory of the wasp is beginning to wear a little thin, or the transformation that a simple defiant sentence, structured by the law of the talion, undergoes in the interpretation of a dream of Freud's: from *Ich habe ihn gelagt, weil er mich gelagt hat* (*SE* v: 484) to *Ote-toi que je m'y mette*. [9] But for Freud the *structure* of the neurosis as established by analysis is that of a transformed grammar. The deformations of morphology and syntax that go under the name of dialect will supply a further metaphor with which to clarify the relations of terms requiring translation. All such analysis will pertain to the structure of language and not to the structure of speech. We are reminded of Lacan's statement that the unconscious is structured like a language (*langage*); perhaps we should add '. . . and not like either *parole* or *langue*'.

Lacan, on the other hand, in contradistinction to Freud, is more concerned to articulate the structure of the analytic discourse, rather than the structure of the neurosis that can be derived from it. The two founding metaphors of his system illustrate this. The first, corresponding to the level of grammar in Freud, is the specular metaphor, which is concerned to structure the layers of images under which the subject *qua* 'optical subject' covers itself, and whose spatial arrangement will be laid out in the time of transference. The second metaphor, again spatial in character, is much more difficult to summarise. Its starting-point is a question: 'From where and to whom/where does the subject speak?' Its assumptions include the declaration of intent: 'I shall show that there is no speech without a reply, even if it is met only with silence, provided that it has an auditor; this is the heart of its function in analysis' (*E* 247/40).

It is the relation, on the one hand, of the subject to its speech, and, on the other hand, of the relation of the subject to the Other, that Lacan is concerned to set out in his increasingly complex and abstract topological models. But it is the emphasis, not to be found in Freud, on the speech of the analysand that distinguishes Lacan's theory. The latter revolves around a rhetoric that is *spoken*: Freud's theory centres upon the analysis of speech that was not spoken but is nevertheless still language. In Freud the key is analysis: in Lacan the object is dialectical. In Freud we are presented with a grammar of relations, between subject and symptom; in Lacan we are to follow a rhetoric of the subject in its relations with the Other.

In fact, Wilhelm Reich, in his study of character analysis, forms the middle term between Freud and Lacan, despite his deviation from the ideals presented by both. As Pontalis points out (1965: 20) Reich showed that there is no structural difference between symptoms and character-traits; they both gain their meaning from the unconscious in the same way. Reich recommended that these traits be taken as the starting-point of analysis, otherwise the same resistance that stems from the character-trait will appear, whatever the 'facet' of the neurosis under analysis. Now Lacan takes this one step further: we must not stop at the character-trait, but take the speech of the analysand as the object of analysis, even that speech whose movement from the empty to the full word will indicate the progress of the cure.

Now, perhaps this is not surprising: didn't Freud say much the same in 1900: *Was immer die Fortsetzung der Arbeit stört, ist ein Widerstand.* ('Whatever disrupts the continuity of the work is a resistance' (translation modified)) (*SE* v: 517)? All we have to do is extend this concept so that the structuration of chains of signifiers indicates the form of neurosis. Indeed, this would be one way of characterising Lacan's theory: the resistance is manifested in the speech of the patient. But we are not yet radical enough. Such a position might still be compatible with a grammatical rather than rhetorical analysis of desire. Safouan recognises this in a most interesting note:

> What distinguishes Lacanian theory is that, in showing the essential dependance of desire on the signifier, the signifier thus imposing, from the beginning, its structure, in so far as it is, in its very nature, the signifier of an absence, we hold desire to be a formation which is born in a constitutive sublimation. (1968: 273n2)

Lacan asserts that desire itself is structured by the signifier from its origin. We can no longer think of the character-trait or the symptom as the bodily articulation of a desire which was there *before* it failed to be spoken and thus lapsed to the level of language.[10] Even such an analytic device, so familiar from Freud's writings, threatens to deflect the focus from the speech of the analysand—its dialectical movement, rather than its analytical reference. The progression from the cathartic cure of the *Studies on Hysteria* to the method of free association takes on a new importance. The move consisted in shifting from an analytic preoccupation with the meaning of a symptom—even if this was not always conceived of in a 'mechanistic' and universalistic manner by Freud, but which, as the *Studies* had witnessed, was founded upon the words spoken by the patient— to a dialectical appreciation of the movement of speech, it being taken for granted that the 'solution' to the question represented by the symptom will somehow or other—perhaps automatically—

'drop out' of the discourse. The psychoanalytic method thus became dialectical, while its theory and its explanation of the structure of a symptom or a neurosis, remained analytic. Thus a tension arose between a grammar and a rhetoric, a tension that seems resolvable only either by formalising the rhetoric as a grammar of speech, or by showing that the grammar of a language is only the first stage in the elaboration of its rhetoric. Either path seems doomed to failure.[11]

There is one theme arising out of what I have said so far that I wish to pursue at some length: the idea that desire is itself structured in an original sublimation. If, as seems plausible, this is the fundamental novelty of Lacan's position, it will probably lead us to the central problem of that theory. Hence, to desire. It is a curious feature of Lacanian concepts that they never stand alone. Once they have been defined, amidst some of the most awe-inspiring qualification, syntactical complexity and ambiguity that it has ever been the good fortune of addicts of the word to encounter, thay are immediately covered over by the interpretation and mutual articulation of related concepts. For example, each of the three concepts 'need', 'demand' and 'desire' never stand by themselves: they only stand in relation to one another. Of course, this has a tactical, maybe even a strategic, value: namely, the avoidance of reference to origins and, in the case of need, demand and desire, the mediation of all reference to biology. But the problem lies not only with biology. It adheres to the continual tendency for psychoanalysis to found its key concepts 'in another place'—in an adjacent science, whether that be biology (*Beyond the Pleasure Principle*), physiology (the theory of stimuli of the *Project for a Scientific Psychology*) (*SE* I: 295–397), anthropology (the murder of the primal father), philology (the primal language), or biochemistry (the 'primal' sexual substances). It is *all* of these extra-territorial references that Lacan would deny. Freud signalled the support he sought from these other sciences by the concept—or the prefix—'primal' (*Ur-*).[12] But he looked not only for support for his concepts, a support which we might compare with that which Lacan requires of structural linguistics and anthropology. As we have seen, Freud hoped to stop the unlooked-for sliding of meaning to which his method gave rise. The discussion of the reality of the *Urphantasie*[13] of the Wolf-man indicates the criteria of architectonic simplicity and fixity that the *Ur-* was intended to secure. The *Ur-* marks the centre of a structure of signifiers that restricts or neutralises the free play of the structure, that marks a point where it is no longer possible to substitute any other element than that which occupies that place (cf. Derrida 1967: 409–10). It is part of the critique of biological thought in psychoanalysis that Lacan puts into motion to deny any privileged status to signifiers derived directly from the series of sexual zones and stages, even though these form the necessary equipment of psychoanalysts, Lacanian or otherwise. The words 'suck' or 'shit' have no special significance for the analyst, unless he seeks to make a fetish out of a word, unless he intends to deprive these words of the privilege that is afforded to them in being words rather than things—that is, of having multiple reference.[14] And if we combine them into a phrase—'suck shit'—we are immediately aware that biology has been shown out of the back door: we are in the realm of the imaginary, a realm made possible by the combinatory power of the signifier (cf. Safouan 1968: 282).

The aim of such a critique is to prevent the reduction of an analysand's discourse to being simply the second-order derivative of a constitutional anality. The critique aims firstly at preventing such reductionism within the method of interpretation, and, secondly, it aims to prevent certain theoretical terms, seemingly borrowed from a domain more 'scientific' than the word-games practised by psychoanalysis, from acting as a temptation to such a reduction. The first part of this critique bears upon the mechanical character that psychoanalysis so often takes on when it puts faith in stock interpretations or stock concepts: the interpreting machine, the translation machine and even the influencing machine of Tausk are indications of this mechanical tendency.[15] But we may well ask whether the second part of the critique, which attempts to deprive the theory of psychoanalysis of all theoretically privileged points, can possibly succeed. Is it possible to acquiesce in the free play of a system without a centre, without a locus into which it is forbidden to place any other term save one?

Certainly Freud's concept of the primal performs the function of such a centre, even if the famous instincts do not afford such a direct entry into the world of symbols as has been claimed for them by Reich or Groddeck (cf. Tort 1974). In the *Project* of 1895 and in *The Interpretation of Dreams*, the primary process, the most important source for the boundary that the concept of primal lays down, hinged around the concept of perceptual identity, that is, 'a repetition of the perception which was linked with the satisfaction of the need' (*SE* v: 556). We note the introduction of the concept of repetition, which places a gap in time—indeed this gap is unbridgeable—between the original perception and its repetition. In the development of the secondary processes—and for simplicity's sake I shall treat these as synonymous with the development of language—the word intervenes between the original perception—the *Urwahrnehmung*—and the searched-for perception. Now to what does this word refer: to the image that has been renounced in the 'present'? Or to the image that was lost forever but is the ground upon which the word can be formed?

On the one hand, the word stands for the object that is searched for and renounced. On the other hand, the word is a monument to a past satisfaction—to the lost object. The differential emphasis between these two is an index of the course of analysis: from the mourning over the lost object to the renunciation of the object towards which the subject's desire propels him. What the concept of regression in language led to was a point in the past when a word was located in the flesh, the mythical origin of language. The compulsive etymologising of psychoanalysis led to the primary units for the determination of the drives, in whose service the words are spoken. There is no gulf between this theory and the theory of symbolism that Jones set out in 1916, when he showed that the origin of all symbols lies in certain limited themes, those of the body, love, life and death (Jones 1918: 129–86). Lacan and Freud agree at this point that the problem of language and the problem of the symbol admit of the same solution, since symbolism owes its origins to previous states of language, or to a regression from conscious verbality.[16] But it is more in the style of Freud to pursue etymologies, believing that they take one closer to that point where the word is made flesh.

Perhaps the problem here *is* the same as that found in the concept of the instinctual representative, which cannot be totally included within the field of language without leaving language hanging in suspense waiting for the pure energy of sexuality to activate it. Does Lacan avoid such problems by discarding the set of imaginary supports that Freud drew upon? In their place he inserts another founding origin: the key-signifier. The signifier precedes the signified, signifiers anteceding the effect of the event, determining a pre-structure that is always inaccessible to the subject, but which can be constructed, one presumes, in the form of a primal scene. Now it is precisely these signifiers that the etymologist is going in search of. And it seems to make little difference if one finds them in the individual or in the history of language. Whether it is a question of phantasy or myth—and psychoanalysis has never deigned to separate these two—the word precedes and determines their structure. Perhaps this boils down to saying that in the word was the beginning.

The concept of key-signifier can be given its due weight as founding cause of the neurosis without necessarily inserting it as cause from outside the system of signifiers. All one has to do is to give to an element of arbitrary choice—in the sense of a random sifting of an indefinite number of signifiers into a pre-formed triadic structure—a place in the determination of neurosis.[17] But in the Lacanian theory, as it developed from its earlier preoccupation with the imaginary to a topology of the symbolic (from the metaphor of the subject as 'eye' to the metaphor of subject as speaker), one element comes to take on more and more importance. I refer to the phallus. And it is this symbol that ties the Lacanian system down, with a 'centre' that allows no other element but the phallus to fill a lack, of which the phallus is the privileged signifier. Let us just survey, briefly and telegraphically, the functions of the phallus.

First, the phallus introduces the infant to desire through its perception of the mother's desire of the phallus. This appears to be the privileged moment of perception for the child, in which it is introduced to its 'lack to be'.

Second, the phallus is the signifier of the signifiers: it represents the general functions of language: 'The phallus is the signifier of this *Aufhebung* (the raising of the signifiable to the function of the signifier) itself, which it inaugurates (initiates) by its disappearance' (*E* 692/287).

Third, the phallus is the key term in the passage 'across' the two great questions that the child is presented with, the two questions which the Oedipus complex codifies: where do babies come from? and what is the difference between the sexes? That the codification of the Oedipus complex takes place around these two questions highlights the historical fact that Freud developed the concept of the Oedipus complex from two sources: the sexual theories of children and the family romance.[18] The centrality of the phallus in the entry into the Oedipus complex is simply a reformulation of the concept of the phallic stage and the clinical arguments of 'Analysis Terminable and Interminable', found distilled in some notes Freud left at his death (*SE* xxiii: 299–300), concerning the fundamental stumbling-block to analysis: the 'being' and 'having' of the phallus (the homosexual position and penis-envy). 'Being' and 'having' represent the intersection of the grammer of the subject with its veiled signification. But it is the phallus that forms the privileged object of these two verbs. Why?

It can be said that this signifier is chosen because it is the most tangible element in the real of sexual copulation, and also the most symbolic in the literal (typographical) sense of the term, since it is equivalent there to the (logical) copula. It might also be said that, by virtue of its turgidity, it is the image of the vital flow as it is transmitted in generation. (*E* 692/287)

We cannot help but be reminded of Franz Bopp's attempt to prove that all verbs in the Indo-European family of languages derive from an original 'copula'—*s*. The phallus thus receives its determination at all three levels: the real, the imaginary (in a manner that reminds us of Stekel's cavalier use of symbols) and the symbolic, in a mode that would have appealed to the etymologising tendency of Freud (see 'The Antithetical Meaning of Primal Words' (*SE* XI: 153–61)).

The emphasis on the phallus as the only object constituted in such a privileged manner—so privileged that it is *the* 'signifier intended to designate as a whole the effects of the signified, in that the signifier conditions them by its presence as a signifier' (*E* 690/285), it is 'where the subject identifies with itself as a living being' (*E* 552/ 196, 'où le sujet s'identifie avec son être de vivant')—is co-extensive with another Lacanian position: the vigorous denial of the viability of a psychoanalysis of pre-Oedipal 'object-relations' (*E* 554/197).[19] All the terms of analysis will take up their positions through the retroaction of the Oedipus complex, whose structure is determined by the exchange of the phallus, that of a lack. When the child enters into the relation between mother and father, it encounters a relation which has *already prepared* the place that it is to occupy, as signifier of a lack (for the mother). The 'ready-made' character of the place of the infant explains the perpetual fascination for analysts of the seduction theory. We find the action of this fascination in Ferenczi's classic paper 'Confusion of Tongues between Adults and Children' (1955: 156–67), which attempted to revive not only the theory of seduction, under the guise of a confusion of desires, but also the concept of the lie, a concept to which we shall return.

What Lacan's theory thus necessitates is the child's *direct recognition* that it *is* the desire of the mother—it is the phallus. (Or not, as the case may be.) It is this recognition upon which is founded its want-to-be (whatever that may be). Once this structure has been established between mother and child, the Oedipus complex is ready to be laid over itself. The phallus is thus the crucial term in Lacan's psychoanalytic theory[20], so crucial that he can build a theory of psychosis (foreclosure of the Name of the Father due to a 'disturbance' of the fastening of the subject under its signifier the phallus) (*E* 553/197), a theory of perversion (Safouan 1968: 275), and a theory of neurosis (the capture or imprisonment of the object to whom a desire is addressed as a question, a question which will ultimately turn around 'the assumption by man (*Mensch*) of his sex' (*E* 685/281), an object that will ultimately refer to the signifier of signifiers, the phallus) around the central lack that the (veiled) phallus covers over.

The phallus is the means by which sex is introduced into a theory that, as long as it remained either a theory of the imaginary or a theory of the Symbolic, had only a contingent relation to that sexual preoccupation which, no matter how one can explain it (away), characterises Freudian psychoanalysis. In fact, if we retrace our steps, we find that it is through the introduction of the phallus that Lacan makes of his theory something more than a rereading of philosophical problems. If the relation of the phallus to the dialectic of 'having' and 'being' is not affirmed and reaffirmed, his system would be philosophy, rather than a recognisable version of psychoanalysis. Thus we can understand the extraordinary scorn, reminiscent of Freud, in which he holds philosophy, when being asked exclusively philosophical questions concerning the subject and consciousness. Lacan's response to such questions is to assert that it is the *resistance of the body to castration* that is the most important concomitant of the division of the subject.[21]

I think we have established the centrality of the concept of the phallus in Lacan's reworking of psychoanalysis. Now let us return to Freud's theory. Firstly Lacan's phallicism facilitates a step forward in the understanding of the development of psychoanalysis. In the period from 1907 to the First World War Freud argued that the first and most important question for the child is: Where do babies come from? (We could re-interpret this, in the light of the aggressive relation to the other baby that emerges when a new baby absorbs the mother's attention, as a question: Where do I (of the mirror-phase) come from?) In contrast, in the 1920s, Freud was emphatic that the first question was: What is the difference between the sexes? This second question tallies well with Lacan's theory: the question (of being) that is presented to all, from the moment of their entry into the Symbolic, is that of their relation to the phallus. But what are we to make of Freud's first position: why is that question important? Can we just subsume it within the realm of the Imaginary, in which the relation to the Other, one's unsexed fellow being, is dominant? In other words, in Lacanian terms, can we redescribe Freud's development as being one in which he mistook the Imaginary for the Symbolic in the period 1905–12, in the same way as he took the Imaginary to be real in the period 1895–7 (the seduction theory)?

If we bring other facts into view this historical hypothesis becomes clearer. For instance, Freud's preoccupation with the sexual theories of children (How are babies born?) and the family romances of neurotics (How can I be big like my parents?) would be evidence of his mapping out of the realm of the Imaginary. His battle with Adler's conception of the couple 'inferior/superior' would also correspond with a preoccupation with the material generated in the imaginary play of the mirror, culminating in the theory of narcissism, which put paid to both Adler's and Jung's theories by laying the foundations for a theory of the ego as an imaginary construct. So far the hypothesis works well. The next set of facts supports it even better. Elsewhere, I have argued that the Oedipus complex was not discovered by Freud until *c*. 1910, in contradiction of most accounts, which refer to the Fliess letters and *The Interpretation of Dreams*, with their references to the Oedipus theme, and thus date its discovery in the period 1897–1900. Part of the evidence for this depends upon Freud's preoccupations and the papers he wrote in the period that I have already mentioned. But there are two other arguments that bear here: Firstly, Freud's realisation that all neuroses stem from various 'transformations' of one 'nuclear complex'; secondly, an awareness that myths and anthropological data can both be explained as permutations of the same universal theme. It is not only *Totem and Taboo* (1912–13) that bears witness to this second argument, but also the theory of family romances and Rank's two books, *The Myth of the Birth of the Hero* and *The Incest-Theme* . . . What these discoveries of the period 1908–14 effect in psychoanalysis is clear: reduction of the possible primary explanations of neurosis. The reduction continued throughout Freud's later work, concluding with the paper often quoted by Lacan, in which Freud brings the problem of neurosis down to the tenacity with which men resist the deprivation of the penis implied by the 'feminine' attitude to their fathers, and women resist the finality of their deprivation of the penis that they expect to receive. We have a strange juxtaposition: the course of analysis opens up a series of significations that had only been dreamt of before, only for the development of theory to restrict once again this field, in the name of explanatory simplicity. [22] The strange equations and over-determinations of Freud's early case-histories—a suitable example would be the phantasy of sucking a penis analysed in Dora's case-history—must be trimmed, cut, simplified until a universal rock-bottom is attained. At the level of the theory of sexuality the movement is even stranger. Freud's discovery that the sexual is not restricted to the genital opened up the whole range of phantasies and explanations derived from non-genital erogenous zones. But, after forty years, in the final analysis, it is the penis that takes the centre of the neurotic stage once again. One way of reading Lacan is thus as follows: he brings to fruition this last conception of Freud's, and does so to the extent of re-interpreting the whole theory of the erogenous zones and the stages of the development of the libido in the light of a phallic supremacy that restricts these stages to being little more than dialects of a language that will and always does have 'in-tersubjective' precedence. Lacan closes again the road to the 'real' world of childhood, the world to which Freud thought he had gained access: the demands of anal and oral satisfaction—which may have existed in reality but for that very reason are of no concern to the psychoanalyst—are only imaginary detours to a con-frontation with the Symbolic and the Signifier of signifiers. For reasons that arise from a reading of Freud and the practice of analysis, Lacan returns its theory to a genital supremacy—and a male genital supremacy at that.

Now the value of Lacan's conception that desire is 'already' articulated by the signifier in an original sublimation is that it refers all questions of desire to the symbolic phallus (the phallus, not the penis), the Name of the Father (not 'the father'), and a death that is metaphorical in the sense that a biological death will not bring to a close the waiting for death that pervades the life of the obsessional neurotic (cf. the Ratman case-history). Desire does not have to be further transformed in order to 'attain' to the level of the symbolic phallus; it is already at that level, since the phallus and desire come into being 'at the same moment'. To place both the phallus and desire together at the origin, as original products of sublimation, places the concept of sublimation at the very heart of psychoanalysis, rather than at the horizon of analysis, as the boundary concerning which the analyst finds it impossible to say more (as it is in Anna Freud's *Das Ich und die Abwehrmechanismen* (1936/1968)).

Let us recall Freud s two examples of sublimation: the arts and the sciences. It seems now that there was more to this taste for the intellectual than the ideal of the nineteenth-century bourgeois. The field of activity of the arts and the sciences is the Symbolic. The arts are certainly recognisable in this description. But to perceive the sciences in this manner involves a certain philosophy of science. It is in this respect that Lacan and Freud would appear to differ markedly. Lacan's theory of science owes much to Gaston Bachelard and Alexandre Koyré. In particular, we recognise Bachelard's emphasis on the *expulsion* of reality from the field of science, to be replaced by the construction of a theory which will be the more 'scientific' the more it is a mathematised set of relations between the constructed objects of that science: '. . . even if experimental science derives its exactitude from mathematics its relation to nature does not remain any less problematic . . . it is clear that our physics is simply a mental fabrication whose instrument is the mathematical symbol' (*E* 286/74).

A mental fabrication: a thought that has been placed, not only on a par with the senses, but has precedence over them, since it is one of the functions of the symbolic universe of science—of its material environment as well as of its technical extensions—to remind its practitioners that their activities have very little to do with reality, despite the protestations of neo-positivistic apologues, who take up a position opposite to that upon which the formalisations of the logical positivists were based, namely, the unbridgeable distance between theory and observation. If we place Lacan's theory of the phallus besides the theory of the necessary foreclusion of the real in the production of thought (*E* 874–5) we shall find that the following footnote from the Ratman case-history, tucked away almost as an after-thought, takes on the greatest significance. Perhaps it also indicates that Freud's philosophy of science was not as simple as has often been made out:

As Lichtenberg says, 'An astronomer knows whether the moon is inhabited or not with about as much certainty as he knows who was his father, but not with so much certainty as he knows who was his mother.' A great advance was made in civilisation when men decided to put their inferences upon a level with the testimony of their senses and to make the step from matriarchy to patriarchy. (*SE* x: 233)

In *Moses and Monotheism*, Freud made it absolutely clear that the 'hominization' of man is made possible by the acquisition of a second 'reality': the mnemic residues of speech allow thought to be placed on the same level as perception (*SE* xxiii: 97ff.). Lacan's theory of the relations between the Symbolic and the Real are indicated in these passages, as they are by two metapsychological theses that Freud laid down:

(1) memory and consciousness are mutually exclusive;
(2) concepts arise *instead of* perceptions (*SE* vi: 134n2).[23]

We can now see more clearly the connection between Freud's unspecified concept of sublimation and Lacan's theory of the Symbolic, with its regal inhabitant, the phallus, and its dimension of desire. I will cite two specific instances of sublimation in order to clarify further its relation to the Symbolic. The first instance is that of Senatspräsident Schreber, whose paranoiacally constructed religious universe was the degraded and distorted version of a wealth of sublimations represented by his juridical 'universe': '. . . the hierarchy of God, the proved souls, the forecourts of heaven, the lower and the upper God' (*SE* xii: 73). The legal world is dedicated to the elaboration of a formal symbolism—categories made universal by definition—and to the articulation of a rhetoric and a dialectic upon that symbolism, which aims at the 'whole truth and nothing but the truth'. A new truth that will make possible an act as purely symbolic as the execution of a member of society by a masked representative of that society; a person will be ordered to return to the place from whence he came.

The second example is to be found at the inception of psychoanalysis. It is the process by which a project that was to 'represent psychical processes as quantitatively determinate states of specifiable material particles' (*SE* i: 245) became a psychology that had no reference to material particles. The passage from the *Project* to Chapter vii of *The Interpretation of Dreams* marks the process of sublimation by which a little piece of reality was denied, foreclosed from the real and made to appear in the Symbolic. It happens before our eyes when we read the *Project*: the neurone becomes an idea. This example indicates to us that it is not a question of reality for science and sublimation; the reality of the brain had to be repudiated before the theory of psychoanalysis was elaborated. In science it is a question not of reality but of truth. With a discussion of this topic I will bring this article to a close.

Sandor Ferenczi had a patient who failed to come to a session one day (Ferenczi 1955: 77–86). The next day Ferenczi asked him why, and the patient strenuously denied that he had not come. After a mutual investigation, they agreed that he had failed to come, but had forgotten that he had not come. But not only had he forgotten that non-event, but he had also forgotten all the things that he *had* done during the day. Slowly they reconstructed a day full of various forbidden activities. Ferenczi classified the patient as a case of split personality, and in so doing realised that for the duration of the analysis the patient had revealed only one side of his personality to the analyst. Another way of putting this was to say that the patient suffered from unconscious mendacity . . . Indeed, Ferenczi eventually explained the patient's acts as being in the service of the compulsion to lie: his split personality represented a desire to lie. Lie built upon lie: his adult lying corresponded to his childhood lying, itself a response to the adult lying to which the child had been subjected. The topic of sexuality lies at the heart of the adult lies. The sexual lies at the core of the mendacity.

But mendacity can be of two kinds, both illustrated by Ferenczi's patient. The first is the lie of silence—the 'hollow of being', the *béance* that figures so much in Lacan's prose—the absence of the patient is the first signifier of mendacity. That this absence appears as part of the psychopathology of everyday life only indicates that the parapraxis lies on a continuum which includes both the lie and the hysterical malingering that elicited so much self-righteous indignation from the men of science of the nineteenth century. The second variety of mendacity is the lie that is spoken without knowing it: unconscious mendacity or unconscious bad faith. And it would appear phenomenologically accurate that the sign of such an experience of unconscious mendacity will be the ever-deepening conviction of truth. It is one of the most important dimensions of psychoanalysis to recognise that the lie opens the way more fully to the truth. As Lacan argues in one of his most stimulating seminars:

> the sign can only present and sustain itself in the dimension of truth. Because, while deceitful, speech affirms itself as true. So for those who listen. For those who speak, first and

foremost deceit demands the support of that truth which it is a question of dissimulating, and, as it develops itself, it supposes a veritable deepening of the truth, to which, if one can say it, it replies. (*Le Séminaire* 1: 289; cf. also 254)

From such a lie one can infer the operation of a 'good memory'—and, as the lie deepens, it brings closer the moment when it will suddenly swing over into a new truth. Such is the course of events to which psychoanalysis both witnesses and trusts.

Of course, what is at stake is the gift of the word, of knowledge. And this is true for the sexual lie, the first lie of the *Project*, often closely connected, as Ferenczi hoped to demonstrate, with the sexual lies that children 'hear'. But this gift has a curious dynamic. In order to know that someone is lying one has to know that the truth is different from that which they say it is; one has to know the truth to know the lie. Of course we could construct more sophisticated models of this process: the consistency theory of truth would lessen the starkness of this statement. But from this paradox arises the peculiar position of the 'facts of life' in psychoanalytical theory. Sexual enlightenment—and the allusion to an eighteenth-century epistemology is clear in both Freud and Lacan—is the central problem for the child. And yet there is no hint that telling a person the truth can yield the state that transcends neurosis. Only the avoidance of truth, the lie, can be explored. The facts of life are as simple and as straightforward as any fact about human beings. And yet there is always a gap between the fact and the knowledge of the fact, the same distance as is marked by Lacan's distinction between the penis and the phallus. For Freud truth would seem to be a simple affair; there are no doubts or questions in his mind about its unequivocal relation to knowledge. Lacan is less unequivocal: there is no resolution, no halt in the questioning of the illusions that are lived by all. True, this is no essential change, but simply a shift in emphasis, parallel to the shift in emphasis from the determination of the signifier by its reference to its determination by its structural relations. Where Lacan arrogantly points the finger at the subject, ironically calling its bluff with cruel tools of mystification, Freud would shrug his shoulders, muttering about the folly of mankind, and hand down to the disciple an empty tablet. The fatal ambiguity in the status of the word—its dual function as sign and as image—perhaps allowed the function of that tablet to become hypostatised. If Lacan is persuaded that the first function of the psychoanalytical theorist now is to remove all holy images from the texts that psychoanalysts hand down to their analysands, then his project becomes more explicable. But the fact that many of his formulations have become catechisms to ward off the dangers of thought indicates the failure of his pedagogy. The Name of Lacan has become just as seductive as any of the more casual images around which people coagulate their hope and fears.

Lacan claims that he has tried to restore irony to its rightful place as the means for continually subverting social relations. Psychoanalysis had lost the ironic edge that gave it power to restore the human right—an inalienable right to alienate truth from the real—to mask and reveal with the same words. The paragon of irony, we should remember, was Socrates, who would both dissimulate and simulate through his simulation of the person who does not know and who thus passes as wise. Wise because he knows that he does not know, or because he does not know that he knows? Is it always the practice of wisdom to ask questions that mutilate themselves in their silent answers? To pick a question at random from Wittgenstein's *Philosophical Investigations*—a book that over-flows with questions that annihilate their own answers, by a thinker whose work bears remarkable similarities to that of Lacan: 'Are we perhaps over-hasty in our assumption that the smile of an unweaned infant is not a pretence?' (para. 249). After all, irony is but a pretence, a piece of mendacity that evokes a recognition of that fact in the other. And so we come back to the sexual lie, and the necessary process of enlightenment as to that upon which one cannot be enlightened since one already knows as much as it is possible to know, namely, nothing.

Let us transpose the context. When Jesus Christ said to humanity, 'Your sins are forgiven', he spoke from the locus of Death, the place that the analyst occupies, the place that Socrates occupies in the Dialogues, and the place that Wittgenstein prepared for himself and for philosophy. And to say, 'I forgive you' is to accede to that little death, the absence of desire, in giving what one cannot give—that is, in loving.[24] To the psychoanalyst, who is continually asked for forgiveness, and meets the demand with silence, the forgiveness that one receives from Christ only implicates one that much more in one's own sin. Perhaps the phrase 'all is forgiven' conjures up more clearly the irony that is involved here. Likewise with the popular refrain, 'we are all equally guilty', an equation that masquerades as a judgement, while obscuring the fact that the terms have already been divided by zero. Yet it would require the arrogance of Freud, when he called little Hans's neurosis his 'nonsense', to escape from the compulsion to construct a calculus of one's own guilt. Such, perhaps, is the arrogance that Freud and Lacan share.

On the ideological field, what brings Freud and Lacan together is their benign scepticism towards belief. Perhaps this is the sense in which psychoanalysts present the face of death to movements that attempt to bind their members together in the service of an idea. Even when confronted with oppression, the analyst replies with a denial, an ironic gesture. This philosophy has been called stoical, but its concrete manifestation is irony, which could be said to be the figure of speech upon which the philosophy is built, just as the aphorisms of Zen and Sufism take the form of the double bind. Such a philosophy is expressed most neatly and quietly in Freud's *The Future of an Illusion*, whose movement is one that passes from dogmatic assertion and anger, to a dignified indication of the irony of the whole project. After all, of which illusion is Freud talking: religion or psychoanalysis? He certainly supplies no answer. From there it does seem a small step from the recognition of the hardness of fate to the glorification of pain. It seems reasonable, using the scholarly apparatus, to redefine the psychoanalytic theory of consciousness as the state of the absence of orgasm. So much talking is a habit, a defence against pain. In the final analysis, one can become addicted to reality as easily as anything else. The Masters could agree that mankind cannot bear very much truth. And, with a curious reversal, a stubborn optimism is the residue of a philosophy of pessimism: the outrageous belief in science that Freud hoarded, the rhetoric of sublimation accorded to the dimension of truth and lies that language introduces for Lacan. One chooses Eros when one affirms the habit of loving, excising the mysterious fascination of masturbation, wherein one hoards all one's love in fantasy, only to find that love is the gift, a shifter, and not the thing itself. As Lacan says, masturbation is an intransitive verb. If we are not to lapse lyrical on the virtues of love, as seems necessary, since 'we know all that already', then we have recourse to the gift of the word, finding recourse in such arcane questions as concern laughing dogs, scheming babies or the facts of life.[25]

NOTES

1. A firm distinction between these terms was not drawn at the time. Cf. the wide scope of the term *Sprachwissenschaft*.

2. The historical change is captured neatly by the history of the name of a journal founded by Lazarus and Steinthal in 1860, and called *Zeitschrift für Völkerpsychologie und Sprachwissenschaft*, discontinued in 1890, and then revived by Thurnwald in 1925, with the new name *Zeitschrift für Völkerpsychologie und Soziologie*.

3. Retained as an important principle for diachronic linguistics by de Saussure; see *Course in General Linguistics* (1972: 223–4/1974: 162–3).

4. Cf. 'Negation' *SE* xix: 233–39. Also a case of Major's: '. . . she showed that *she didn't know that she knew*, a formula which implies that the repressed representation found its transcription in a mode of symbolisation' (Major 1977: 151).

5. Timpanaro makes some very interesting comments about the necessity for the hypothesis of the 'polyglot unconscious' in *The Freudian Slip* (1976: esp. 80–1, 90).

6. The retroactivation of meaning takes place upon two temporal levels: the first, by which meaning is read 'backwards' in language, perhaps depends upon the structure of grammar; the second, *Nachträglichkeit*, depends upon a more important temporal relation, standing outside of language and perhaps to be identified, as Freud did in the *Proton Hysteron* of the *Project for a Scientific Psychology*, with a biological time of maturation.

7. According to the principle, 'where there is a *Sprache*, there is a *Volk*'. See note 3 above.

8. Laplanche and Pontalis (1968: 9–10):

[Freud] invokes [primal realities] less in order to provide a reality which escapes him in individual history, than to assign limits to the 'imaginary' which cannot contain its own principles of organisation . . . However we should not be in a hurry to replace the phylogenetic explanation by a structural type of explanation . . . [The original fantasy] is characterised by certain traits which make it difficult to assimilate to a purely transcendental schema, even if it provides the possibility of experience.

9. Note that the French phrase, as quoted by Freud, is not idiomatically correct; it should read, *Ote-toi d'là, que je m'y mette*.

10. As I expressed myself in a previous discussion of Lacan's work, in the *Times Higher Educational Supplement*, 4 November 1977, p. 12.

11. Cf. Felman (1974: 42):

It would seem that Lacan's scientific programme is to reduce the rhetorical mystifications, by way of the unconscious, to the rigour of grammar. The unconscious as practice and psychoanalysis as science consequently model themselves on two different epistemologies and part company with each other in the same way as grammar differs from rhetoric.

As is obvious, I would characterise Lacan's treatment of rhetoric differently, but the tension still remains.

12. Cf. Green (1967: 367–8): 'Here we encounter once again the weaknesses of a strictly ontogenetic position, which . . . accords preeminence to the remotest and oldest. Primitive and primordial become equivalent. And one understands that the fascination of the German *Ur* . . . invited this conjunction.'

13. Not found in Freud as such; cf. Laplanche and Pontalis (1968).

14. The lack of privilege that Lacan affords to the words that take on a special place in Klein's theory, or in Ferenczi, can be gauged from his discussion of a dream analysed by Ella Sharpe. Sharpe's analysis made much of the explicit sexual references in the dream: 'her vagina gripped my finger' etc., and erected a set of 'Kleinian equations': mother's breast equals father's penis. Lacan circumscribes the importance of such terms and equations, preferring to take as the key point of the dream-text: 'One can say "I masturbated her" and that is correct but it is all wrong to use the word transitively,' a phrase that gives Lacan the opportunity to state: '. . . the whole of the dream analysis rests, according to us, on reestablishing the intransitivity of a verb' (1959–60: 330ff.).

15. Cf. Major (1977: 55ff.) on the interpreting machine; Besançon (1971:58) on the translating machine; Tausk (1933: 519–55) on the influencing machine.

16. Cf. Freud, letter to Jung dated 14 March 1911, 'Can you do anything with this formula: the symbol is an *ucs.* substitute for a *cs.* concept; symbol formation is the initial stage of concept formation, just as repression is the forerunner of judgement?' (Freud 1974: 405).

17. Cf. *Le Séminaire* I and the introduction to the seminar on the purloined letter (Lacan, 1956).

18. This point is documented in detail in Chapter III of Forrester (1980).

19. Cf. also the remarks in *Le Séminaire* I (95ff.) *vis-à-vis* Kleinian theory.

20. Leclaire (1966: 60):

Dr Leclaire stresses the importance of marking the necessity of a foundation (*butée*), which allows the analyst to orientate his evasive movement (*son mouvement de dérobement*) and to ground his choice. This foundation, must one look for it in biology, as Freud did, in the reality of seduction or of the primal scene? . . . An attempt will be made to show, in answer to this problem of foundation, that what must take its place (*tenir lieu*) is the phallic reference.

21. Lacan (1966b: 8):

It isn't to consciousness that the subject is condemned but to his or her body which resists in a multitude of ways the realisation of the division of the subject. That this resistance has served to house all sorts of errors (amongst them the soul) does't prevent this division from lodging effects of truth in the body, such as that which Freud discovered under the name to which his disciples still hesitate to assent: castration.

22. Lacan recognises this particular development in Freud's thought. Cf. Lacan (1956–7: 851): 'one must remember the central position of castration in Freud's thought—but it wasn't more than one key amongst others for him at the time of Little Hans.'

23. Note found in the margin of the 1904 edition of *The Psychopathology of Everyday Life*. These two theses concerning memory, consciousness and perception

are discussed at some length in Chapter IV, Section 1 of Forrester (1980).

24. Lacan (1956–7:604)'. . . when it comes down to it there is no greater sign of love than giving what one hasn't got.'

25. The earlier version of this paper, that read to the seminar, owed much to discussions with Nick Totton.

3 On Language and the Body*

PAUL HENRY

> What is massively, definitively absent is the body. Absent insofar as the body is that which does not lie, that which cannot itself represent, fictionalise itself. As is proved precisely by death and the sexual act. (Christian Zimmer, 'Comment meurt-on à l'écran? Un livre de Gérard Lenne', *Le Monde*, 26 June 1977.)

One of the most remarkable aspects of Chomsky's concept of competence is the transformation it introduces into the represen-tation of the relations between language and the body. By positing that something fundamental in language is not learnt, this concept freed linguistics from the behaviourism inherent in structuralism while at the same time opening the way to a systematic theory of syntax in linguistics, breaking with grammar and rhetoric. But Chomsky's undertaking has remained dominated by a basic psychological principle: in man, everything which is not learnt comes from the body. Chomsky speaks of the innate genetic bases of linguistic competence, conceives the latter as a 'mental organ'. In other words, it is in the guise of the psychological duality of body and mind that, even in Chomsky, linguistics meets the body. Paradoxically it seems nonetheless that it only thus meets it the better to be rid of it and to establish itself in the dimension of the subject, the dimension which is properly that of language. It is by proxy of the notion of knowledge (*savoir*) and more precisely of a knowledge supposed to lie in the body, at least in its foundations, that the autonomy and specificity of the concept of competence is speculatively guaranteed.

Linguistic competence is, to begin with, a knowledge which is set

---

* *Translated by Ben Brewster.*

to work, at a first level, to identify any verbal sequence as belonging or not belonging to *langue*. In other words, the question of this special knowledge is Why is *langue* as it is and not otherwise? (cf. Milner 1978). This has nothing to do with the body. All that underpins it is the fact that there is no possible language without the possibility of a demarcation between what belongs to *langue* and what does not. Although there is no assignable frontier demarcating that part of the 'verbal' which is related to *langue* and that which is not, nothing belongs to language if it has no relation to *langue* (cf. Henry 1977). This is a version of de Saussure's 'It is *langue* that constitutes the unity of language.' The definition of *langue* as simply constituting this unity makes it all the less amenable to any empirical registration, as Chomsky makes explicit when he speaks of 'linguistic intuition'. This just means that there is no *a priori* formal criterion enabling one to decide whether a verbal sequence belongs to *langue* or not. It is to say that *langue* escapes the order of representation, being confined to the order of what is only representable, at best representable. From here to making *langue* the object of a knowledge is but a step, precisely the step by which the concept of competence is formed.

But what is added to this by presupposing behind this knowledge an organic reality, by linking it to the body and speaking of a mental organ? On the one hand, it restores this knowledge to an order of representation, indeed, a very specific order of representation, the one in which there is no reality not relatable to the body. The idea of a 'mental organ' attests to a certain reality of the linguistic knowledge, a reality independent of 'intuition' and the subject. But one must admit that this reinscription in the order of representation and of reality remains purely speculative. It is meaningless as it contains no specification. To speak of the innate organic bases of competence is to state something about its being but nothing about its form. It has no implications from a linguistic point of view, and the idea that something might be deduced about *langue* from a knowledge (*connaissance*) of cerebral organisation remains a chimera. It is as much a chimera as to wish to deduce phonology from the physiology of phonation. In a certain manner, Chomsky's 'mental organ' is analogous in more than one respect with Descartes's 'pineal gland', despite all the studies of the anatomical locations and physiological processes at work in language activity. It is to wish to seek what is real about *langue* in the body and all that one can say is that it is not there.

This being so, what function does the organic reference for *langue* have? Precisely because it is meaningless, because it introduces no specification, it seems to be one of the most effective ways of resisting all reductionism, a much more effective way of attesting to what is real about *langue* than any other psychological or social specification of the subject of linguistic knowledge (*savoir*). For it is certainly the subject that is surreptitiously reintroduced by the organic reference, a subject reduced to the body, itself reduced to its anatomical, neurological and physiological reality. For Chomsky, the body is the unifying principle of the subject it represents, the subject of linguistic competence. An imaginary, organic unity, supported by the phantasies linked to the body, phantasies of the ego, of its irreducibly imaginary unity and identity. In other words, the body is the imaginary representative of the subject-ego in the theory of grammar and more widely in the Chomskyan theory of language. Beyond the phantasy, it is positivism which returns here in the form of the principle of a unitary language of science surpassing the psychological opposition between the bodily and the mental. To sum up, it is a matter at once of placing oneself in the field of science, the field dealing with the body as an organism, and of settling on behalf of linguistics a question which constantly recurs in it, that of the unity and identity of the speaking subject, the support of the unity of language.

From here we can measure how far apart are the point of view of the linguist, striving to contain language in a unity, an organic unity in this case, and that of psychoanalysis, for which only in phantasy could the body be a principle of unity and identity. Up to a point it can be said that for linguistics, too, the body is what is massively absent, all the more so in that it is referred to via a unitary representation which masks the fact that it is fragmented and full of gaps (*béance*). It remains to be seen why linguistics finds it so difficult to get rid of psychologism, why it appeals, almost irresistibly, to such representations of the body. It is not enough to invoke a positivism dominant in scientific practice. It must be realised that the place of this representation is inscribed in linguistics itself, in the form of questions which cannot be answered in it. Linguistics can ignore the body so long as the question of the unity and identity of the speaking subject does not re-emerge in it, so long as it can deal with *langue* and not with language. But we know that such questions do arise once the unity of language is lost, or, what amounts to the same thing, once the unity and identity of the speaking subject come into contradiction with the development of linguistic description, a distinction has to be made between 'subject of enunciation' and 'subject of the enounced'. The identification of the 'subject of enunciation' refers to the subject as a speaking being, not just as the support for a specific knowledge (*savoir*). The 'subject of enunciation' is the one who speaks in so far as he or she is different from any other subject, it is the subject in its unity and identity. This brings up questions about what the subject knows or does not know, about the reasons why he or she says this and not that, reasons which are no longer linguistic reasons at all, a knowledge (*savoir*) which is no longer the knowledge demarcating what belongs to *langue* and what does not. That reference to the body could be supposed to provide the support for a representation of the identity of the subject is, after all, the real problem. It presumes that within the representation of the body *langue* has been detached as a part, as a specific organ. All bodies are made up of different organs related to one another, but for all that each constitutes a unitary system, a whole, a unity of its parts, irreducibly different from any other body. Here the universal and the particular come into conjunction. But that *langue* could be conceived of as detached from the body, as a part on its own, 'a storehouse in the brains of individuals filled through their active use of speaking', as de Saussure put it, or as a specific mental organ, is not something which goes without saying.

The construction of this representation is the result of a historical process which has played an essential part in the development of linguistics: the constitution of national linguistic units. This seems to me to have been one of the historical preconditions for the emergence of linguistics as a science. The constitution of national linguistic units, which is not unconnected with the legal bases of the bourgeois states, led to the abandonment of a representation of *langue* with a privileged relation to the body, as the 'mother tongue', for a new representation of *langue* as the national language, part of the 'body' of the state and no longer of the body proper, replacing the various dialects which were still representatives of the original *langue*, of one's own tongue. This detachment of *langue* from the body, even if we must locate it entirely in the ideological register, was surely the necessary precondition for the development of a new approach to language which located *langue* in the mind rather than in the body. This is not affected by the fact that, since then, for the reasons given above, or others, it does not much matter, attempts have been made to re-establish a link between language and the body. I would suggest that something of the corporeality of language was changed by that very fact, so that now this corporeality can only be thought indirectly, via representations that were worked out by biological science between 1750 and 1850.

If one wants to find out something about the corporeality of language now, one cannot turn to physiology, neurology or anatomy. All they can do is mask that corporeality, make the body seem even more absent from language. But the corporeality of language is attested by the whole analytic experience. This is all the more remarkable in so far as Freud's point of view was neurological, too, in so far as he, too, wanted to turn psychology into a natural science. Perhaps it is because Freud was quite peculiarly pre-occupied with death that he was brought to go beyond this point of view, without ever explicitly abandoning it. It was not so much sexuality as death that obsessed Freud, and that obsession forced on him a quite unique point of view on the body and language.

The uniqueness of this point of view is clear once we look at his characterisation of unconscious desire as eternal and indestructible. Such a desire cannot find a place in a biological representation of the body. And we know that the eternity of unconscious desire, its indestructibility, the irremediably lost character of its object, are the core of the death drive, and that the latter attests to the corporeality of language. I say *corporeality* of language rather than talking of language's hold on the body or the presence of the body in language, which would still be to think of the body and language as dissociated. If one accepts that death, along with sexuality, is what escapes representation in the body, one must take the consequences and accept that, in death as in sexuality, body and language cease to be dissociable. What Lacan is stating when he says there is no such thing as a 'sexual relationship' (*rapport sexuel*) is precisely that sexuality escapes representation, which presupposes the production of a difference within a relationship (cf. *Le Séminaire* xx: 49–59; Heath 1978: 59, 63). In doing so he has added to Freud's main proposition about death by insisting, not so much on the dimension of language, as on what he has identified as being that of the signifier. The signifier is not of the order of representation, being simply what is wanting in its place, pure difference, to use de Saussure's terms. From the point of view of the signifier, body and language are not dissociated. That Lacan insists nonetheless on the fact that the concept of the signifier derives from linguistics does not affect this.

4 Representation and Pleasure*

MOUSTAPHA SAFOUAN

To the question: how is the reality principle produced from its supposed opposite, the pleasure principle? Freud gave an answer which has become, as it were, an 'official version'. It can be summarised as follows.

At the beginning of existence, the psychical apparatus is subject only to the pleasure principle, which means not just that pleasure is the only aim it pursues, but also that only what is agreeable constitutes an object for it at all: for the apparatus does not just tend to discharge its tensions when the object is there, but also to hallucinate its presence in response to those very tensions. The discharge that occurs in this case unfailingly generates disappointment. From here on another principle comes into play, which is this: it is not enough that an *x* be agreeable for it to be constituted as an object; another property is required of the object, it must be real, an understandable enough condition. For if it is true that everything perceived is not real, if reference to perceptual exteriority is no longer sufficient to define the reality of the object, it is none the less the case that every real object is an object of perception, and that, assuming satisfaction does not fall from the sky, it is in the perceptual field that the subject has to recognise the real object. Thus a new faculty develops: that of attention, which is directed at the 'agreeable' in the suspicion that it may be no more than a lure, a hallucination. Information received from outside thus acquires as much importance as the internal sensations of pleasure or unpleasure. Then memory is added to attention: the characteristics of the object are not just observed but also recorded. It is precisely the

* *Translated by Ben Brewster.*

comparison between the characteristics of the real object retained in the memory and those of the object which now presents itself as the same but may only be a semblance, it is this comparison that determines what answer be given to the question: to wait or to wait no longer?—i.e. the question as to whether the apparently agreeable object is also truly satisfying, in other words, real, or not. This genesis of the reality principle presupposes that the apparatus is learning to arrest its primary tendency to discharge: the aim is no longer to reduce all tension to zero (pleasure at any price, so to speak) but to maintain constant or nearly constant a minimal energy level. Moreover, in so far as the human being, born prematurely in total impotence, becomes capable of performing the 'specific action' that introduces into the external world such changes as are necessary to find the object, discharge becomes action. This transformation is possible thanks to the intervention of thought as proleptic, experimental action, an action in miniature, as it were, which requires expenditure of only the minimum of energy held in reserve (one thinks of the child learning to cool its food before eating it). A substitution parallel with the one in which action replaces discharge is to be found in the fact that the mechanism of repression—the psychical apparatus immediately withdrawing cathexis from anything painful—is replaced by the function of judgement—which presupposes a certain tolerance for what is painful, until it has been decided whether the painful object is or is not useful with respect to the aim, which is to find the real object or bring about its presence.

Despite what might be called its 'popularity', this official version of the genesis of the reality principle out of the pleasure principle raises many objections, both logical and textual.

Logical ones first: for if it were only a question of describing an evolution, as seems to be Freud's aim, hallucinatory activity should disappear leaving no other trace but the dream—which is a phenomenon that occurs during sleep, i.e., when our relation to the outer world is very weak, and should therefore not seriously disturb our relation to that world. The general tendency to avoid unpleasure and seek pleasure would have to be considered a stifled tendency, since no one claims it goes so far as to make us project into the outer world what is not there, in other words, so far as to force us into hallucination in the psychiatric sense of the word. If this version were all we could get from Freud, he would by no means have described the loss of the function of the real, but on the contrary the path that leads to its *domination*, and we should have to locate ourselves in the midst of a human race of producers producing useful objects, objects answering to their needs.

The *textual* ones next: for as we read further in *Formulations on the Two Principles of Mental Functioning* we meet surprise after surprise. First we learn that thought, which has been presented to us as a result of the intervention of the reality principle, constitutes on the contrary the privileged field of our sexuality: the latter finds its 'satisfaction', if one can so express oneself, not in real objects but in phantasies. We then learn that what repression strikes is precisely these phantasies, which constitute the specific sources of our pleasure. Finally we learn that the reality principle is powerless here, that no reality test will correct these phantasies, which thus enjoy an undisputed sway over our existence and over our perception, since repression strikes them even before we have had time to recognise them. All these surprises can be summed up by saying that it is really in representation and not in hallucination that appetition finds its 'realisation' or even its primary object. But with such a claim, the meaning, if not the nature of pleasure itself changes. Let me explain.

According to the official, but misleading version of Freud's thought, unpleasure is the effect of the tension aroused in us by stimuli received from within our own bodies; i.e., needs. Only a real object is capable of reducing these tensions or satisfying the respective needs, and pleasure is the effect or sign of such satisfaction. These same tensions lead us to hallucinate only in so far as we find, or think we find, in our hallucinations such an object. For us, in principle, the object is a real object, even if it is not always real in fact; and it is in the order of the real that we seek it. As a result, in this perspective, pleasure is a 'pure' pleasure, a pleasure to be sought as unpleasure is to be avoided: there is no mixture of the two. In saying this I am not trying to rule out the existence of pleasures which lead to unpleasures, or unpleasures rewarded by pleasures; such possibilities are widely attested in experience and in no way inexplicable in the perspective that I have called the official version. On the contrary, I would go so far as to say that that version is designed to justify them. I use the term 'mixture' in the Platonic sense of the term: what is ruled out is the possibility that pleasure and unpleasure might partake of one another, that pleasure might also be unpleasure and unpleasure pleasure; for such a mixture would be as much as to mix fullness and void! But it is precisely this impossibility, this contradiction that I believe contains what can be called the secret of the pleasure principle for Freud. It is really the existence of this contradictory mixture that Freud affirmed when he affirmed the essential link between the appetition of the *Wunsch* and representation. To prove this we must examine more closely the nature of representation, or, more precisely, the nature of what the German language designates by the word *Vorstellung*.

This term has played a considerable part in German philosophy, endowing it with resonances to which Freud could not but have been responsive, if only because he attended the lectures of the man who launched this term on its career, Franz Brentano.

Brentano was looking for a property distinguishing mental phenomena from physical phenomena, and he found it in what the Scholastics called *inexsistentia*, which means not 'non-existence' but 'existence in', the existence of the object in the mind or as it presents itself to the mind, as the latter knows it and experiences it. Hence Gandillac's French translation of *inexsistentia* as *présence* is quite correct:

> Every mental phenomenon [wrote Brentano] is characterised by what the Scholastics of the Middle Ages called the intentional (or mental) inexistence (*die intentionale Inexistenz* in German, *la présence intentionnelle* in Gandillac's translation) of an object, and what we might call, though not wholly unambiguously, reference to a content, direction towards an object (which is not to be understood here as meaning a thing), or immanent objectivity (*die immanente Gegenständlichkeit*). (1973: 88; French translation 1944: 102)

It follows that, for Brentano, the task of psychology became to study the different ways in which the mind is directed towards the object, the different modes of intention (*intentio*). Brentano maintained that there can only be three of these: the most basic is *Vorstellung*, an untranslatable term of which 'idea' and 'representation' are inadequate renderings.[1] Every time we see a colour, hear a sound, construct an image or understand the meaning of a word, we experience a *Vorstellung* in Brentano's sense. Then comes judgement, which is distinguished from *Vorstellung* in that when we judge we accept something as true or reject it as false. Finally there is the phenomenon of love and hate, in which we accept something as good or reject it as bad.

Of these three kinds of experience, *Vorstellung* is logically the first in the sense that judging is judging something, just as loving or hating is loving or hating something.

These premises gave rise to a problem which is not unlike the age-old debate between realism and idealism (cf. Moreau 1958: 9). If consciousness is defined by intentionality as consciousness *of* something, of an object, must the object be defined by that very presence to the consciousness that the subject has of it, or is there beyond the immanent object the transcendent object, the thing in itself, outside that relation to consciousness?[2]

This question led some philosophers, notably Twardowski,[3] to distinguish between two terms: *Inhalt* and *Gegenstand*, which Brentano used indiscriminately to designate the 'something' which enjoys intentional presence in consciousness and towards which consciousness is directed. In fact, as Findlay emphasises (1963: 8), Twardowski was convinced, as was Mill, that when people use the word object independent of them and not of the *Vorstellung* or representation they have of it. But he reckoned that in order to go beyond ourselves in this way we have to form in our minds an image or sign of the object towards which we direct our thought, as there must also be a link (*Bindeglied*) which will make it possible for our idea to refer to one definite object and no other. Hence three things must be distinguished: (1) the representation (*Vorstellung*) as an act of consciousness; (2) the object presented to us by means of this act; and (3) the content which exists *in* our idea, and *through* which, as intermediary, the reference to the object takes place.

It is hard nowadays to accept the mediatory role thus attributed to the image; however, in order to sustain the distinction he had introduced between the image or content of a representation and its object, Twardowski invoked, among other arguments, one which is very important because of what Meinong then made of it. This argument can be summarised as follows: if someone utters a true judgement denying the existence of a given object (e.g. that of the winged horse Pegasus), he must have an idea of the object whose existence he denies. Hence the idea exists, whereas the object does not.

Once accepted by Meinong (1899), this argument led to a distinction between three sorts of non-existent objects: those whose non-existence is just an empirical fact, like golden mountains; those whose existence would imply a contradiction, such as the square circle; and lastly those which can be said to subsist (*bestehen*) but without existing in the manner of a tree or a horse, such as numbers and relations. According to Meinong, not only are there facts of non-existence, but those facts exist independently of thought. For example, it is a fact that no automobile vehicles existed in 1700, although no one at the time thought of this lack. This envelopment of existent objects by non-existent ones led Meinong to his doctrine of the 'pure object', pure in so far as it is sustained beyond being and non-being. This does not mean that it has neither being nor non-being, which would contradict the law of the excluded middle, but simply that the fact of being or not being has nothing to do with the object as object. Whether an object is or is not, that does not affect what it is; the roundness of the round square is not affected by its non-existence. It is in this sense that it can be said that the pure object is an *Ausserseiend* or possesses an *Aussersein*.

Despite its attractive character, this theory, which amounts to an affirmation of the principle of the independence of *So-sein* with respect to *Sein*, the principle according to which it is a fact that a round square is round, provoked serious objections, notably from Russell, who pointed out that this principle has the disadvantage of limiting the validity of logical principles. So, to overcome these objections, E. Mally, a student of Meinong's, proposed a theory which rejected the principle of the independence of *So-sein* with respect to *Sein*, and rested on a more rigorous analysis of the relation between the object and its determinations (1912). On the view of Mally every determination determines an object, but not every determination is satisfied (*erfüllt*) by an object. The determination 'being two-legged' determines the abstract determination 'biped', which is usually called a concept, but it is satisfied by nearly every human being. The object which satisfies a certain determination is really characterised by that determination, but the determinate of a certain determination need not really possess that determination. The round square is not really round, nor is it a square at all; the only properties it really possesses are those of being determined by a certain determination and by all its implications. The possession of these properties is, of course, not contrary to the laws of logic. Nor is it necessary to deny to the round square as a pure determinate every vestige of being; it is to be found among the formally possible combinations, but its determinations can never be satisfied. As Findlay remarks (1963: 112) with these modifications the whole notion of *Aussersein* changes; it is no longer a realm of full-blown objects unfortunately deprived of being, but something more nearly analogous to a space of points, which may or may not be occupied by actual objects. The round square is not really a round square but a locus in this space, concerning which we can say *a priori* that it will never be filled. The end result is thus the idea of a space made up of points which represent, in Mally's terminology, the 'determinates' in which we recognise, as Bentham would say, 'fictitious entities' which are produced only by the signifier and the combinations it authorises in its very nature as a signifier before reality comes into consideration at all. They are fictions which, as it were, come out of our mouths and settle in the space discussed by Mally, which space is in the last analysis that of discourse.

This recognition of the power of the signifier, a power which lies in the fact that it is the existence of language that constitutes the being of things (in the first place in the sense of being as a verb), surely enables us to solve the paradoxes about the existence of non-existent objects. Here we should recall Russell's response to the problem of non-being posed by Meinong:

> Being is that which belongs to every conceivable term, to every possible object of thought—in short to everything that can possibly occur in any propositions, true or false, and to all such propositions themselves. . . '*A* is not' implies that there is an *A* whose being is denied, and hence that *A* is . . . Numbers, the Homeric gods, relations, chimeras and four-dimensional spaces all have being, for if they were not entities of a kind, we could make no propositions about them. Thus being is a general attribute of everything, and to mention anything is to show that it is. *Existence*, on the contrary, is the prerogative of some only among beings. (Russell 1937: 449, my emphasis)

Now this response, which makes being an attribute of anything whatever or, in contradiction to Aristotle's view, makes everything whatever a subject of being, is based on a confusion. It is true in the sense that the *signifier* I write (or pronounce), the letter '*A*' must exist for me to be able to add '*is not*'; but it is false in the sense that the signification conveyed by it (if it has one) does not have to *be* in the same way. There is no contradiction in saying the unicorn *is not*, if by that I mean the figure summoned up when the word 'unicorn' is pronounced and not the word itself. In a word, the problem formulated since antiquity in the terms: 'Not being is not, since for me to be able to talk about it, it must be; but if it is, it is not non-being' is strictly speaking a fallacious one. For, far from a being (in the first place in the sense of being as a noun) having to *be* for me to be able to talk about it, I must first talk about it for the question whether an object exists which corresponds to or 'satisfies' what I say to arise.

It will perhaps be objected that this not always or necessarily the case, for after all, all objects are not unicorns, square circles or golden mountains; in what I say there are utterances (*paroles*) that so to speak take up words that could be said to be dictated by things themselves, words made to designate objects, and objects which really, physically, exist, words 'already satisfied', so to speak. Such as the sun—to go back to Twardowski and Stuart Mill. But it is not hard to fend off this objection, for, to maintain with Aristotle [4] and against the Sophists and Russell that being is not a universal attribute does not mean that nothing exists. But the existence of real things by no means implies, as this objection assumes, that language is made to designate them. A famous Egyptologist, Sir A. Gardner, took this conception to its ultimate conclusions, attempting to translate all the elements that constitute the parts of speech: prepositions, adverbs, adjectives, etc., in terms of nouns, since for him language had to reflect, or have originally reflected, individual substances (a house, a man, etc.). The forced character of the devices he had to employ to bend language to this designatory conception suffices to prove the literally meaningless nature of the attempt; for it amounts to a desire to remove meaning leaving only substances whereas these substances only *are* (i.e. can only be said to be) in so far as they inhabit language, just as man does. [5]

However, I can take advantage of the objection by noting that if, with Mill or Twardowski, one argues that someone who speaks of the sun is thinking of the real object that exists independently of his thought, that is to say that the discourse of the subject in question is subtended by that subject's belief in the existence of the sun and that it is in this very belief that the sun *is for the subject* before it exists in real space. This is so true that it sometimes happens that the subject is seized by a fear that the belief will be belied. Consider someone who, in relation to the question of induction, wonders: How can I be sure that the sun will rise tomorrow? In fact, who doubts the regular movement of the sun or the reliability of its habits? It is not the sun that is at issue here but the assertion that it will rise tomorrow too, in so far as that assertion postulates as such, as an assertion, some belief. This is not to deny the existence of the sun in real space; but real though it be, it does not exist for the sunflower. From which I draw these conclusions:

1. That of all the things in the world the signifier is the one whose real and material existence is the most certain, since without it there could be no question of existence or non-existence.

2. That discourse, in so far as it constitutes the concrete form in which the signifier exists, constitutes what Mally called a space of points or places.

3. That these places or *topoi* in which we recognise Mally's 'determinates' are things said, or things in so far as they are first of all things said, or are as yet no more than things said.

If we now agree that *Vorstellung* or 'representation' is the most appropriate term for these objects immanent to discourse and hence to consciousness, since consciousness is for Freud, in his *Project for a Scientific Psychology* (*SE* 1: 283–399) what is linked to utterances (*paroles*), it follows that in its ordinary sense the opposition between 'word representation' and 'thing representation' is an opposition based on the miscognition of the fact that 'it is the straw of the word which first bore the grain of the thing' as Lacan has elegantly put it.

If we remember further that representation is the domain dominated by the pleasure principle, i.e., if pleasure is already to be found in fictitious entities whose presence is strictly speaking the presence of absence, the deduction of the reality principle from the pleasure principle must be as difficult as that of the existence of God from its concept. Indeed, if this is so, what motive does the subject have for asking whether an object exists? Rather it constitutes a reason for not asking it. And if the truth of pleasure is that it is pleasure in absence, in other words in privation, does that mean that pleasure is unpleasure? An affirmative answer is unavoidable. Indeed, the question I have just raised is not unrelated to the one Plato put in Socrates' mouth in the *Philebus*: 'Well then. Consider someone being deprived for the first time. Could he have any contact with replenishment from either perception or memory of something he is neither undergoing at the moment nor has ever undergone before?' (35a, English translation 1975.)

This question leads Socrates to distinguish between desire and pleasure. Desire is not a search for pleasure. Pleasures and pains have their seat in the body, whereas desire is in the soul, the function of a memory older than any reminiscence conceived as the recall of a sensation or perception. But we are no longer able to accept this solution since the soul is no longer a reality for us, its concept is no longer valid currency. On the contrary, we begin to answer our question when we propose that, far from being the image or reproduction of the object, the representation or 'determinate of the determination', as Mally would have said, is a production of its absence.

Indeed, absence and presence are generally regarded as two things one of which excludes the other while at the same time implying it. The fact that Peter is present *here* implies his absence *elsewhere*, just as his absence here implies his presence elsewhere. So much for the mutual implication. It remains that absence and presence have so far been envisaged as attributes of Peter, and it is in such a perspective that they appear to be two equivalent or rather symmetrical things, and one can say that presence, i.e., the presence of a particular object, stands out against a background of absence, as absence does against a background of presence. But so far I have precisely said nothing particularly significant. What is more interesting is to consider them in their relation to one another directly and not via the object whose attribute they are supposed to be.

For this, let me quote another passage from the *Philebus*: Socrates asks his interlocutor, Protarch, to 'take any three things now, say one gold, one silver, one neither, just to have fine names' (43e). Of the three objects named in this passage, what is the difference between the first two and the one called 'neither' or 'none'? It is this: one cannot put one's hand on the last one. Yet it is still true that stating 'silver' or 'gold' does not put any money in my pocket. This nomination produces something named for which it remains to be seen whether there is an object satisfying it or not. If this were not the case, the question as to whether I have any or not, i.e. the question of the existence of the money in the perceptual field, would not arise. In a word, Plato has given us the proof that it is by no means necessary that the object first exist for it then to be named. The signifier puts the subject 'in contact' with the signified without prejudging its existence. The principle of error resides not in the tendency to hallucination but precisely in language, i.e., rather curiously, in the very instrument which gives our action on the real its familiar effectivity; and it is not just a joke to identify Plato's 'neither . . . nor' here as the very structure of the object of desire according to Lacan.

In the light of these considerations, let us go back to the example of Peter from which we began. If I ask: 'Is Peter here?', it is clear that, beyond the real presence of Peter which excludes his absence, as well as his real absence which excludes his presence, the very statement of the question would be inconceivable if there were not the Peter constituted by Peter's absence, the one we might call the 'Peter of always', I mean his nominal being, the one conferred on him even before his birth. And we know the shattering, even traumatic effect on the subject of learning it has been born without a name, or that its birth had put its parents in a quandary because they had not chosen a name *for it*. It will be said that this is because it sees in the fact a suggestion that its birth was unwelcome, or represented an event they would prefer had never occurred. This is not untrue, but what does it say about the structure of subjectivity if not that no subject can bear the reduction of its being to no more than its flesh and blood reality? Heidegger described *Dasein* as a dereliction. In truth, as things present themselves immediately or ordinarily at the level of the 'inauthenticity' of *Dasein*, the subject has no difficulty accommodating itself to its being-there, better, it forgets it, but it does not forget the name in which it will retain an ineradicable 'presence' beyond the eradication of its reality. If you cut the subject off from that background of non-being from which it is born as a child of discourse and in which runs its reality or being-there, its *Dasein*, the result will not be dereliction but certainty: the certainty of a life which is verily defined by death. For, I ask you, what is it that is signified in the being-there of that purely fleshly being except the fatality called corruption, death and decomposition? What is life as such if it is not the very way death gains in presence? At any rate, that is a point of view.

But life for the speaking being does not find its respiratory element in the proper name alone. For a less pathetic example, allow me to offer a personal anecdote.

I have a woman friend who lives abroad; we meet every few years, which enables us to discuss what we have each been doing. Learning that I was working on feminine sexuality, she demanded: 'What do you know about that?' 'That's what we'll find out.' 'And why are you working on it? What is it you want to know?' My friend's intelligence is not in question, but not being an analyst, it did not occur to her that one does not write just about the things one wants to know, why not also about the things one would have preferred to remain ignorant of? But anyway, as it is the elementary law of conversation to steer clear of high-temperature zones, I ventured the answer that I was perhaps trying to find out whether a relation between the sexes was possible that would be a relation between equals. 'What's that you're saying? I want a being (*un être*) superior to me!' 'But Hilde (that is my friend's name), there is no being superior to you.' I am not exaggerating if I describe the effect of this answer on my friend by saying that she was suffocated by it. In other words, it was enough that my friend be deprived for a moment of her *deficiency* (for what is this notion of a being superior to her if not the very idea of her own deficiency?) for her presence, reduced to its reality, its being-there, to become the most oppressive thing in existence!

To speak of a pleasure linked to representation is in the end to say something we all know, i.e. that the human being is easily satisfied with words (*se paie de mots*). The subject finds a pleasure in representations to the extent that it finds in them supports for its identifications. Of course, this identificatory gain, this gain in quiddity, does not give rise to any gain on the plane of being. The function of identification is rather to give direction, *intentio*, to our lack in being. More precisely, thanks to identification, being is installed and ordered as a having to be, a 'to-being' (*à-être*). No matter that the subject, which is not born with the solution to ontological problems at hand, will defend its identifications as its very being. Besides, it would be a mistake to imagine this having 'to-be' in the sense of a more plenary realisation of being; the very one that impels us to speak of a supreme being—a notion which is meaningless save for those who imagine there is more being in a pyramid than in a grain of sand. This having to be opens on to another horizon, where what is at stake is not being but knowing. But here I am touching on psychoanalysis's particular contribution, on the question of repression.

It will be recalled that Freud began his *Formulations* with the remark that the introduction of the notion of repression enables us to explain the loss of the *fonction du réel* (function of the real) produced in neurosis, but that he went no further than a summary 'definition' of repression restricted to a comparison between it and Griesinger's hallucinatory psychosis. A comparison whose paradoxical, if not unacceptable, character I have emphasised, and with good reason. For, a few pages further on, when he wanted to explain what becomes of repression after the introduction of the reality principle, he described it as a mechanism which aims to exclude 'from cathexis as productive of unpleasure some of the emerging ideas (*Vorstellungen*)' (*SE* xii: 221). There can be no doubt that this exclusion 'from cathexis' means exclusion 'from consciousness'. Moreover, in the article he devoted to this concept a few years later, 'Repression', Freud wrote in so many words: 'The essence of repression lies simply in turning something away, and keeping it at a distance, from the conscious' (*SE* xiv: 147). Now, to deny a reality or an event and to exclude them from knowledge or the conscious are not the same thing at all.

Take the example most frequently used to illustrate Griesinger's hallucinatory psychosis, that of the girl who loved in good faith and whose lover, contemptuous of his promises, would not marry her. She refused to acknowledge the fact, she did not believe in the lying Other, and, mad, she went on wearing her wedding dress. What the subject is denying here is the *event* which has happened to it, i.e. the fact that it has been betrayed. But heaven betrays us sometimes, for example, by carrying off one of our loved ones. And it sometimes happens that the subject does not have these resources of negation and hallucination, as it were. It visibly fades away, it becomes no more than a single long complaint. Only it is a complaint . . . without any truth in it. Not that its pain is pretended—far be it from me to cast doubt on the subject's sincerity—on the contrary, I would say that here not only is the subject saying what it thinks, but it is also thinking what it says— which to my mind is no less a sign of a serious inadequacy in the subject's relation to the symbolic order. Let us now consider what happens 'normally', i.e. in more or less neurotic structures. It is rare for a subject to forget the date of its birth. But the date of the death of someone near or dear is often forgotten. The death itself is not forgotten, but the date is shrouded in some uncertainty, in a doubt as to the day, the month or even the year. Such a doubt alerts us to the fact that a certain truth is hidden here, in the subject's relationship to the event or the memory he retains of it. What truth? Only analysis enables us to tell in each case. For example: that I was also waiting for that date as the date of my own *true* birth: the first has always been bungled; it is 'traumatic'. In other words what repression keeps at a distance from consciousness is not the event which is 'productive of unpleasure' or the memory it leaves, but, in so far as such an event coincides or telescopes with a

Wunschvorstellung, a representation of desire (in my example, something which might be stated as 'may he die'), that representation sends us, as it were, an official delegate, not just a *Repräsentanz*, but a *Repräsentant*, as Freud customarily wrote initially, which represents what? My relationship to that very representation. The unpleasure motivating the repression is not in the repressed representation. The unpleasure is in the ego if it learns of, or every time it threatens to approach, the repressed. Not only is the repressed not an element productive of unpleasure, it is even a representation productive of pleasure . . . so long as it is unknown. In my example, this is the representation of the 'true birth', which we can add, as indicative of the lack in being, to the other two: the proper name and the superior being.

This is not unproblematic. For when, in *Formulations*, Freud wrote, 'In the realm of phantasy, repression remains all-powerful' (*SE* XII: 223), this was as much as to say that, *from his point of view*, repression, contrary to what he had written at the beginning of the article, does not conform to the pleasure principle. As we know, he took this problem up again later in the article he devoted to repression. But that text's conclusion seems even odder: for it confirms on the one hand that the *Wunschvorstellung* or *Triebvorstellung* is productive of pleasure, but that on the other, its satisfaction, the satisfaction of that representation, produces unpleasure, even that maximal unpleasure that is anxiety. But if this is so, would not the pleasure principle better be called the 'principle of privation'?

NOTES

1. In philosophical contexts, *Vorstellung* is often translated into English as 'presentation', and the translators of the *Standard Edition* use 'presentation' when Freud is appealing to the philosophical use of the term, 'representation' or 'idea' otherwise. Here I have followed French usage and translated it as 'representation' throughout—Translator's note.

2. Unlike Brentano, I rather favour the interpretation Geach has recently given of St Thomas Aquinas's *esse intentionale*, according to which this *esse* is *not* a relation (cf. G. E. M. Anscombe and P. T. Geach 1967: 95). On the subsequent development of Brentano's thought about the above posed question, or rather on the difficulty of tracing it, see Lucien Gilson (1955).

3. K. Twardowski, *Zur Lehre vom Inhalt und Gegenstand der Vorstellungen.* (1894). In his book *Meinong* (1974), Reinhardt Grossmann has announced an English translation of this work which has not yet, to my knowledge, appeared.

4. See Pierre Aubenque's admirable *Le Problème de l'être chez Aristote* (1972).

5. 'If men inhabited language, there would be no housing problem,' it has been wittily said. It is just that they do not inhabit language alone.

5 Lacan's Philosophical Coquetry

TONY CUTLER

PHILOSOPHICAL CONCEPTS AND PSYCHOANALYTICAL THEORY

Let us take as our starting-point Freud's short paper 'Negation' (*SE* XIX: 235–9), a paper which provoked a famous exchange between Lacan and the great Hegel scholar Jean Hyppolyte. (cf. *E* 369–99 and 879–87). Freud's paper begins by referring to a common experience in psychoanalysis: the patient's statement of repressed material in the form of a negative statement:

> The manner in which our patients bring forward their associations during the work of analysis gives us an opportunity for making some interesting observations. 'Now you'll think I mean to say something insulting, but really I've no such intention.' We realize that this is a rejection, by projection, of an idea that has just come up. Or: 'You ask who this person in the dream can be. It's *not* my mother.' We emend this to: 'So it *is* his mother'. In our interpretation, we take the liberty of disregarding the negation and of picking out the subject-matter alone of the association. (*SE* XIX: 235)

Freud seeks to use this observation not in the elaboration of the technique of psychoanalysis but as an index of an epistemological thesis. The paper presents an analysis of the stages in the development of the faculty of judgement; it provides an account of the genesis of judgements. On this genetic account the subject begins 'at first' by confusing evaluative and existential judgements. That is to say that the subject's judgement of the goodness or badness of a perception governs the judgement of its existence, i.e. position within the 'real' is determined by valuation:

> the original pleasure-ego wants to introject into itself everything that is good and to eject from itself everything that is bad. What is bad, what is alien to the ego and what is external are, to begin with, identical. (*SE* xix: 237)

For there to be a *distinct* question of the reality of 'something of which there is a presentation' (*SE* xix: 237), it is necessary to give an account of how the exclusive domain of the pleasure principle is 'superseded'. This question of reality arises because of the loss of an object: ' . . . a pre-condition for the setting up of reality-testing is that objects shall have been lost which once brought real satisfaction' (*SE* xix: 238).

We are here dealing with an origin in the form of continuity, in other words, the *differentia specifica* lies not in the modality of judgement but rather in the conditions under which judgement is made:

> The study of judgement affords us, perhaps for the first time, an insight into the origin of an intellectual function from the interplay of the primary instinctual impulses. Judging is a continuation, along the lines of expediency, of the original process by which the ego took things into itself or expelled them from itself, according to the pleasure principle. (*SE* xix: 238–9)

The distinction thus effected enables existence and valuation to be separated and consequently allows for the observations at the beginning of the paper to be explained, since the repressed material is, by definition, not nihilated, but negated, thus the simultaneity of de-valuation and existence depends upon negation:

> The performance of the function of judgement is not made possible until the creation of the symbol of negation had endowed thinking with a first measure of freedom from the consequences of repression and, with it, from the compulsion of the pleasure principle. (*SE* xix: 239)

It is worth examining in some detail the logic of Freud's argument in this paper. The argument constructs an origin and

indeed an origin that finds its place in a logical progression. At the
outset the lack of distinction between evaluative and existential
judgements is implicitly referred to the absence of the utility of the
distinction. It is with the loss of the desired object that the initial
state of affairs is transformed. Freud's argument thus takes the
following form:

1. Since an object of satisfaction has been lost it follows that there
must be a distinction between a valued object and its existence, i.e.
valuation does not, by definition, imply existence, in this case
external to the ego.
2. Consequently objects external to the ego may be valued or de-
valued.
3. Conversely de-valued objects are not denied existence by
virtue of their devaluation.

The function of judgement responds therefore to the loss of a
desired object as to a premiss, in the form of an 'if *a* then *b*' where *a*
takes as value the loss of the desired object.

How are we to characterise this problem of origin which Freud
poses? An answer can be found by considering the two possible
solutions which psychoanalysis has investigated. Both take the form
of a passage 'back along' a temporal linear chain. On the one hand
one could consider the history of the individual and search for the
precipitant of the function of judgement, the loss of the desired
object, with reference to the Oedipus complex. The other possibility
is to look for the origin of that interdiction itself and to refer to the
history of the species and in turn to the pre-existing environment of
the species. The second option may now be unfashionable but it
does attempt to respond to the question of where the origin of
judgement should be situated and it was, of course, a possibility to
which Freud devoted a great deal of study. For Freud the 'origin of
culture' was a valid object of investigation.

Both these arguments fall into an infinite regress which can only
be halted by recourse to a concept of origin which is both explicitly
teleological and epistemological. If the point at which the regress
must stop is to be identified it must be by reference to a constructed
cut-off point. If we are concerned with the origins of knowledge then
the cut-off point will be the point at which knowledge departs from
'non-knowledge', the cut-off point will thus depend upon an
epistemological distinction. This, of course, implies a circular

argument, knowledge is knowledge by reference to the origin or cut-off point and the origin is where it is because it is the point at which knowledge begins.

Lacan seeks to make use of the argument in Freud's paper by invoking a distinction relevant to psychoanalytic diagnostic categories, in particular to psychosis. The insertion of this category within a problematic of the origin of knowledge involves, therefore, the implication for Lacan that psychosis is a kind of 'non-knowledge'. Lacan defines psychosis as a deviation from a process of the genesis of knowledge and it thus becomes a species of non-knowledge. Of course, this is unexceptional: psychiatric categories have often been defined with reference to a point on a scale of knowledge which marks their deviation from a norm.

A number of serious implications follow from such a position. If diagnostic categories are 'forms of knowledge' then the category designates a particular 'subject of knowledge'. In turn if the category has an epistemological foundation then it embodies a concept of 'knowledge' defined as universal, i.e., the 'form of knowledge' has a determinate relation to all other 'forms of knowledge'.

When this schema is applied to a determinate case then the subject and the diagnostic category necessarily become identical; the identity simply arises from the elements of the schema. A subject must therefore embody a diagnostic category since the latter is, by definition, universal. In turn since the knowledge of 'non-knowledge' arises from an origin which is universal for every subject or case then each subject must be identified by a diagnostic category (including 'normality') since that diagnostic category is in turn defined by reference to that origin.

The applicability of these arguments to Lacan's theoretical position may be traced in relation to his analysis of psychosis. In this analysis Lacan's key term is repudiation or *foreclosure*, which is his translation of the Freudian term *Verwerfung*. Foreclosure is to be distinguished from repression and is used in particular in Freud's case study, *From the History of an Infantile Neurosis* (*SE* xvii: 7–122), better known as the case of the Wolf Man. The distinction between repression and foreclosure depends on the question of the existence of castration for the subject and the correlative question of the register of the (re)appearance of castration. In both normal and neurotic cases the existence of castration is 'accepted' and, simultaneously, this 'acceptance' is the moment of formation of the symbolic for a given subject. The psychotic case is differentiated, however, by the repudiation or foreclosure of castration and its (re)appearance in the register of the real, not the symbolic.

Foreclosure or *Verwerfung*, for Lacan, corresponds to what is opposed to the primary affirmation or *Bejahung*: ' . . . it is exactly that which opposes itself to the primary *Bejahung* and constitutes as such that which is expelled' (*E* 387).

Lacan's reference point is to the passage in the paper 'Negation' where Freud traces the origin of judgement to the oral instinctual impulse:

> The attribute to be decided about may originally have been good or bad, useful or harmful. Expressed in the language of the oldest—the oral—instinctual impulses, the judgement is: 'I should like to eat this', or 'I should like to spit it out'; and, put more generally: 'I should like to take this into myself and to keep that out.' (*SE* xix: 236–7)

Verwerfung is here equivalent to the expulsion. There is an obvious point that follows from our initial discussion, namely that the *differentia specifica* of psychosis is situated by Lacan at a level which in Freud's paper is prior to the functioning of judgements of existence. For this reason the definition of psychosis can be seen in terms of a modality of knowledge, or, as I shall try to show, non-knowledge.

For Lacan *Verwerfung* signifies that castration is not repressed but expelled 'into the real', outside the symbolic; such an expulsion necessarily implying a denial of existence. When Lacan is discussing Freud's theses on negation, he uses as an example of foreclosure (*Verwerfung*) an incident taken from the case of the Wolf Man. The incident concerns an experience of hallucination at the age of five which the patient describes as follows:

> When I was five years old, I was playing in the garden near my nurse, and was carving with my pocket-knife in the bark of one of the walnut-trees that come into my dream as well. Suddenly, to my unspeakable terror, I noticed that I had cut through the little finger of my (right or left?) hand, so that it was only hanging on by its skin. I felt no pain, but great fear. I did not venture to say anything to my nurse, who was only a few paces distant, but I sank down on the nearest seat and sat there incapable of casting another glance at my finger. At last I calmed down, took a look at

the finger, and saw that it was entirely uninjured. (*SE* XVII: 85)[1]

Freud comments that the hallucination relates to a 'current' in the patient's psychic processes which questioned the reality of castration (*SE* XVII: 85).

The expulsion/foreclosure of castration cited here responds to a rigorous necessity for Lacan. Because it is simultaneous with a non-entry to the Symbolic, the denial of existence corresponds to a (re)appearance of castration in the register of the real: . . . *that which hasn't come to light in the symbolic, appears in the real* (*E* 388).

What is the basis for this rigorous link between real and symbolic? We can only understand it by referring to the epistemological theses embodied in Freud's paper 'Negation'. Because the question of differential relations to the real is basic to the logic of Freud's argument then necessarily entry/non-entry to the symbolic, as it determines the formation of the subject, also necessarily determines the subject's relation to the real. The differential relation at issue in this case is that which opposes the 'mediated' relation which constitutes the real of normality and neurosis to the 'immediate' relation of psychosis. This latter relationship could well be expressed in the terms in which Hegel discusses the ego in the case of sense-certainty:

> Consciousness, for its part, is in this certainty only as a pure 'I'; or I am in it only as a pure 'This', and the object similarly only as a pure 'This' . . . the 'I' does not have the significance of a manifold imagining or thinking; nor does the 'thing' signify something that has a host of qualities. On the contrary, the thing *is*, and it *is*, merely because it *is*. It *is*; this is the essential point for sense-knowledge, and this pure *being*, or this simple immediacy, constitutes its *truth*. (Hegel 1977: 58–9)

The formation of psychosis, a point to which we shall return, is a process of nihilation of individuality and therefore plays on the opposition between an in-itself and a for-itself, thus the correspondence between the nihilation of individuality, and the ontological status of 'pure being'. Similarly, the correspondence pure being-immediacy of the object is necessarily posited since the hallucination is an event rooted in its individuality and is, consequently, dis-associated.

We can understand the account of the formation of psychosis if we recall that to postulate an origin, a cut-off point, it was necessary to have recourse to epistemological criteria to define the cut-off point. In so far, therefore, as psychosis is an 'epistemological deviation' then the source will be found in a failure to cross the divide which separates knowledge from non-knowledge. We might be tempted to refuse the use of this term 'non-knowledge'—to dispute the authority on which it bases itself. It could be argued, for example, that, even if we accept the role played by epistemology, psychosis at least involves a 'knowledge' not simply definable by, or subject to evaluation in terms of, a general standard. The rigour of the problem of the origin would lead to a different conclusion. Psychosis is *before* the cut-off point. As such it is comparable to the later points in the development both as temporally prior *and* as logically inferior. Lacan tells us that this problematic of the origin is to be thought through a dialectic 'which obliges us to understand the ego (*moi*) from beginning to end in the movement of progressive alienation which constitutes self-consciousness in Hegel's phenomenology' (*E* 374). The latter reference should, however, be taken as proving no more than what Lacan's concepts already tell us.

The link between temporal anteriority and logical superiority is inescapable. And this because the early stage is, by definition, only knowable from beyond the cut-off point. In the climbing metaphor so beloved of epistemologists, to see the bottom of the slope *as it is* we require the vantage point. Yes indeed, the climb was worth while even if it engenders a feeling of *déjà vu*. The very notion of the cut-off point implies the distinction in the levels of knowledge concerned. For this reason Lacan takes over the Hegelian paradox that the 'knowledge' of the psychotic is necessary with reference to the total process (i.e. from the standpoint of its end), but that in itself it dissolves into a non-knowledge whose self-subsistence is a contradiction in terms since it requires the supplement of its determinations which only appear 'later' in the process of knowledge. Precisely, therefore, psychosis represents an arrested knowledge and thus, in its self-subsistence, a 'non-knowledge'.

The origin of this 'non-knowledge' is the non-access to the beyond of the cut-off point. The terms of this non-access merit serious consideration. We have a case of the genesis of a subject[2] and this genesis entails that we have a further correspondence, namely that between ontological status and knowledge. To study the origin is to study an effect of the determination of the ontological status of the subject. The opposition in question is that between a dyad and a triad. The case of psychosis is that of the dyad, a dyad involving the ontological relation between mother and child. It is not strictly correct to situate this dyad as arising out of itself in terms of a genesis from the mother-child relation as, for example, Lemaire implies when she argues:

> The maternal attitude is determinant here . . . if the mother treats her child as the complement of her own lack, as the phallus with which the child is in any case trying to identify, if, therefore, the child is everything to her and merges with her in a diffuse union, then the child cannot dispose of his own individuality. (1970: 375–6/1977: 234)[3]

The assertion of the symbolic is not simply guaranteed by the mother since certain determinants require reference to the place of the father as Lacan himself makes clear (*E* 578–9). Nevertheless the crucial role of ontology is indisputable. The mother's claim on the being of the child nihilates the individuality of that being, correspondingly that nihilated being is immediate 'knowledge', non-knowledge in its self-subsistence.

It is, of course, possible to argue that the ontological basis is merely apparent and that the dyadic and triadic relationships are not constitutive but rather depend upon prior 'structural' conditions. This in turn might refer us back to Lacan's well-known paper on 'The Mirror Stage' but such a reference does not invalidate the argument outlined above. Talking of the mirror stage, Lacan tells us:

> This jubilant assumption of its specular image by the child at the *infans* stage, still sunk in its motor incapacity and nursling dependence, would seem to exhibit in an exemplary situation the symbolic matrix in which the *I* is precipitated in a primordial form, before it is objectified in the dialectic of identification with the other, and before language restores to it, in the universal, its function as subject. (*E* 94/2)

The precondition for the access/non-access to the Symbolic is itself a stage in the genesis of the subject. Furthermore this stage is equally defined in ontological terms. We have an additional dyad here from which the third term is absent, and the dyad's eternalisation will be determined by the condition of access/non-access but those conditions will seize on a moment of being and 'freeze' it. These considerations should make it clear that Lacan's philosophical terminology cannot be dealt with as an affinity at the level of phrases subsumable under the famous/infamous 'coquetry' (a term only meaningful within an epistemological reading) but with concepts which must be taken at the letter.

What then of the famous *differentia specifica* of Lacanian theory, 'the unconscious structured like a language'—that which 'everyone knows' when this 'everyone' is an imbiber of 'introductory' works on 'structuralism'?, What is at issue here is the place occupied by the structure of language. If our previous arguments are correct then we should expect the operation of language in Lacan's theory to be subordinated to a dialectic of being. In one sense this is obviously true since the access to language works through an ontological process, and since language exists as it were 'at the gate' it functions as an articulation of a result not as a determinant. The correspondence goes further, however, because the conception of language identified with the Lacanian concept of the Symbolic is that of de Saussure. For de Saussure language is a system of differences, in other words a system autonomous by definition from the *parole* which is, in turn, its realisation. Access to language is the access to a universal as condition of existence of the particular.

Saussurean linguistics is a malleable tool for such purposes in so far as it combines an empty set of differences and a pre-linguistic social contract which determines meanings. Within this space ontology has asserted itself more recently in the attempts to 'solve' the problem of 'arbitrariness' by reference to linguistic realism in the case of Jakobson (1971a) or sociological realism in the case of Lévi-Strauss (1970).[4]

The ontological architecture which has been discerned can be related, in turn, to the agency of entry into the Symbolic: the Name of the Father. It is perfectly clear that the Name of the Father does not imply an empirical father of a given type, or, indeed, an empirical father at all, that is to say that the concept does not refer, *in any simple sense*, to an interpersonal relation. However, the variability of personages at the sociological level does not, of itself, destroy the problem of interpersonal relations. For if the Symbolic does not require empirical personalities as its support, it does nevertheless require personifications. If we look again at the Lacanian delineation of psychosis, it is evident that the mother's relation to the child as extension of her own being is a case of dual destruction of personification. The destruction of the individuality of the child is posited as the effect of the subsumption of the latter under the being of the former through the mechanism of the 'freezing' of the being of the latter. In turn, for this destruction of personification to take place a second must accompany it: the destruction of the personification embodying interdiction. We thus return to determination at the level of empirical subjects since it is a question of the practice of the mother, the mother in respect of the father, or the mother in respect of the role of the father. Of course, there is no question of a simple identity between subject and personification, and equally for Lacan there are ruses by which the authoritarian father subordinates himself to family, nation and order, although by the inevitable ruse of the ruse such abasement may completely vacate the place of symbolic authority (*E* 575–83). However, such ruses are meat and drink for the sophisticated existentialist. A humanist position by no means requires that intention and effect be identical. On the contrary, since the alienation of intention is a central theme of existentialist pessimism, any unity of intention and effect could only be the basis for a facile bovine optimism or humanist misanthropy. The *sine qua non* of humanism is not the unity of intention and effect but only the starting-point in intention with the consequent centrality of interpersonal relations.

If we take stock of what we have tried to prove, we can say that the Lacanian invocation of philosophy, which we have traced from its foundation in Freud's paper 'Negation' to its usage in the definition of psychosis, produces a set of structured discursive relations:

1. The problem of the genesis of the subject as a set of relationships structured by an end relation between subject and real.

2. The deviation from this genesis producing the correspondence between the non-subject and non-knowledge: the psychotic.

3. The origin of psychosis in the freezing of the subject at a given stage of being.

4. The subordination of the psychotic subject under the being of the other.

5. The linguistic as the effect of the ontological in two senses:

(*a*) the linguistic is situated at the cut-off point;

(*b*) the correspondence between the characterisation of language in the argument and the epistemological role of universality with its ontological correlate.

6. The determinate role of personifications in the definition access/non-access to the Symbolic.

PHILOSOPHICAL CONCEPTS AND PSYCHOANALYTICAL PRACTICE

We can now turn to our second problem: the effect of philosophical concepts on the definition of analytic practice. Generally the effect is to produce a deductive schema whereby the individual case is subsumable under the diagnostic category/subject concerned. The identification of the subject and the diagnostic category derives from the generality and the unitary character of knowledge as defined by epistemological concepts. Since the case refers to a 'modality of being', it can be considered as a unity, i.e., we talk of 'neurotics', 'psychotics', 'schizophrenics', etc. Further, since the genesis is concerned with knowledge and deviations from knowledge then there will be a necessary generality to the diagnostic category such that the case will be a realisation of the category concerned.

It is necessary to state that when we look at Freud's work this issue of the relation between a general corpus of theory and the determinate case is unresolved and what we will say will do no more than touch on the problems engendered by it. The problem may be clarified by starting from a hypothetical question: why does psychoanalytic theory and practice not follow the strictly deductive schema outlined above? And, correlatively, why is there not a 'preventitive' Freudian therapeutics?

An analogue of the problem was faced by Freud in *The Interpretation of Dreams* (*SE* IV and V). In his opening discussion of the literature on dream-interpretation, Freud summarises the interpretative methods of 'dream-books':

> Suppose, for instance, that I have dreamt of a letter and also of a funeral. If I consult a 'dream-book', I find that 'letter' must be translated by 'trouble' and 'funeral' by 'betrothal'. It then

remains for me to link together the key-words which I have deciphered in this way and, once more, to transpose the result into the future tense. (*SE* IV: 97–8)

In his criticism of this mode of analysis Freud focuses on the fragmentary or atomistic relation between symbol and meaning:

> The essence of the decoding procedure, however, lies in the fact that the work of interpretation is not brought to bear on the dream as a whole but on each portion of the dream's content independently, as though the dream were a geological conglomerate in which each fragment of rock required a separate assessment. (*SE* IV: 99)

In fact this objection implies an objection to the possibility of a book decoding dream symbols since for Freud the unity of the dream is established by the wish fulfilment and, naturally, the wish is in no way deducible or general. However, it is the case that Freud does use general notions of dream symbols, invariant relations between symbols representing the sexual organs, for example (cf. *SE* V: 355–7). In the latter case the pertinence for the differential treatment of the dream-book and of the representation of the sexual organs in dreams is not clear.

We have already tried to indicate that a philosophical basis to psychoanalytical theory such as that suggested by the Lacanian position contains the implication of a broadly deductive relationship between theory and case. We have already indicated that Freud is ambiguous on this question. Our object will not be to 'solve' this problem since the treatment required would have to be vastly more extensive than is possible within the present work. We will, however, address two problems:

1. Does the material in a case study lend itself to treatment in terms of a genesis of the subject?
2. What role in the case study is played by statements referring to a general theoretical framework from which the interpretation of the former may be deduced?

The term 'case' has been used advisedly since the material for discussion will be drawn from the case of the Wolf Man alone. This is not presented as a 'representative' case but as an exemplar of the theoretical problem under consideration. Let us begin by looking at how Freud elaborates the determinants of the Wolf Man's psychic formation. Early in the study Freud seeks to explain the determinants of the sexual aim of the Wolf Man. After phantasising an attempted seduction of his sister, the patient explained that the situation was, in fact, the reverse and that he had been seduced by his sister. While this explanation is clearly not exhaustive, the seduction by the sister constituted the formation of the sexual aim of the Wolf Man: 'His seduction had given him the passive sexual aim of being touched on the genitals. . . .' (*SE* XVII: 24). The pursuit of this sexual aim led through a further sexual object, his attempts to seduce his nurse:

> How did the boy react to the allurements of his elder sister? By a refusal, is the answer, but by a refusal which applied to the person and not to the thing. His sister was not agreeable to him as a sexual object, . . . But he tried to win, instead of her, another person of whom he was fonder . . . He therefore began to play with his penis in his Nanya's presence, and this, like so many other instances in which children do not conceal their masturbation, must be regarded as an attempt at seduction. His Nanya disillusioned him . . . (*SE* XVII: 24)

This, in turn, led to the adoption of his father as the sexual object:

> The object of identification of his active current became the sexual object of a passive current in his present anal-sadistic phase. It looks as though his seduction by his sister had forced him into a passive role, and had given him a passive sexual aim. Under the persisting influence of this experience he pursued a path from his sister *via* his Nanya to his father . . . (*SE* XVII: 27)

The means he used were fits of temper which were designed to bring forward chastisement from his father: '. . . their purpose was masochistic. By bringing his naughtiness forward he was trying to force punishments and beatings out of his father, and in that way to obtain from him the masochistic sexual satisfaction that he desired' (*SE* XVII: 28).

The psychic formation of the Wolf Man was determined by the formation of the sexual aim and the chain of objects leading to the father combined with his witnessing sexual intercourse between his parents, an event recalled in a dream which makes up the centrepiece of the whole analysis (*SE* xvii: 29–47). On at least one occasion, the child witnessed his parents' intercourse *a tergo* (from behind), the significance of this being that the child was able to clearly see the father's and mother's genitals. This material was not psychically decisive at the time of the event (when the patient was one and a half years old) but became so later in relation to the passive sexual aim *vis-à-vis* the father. Freud evaluated its significance in the following way:

> What was essentially new for him in his observation of his parents' intercourse was the conviction of the reality of castration—a possibility with which his thoughts had already been occupied previously . . . For now he saw with his own eyes the wound of which his Nanya had spoken, and understood that its presence was a necessary condition of intercourse with his father. (*SE* xvii: 45–46)

What emerges clearly from this case is its fundamentally anti-teleological character. The formation of the sexual aim and the displacement of sexual objects are both ascribed to a specific determinant. The same is true for the effect of witnessing the parents' intercourse. There is no *necessary* link binding these determinants together: it would have been possible for a different sexual aim to have been formed or a different sexual object to have been adopted. Furthermore, the effect of witnessing the act of intercourse only drew its significance from the specific combination of sexual object and sexual aim, and, of equal importance, the witnessing, with its crucial role in forming the ambivalence, was in no way deducible from the sexual aim and object.

If we have demonstrated that Freud's analysis of the Wolf Man does not involve a genesis with its corresponding teleology, is, nevertheless, this end result a subject/diagnostic category? In partial response to this question, it is worth noting that the episode extracted from the Wolf Man case as a paradigm of 'psychosis' is read out of context. In the case study Freud interpreted the hallucination of the amputated finger not as proof of the patient's psychosis but rather of the complex and ambivalent nature of the Wolf Man's psychic formation:

> In this connection, once again, he behaved in the manner which

was so characteristic of him, but which makes it so difficult to give a clear account of his mental processes or to feel one's way into them. First he resisted and then he yielded; but the second reaction did not *do away with* the first. In the end there were to be found in him two contrary currents side by side, of which one abominated the idea of castration, while the other was prepared to accept it and console itself with feminity as a compensation. But beyond any doubt a third current, the oldest and deepest, which did not as yet even raise the question of the reality of castration, was still capable of coming into activity. (*SE* xvii: 85)

These conclusions coincide with the reversal which the Wolf Man practised at the beginning of his analysis when he phantasised the seduction of his sister. Freud interpreted this reversal as 'meant to efface the memory of an event which later on seemed offensive to the patient's masculine self-esteem, and they reached this end by putting an imaginary and desirable converse in the place of the historical truth' (*SE* xvii: 20). The case study does not, therefore, sustain the second central element of the deductive schema: the identity of the subject and the diagnostic category.[5] The final question to pose in relation to the deductive schema is the role played by general theoretical statements in the interpretation. The latter may be characterised as statements which are 'applicable to any case', that is to say that they can be applied deductively in the case according to determinate ground-rules of identification. We shall take a selection of these applications and seek to demonstrate that they do not function in fact as means of validation of the interpretations which are deducible from them unless there is specific references to other elements in the case study material. The fact of these specific references makes any notion of 'applicable to any case' nonsensical.

We can first examine the link which Freud tries to forge between the dream and the child's observation of the parents' intercourse. In defence of the interpretation that some of the latent material of the dream referred to a real event, Freud invokes an argument which makes appeal to the Wolf Man's observation that the dream had a marked sense of reality:

We know from our experience in interpreting dreams that this sense of reality carries a particular significance along with it. It assures us that some part of the latent material of the dream is claiming in the dreamer's memory to possess the quality of reality, that is, that the dream relates to an occurrence that really took place and was not merely imagined. (*SE* xvii: 33)

The relevant material in the case study which would sustain this argument are of two types, evidence of a direct nature and material of a cross-referential character.

In the first case the strongest evidence for the reality of the observation of intercourse stems from an admission made by the patient that the mother and father had intercourse on three occasions. This admission came in the form of an incorrect attribution of this figure to a result of Freud's analysis:

> Why three times? He suddenly one day produced the statement that I had discovered this detail by interpretation. This was not the case. It was a spontaneous association, exempt from further criticism; in his usual way he passed it off on me, and by this projection tried to make it seem more trustworthy. (*SE* xvii: 37n5)

Much more indirect is the interpretation given by Freud of the fact that the patient was subject from the age of ten onwards to fits of depression which reached their peak around five o'clock in the afternoon. The inferential link made by Freud is that the observation of intercourse may have taken place during a late afternoon siesta on the part of the parents (*SE* xvii: 37).

There are, necessarily, further cross-references within the material interpreted. For example, the patient's fear of wolves only related to representations of wolves in an upright posture and did not extend to a fear of pictures of wolves in general. His fear was thus associated with the posture assumed by the father in intercourse from behind. Similarly, the patient's later object choice was associated with the position adopted by the mother in the 'primal scene':

> The most striking phenomenon of his erotic life after maturity was his liability to compulsive attacks of falling physically in love which came on and disappeared again in the most puzzling succession. These attacks released a tremendous energy in him even at times when he was otherwise inhibited, and they were quite beyond his control . . . this compulsive love . . . was sub-

ject to a definite condition . . . It was necessary that the woman should have assumed the posture which we have ascribed to the mother in the primal scene. (*SE* xvii: 41)

The material so far considered merely selects from the rich and dense interplay of cross-references. To take another example: the wolves which appear in the dream are traced to a story told to the patient by his grandfather. However, in the story the wolves are beneath the tree while in the dream they are in the tree. Their presence is explained by Freud as the result of a complex wish-fulfilment in which the sexual desire finds its representation within a dream already subject to the child's desire for the Christmas presents he is about to receive. From the 'inverted' position of the wolves, Freud infers a systematic inversion within the dream: 'Their relation to the tree has therefore been reversed in the dream; and from this it may be concluded that there are further reversals of the latent material to be found in the content of the dream' (*SE* xvii: 43n).

The basis of the inference is rather unclear but it could be postulated in a rule whereby the identification of inversion of latent material should be taken as a sign that inversion will be systematic. However, once again the rule is not required by the argument. The first inversion is not, in fact a deduction from a general rule, rather it is the product of Freud's analyses of the complex wish that articulates the dream. The inversion is derived from one of the components of the complex wish. It is this cross-referential character that characterises the interpretation of further inversions. Thus, for example, in the dream the wolves closely observe the patient whereas in the postulated latent material it is the child who closely observes the intercourse. The validity of this argument refers us back to the question of the reality of the event. Another example is the transformation of the tail-less wolf of the story to the wolves with foxes' tails in the dream. These over-compensating tails refer us to the sexual wish that the choice of sexual object can be made (and this condition breaks the dream by pushing it to its limits) without castration. So, once again, the 'inversion' is determined by internal reference.

A final example: in the dream the wolves are in a 'big walnut tree'. Freud comments: 'Moreover, as I have often been able to satisfy myself, a high tree is a symbol of observing, of scopophilia. A person sitting on a tree can see everything that is going on below him and cannot himself be seen' (*SE* xvii: 43n). Again we are referred back to the observation of intercourse and, in turn, to the system of internal proof related to it. In this example intercourse *a tergo* (from behind) combines for the observer the possibility of 'seeing everything' and 'not being seen'.

CONCLUSION

We have tried to do two things. On the one hand, to show the chains which a rigorous philosophical reading will produce, the chains of the deductive schema in which the case study and analytic practice are the unwitting tools of a logos. On the other, we have sought to investigate, if only descriptively, the 'residuum' of the case study, the nature of its theoretical character. This has taken us on to a different terrain from that of Lacanian theory. Can we conclude that in the case of Lacan we have simply been dealing with philosophical coquetry? Well, coquetry may get 'out of control', the point comes where the averted eyes may meet . . . let us just say that a philosopher might decide that this 'coquetry' of Lacan's is indeed a case of true love.

NOTES

1. The dream referred to in the first sentence of this quotation is the centrepiece of the case study. See below.

2. Hyppolite's opposition genetic/mythical is not pertinent here since both would be included in my concept of genetic.

3. The essential point to grasp is that Lemaire's reference to the father assumes that he is completely mediated by the mother, Lacan does not make this mistake.

4. For the initial discussion of this problem cf. Benveniste (1966: 49–55/1971: 43–8).

5. This conclusion could be sustained theoretically with reference to the presentation of the concept of component instincts in *Three Essays on the Theory of Sexuality* (*SE* vii: 167–9).

6 The Concept of a Constitutive Subject

CHARLES LARMORE

I

Against all appearances, the concept of a constitutive subject does not belong solely to the more arcane regions of modern philosophy. Kant's transcendental philosophy did, of course, introduce the concept and provided the impetus for later attempts to think through explicitly and systematically all that that concept involves. The vast quantity and difficulty of the writings that Husserl left behind testify to the unending rigour that he thought such a task required. But the concept of a constitutive subject is not just a philosophical one, any more than perhaps any philosophical concept. For the concept embodies a response to a problem that arose along the borders between philosophy and the other domains that, in the early modern era, underwent profound revolutions. The problem was how we should make sense of the fact that man finds accessible large new areas of experience, unhoped-for discoveries, and the thorough reorganisation of his economic and political way of life, once he resolves to lay down, on his own, the conditions for experience, instead of permitting them to be dictated by the world outside. This is the problem to which Kant explicitly addresses his *Critique of Pure Reason*, as he indicates in the preface to the second edition: '. . . reason has insight only into that which it produces after a plan of its own.' Truly scientific knowledge appeared possible only through the experimental manipulation of nature that is guided by the critical elaboration of hypotheses we propose ourselves, rather than through the passive observation of what nature itself happens to offer to view. Economic development and prosperity seemed to hinge upon men ceasing to honour the external claims of tradition and family and seeking to satisfy their own individual needs and gear their economic activity toward maximal efficiency. Social justice was thought to arise from the exclusion of traditional obligations and of the idea that right depends upon divinely guaranteed principles; a just society is one that all of its prospective members freely contracted to make. Man appeared to become fully man only when he settled in advance upon the forms through which he would encounter the things in the world. The history of man prior to these revolutions (the Scientific Revolution, the Economic and later Industrial Revolutions, the various political revolutions) looked like an age of self-imposed bondage, for all along man must have possessed the capability to shape experience. Thus, according to Kant, what men had considered to be the demands made by the external world had been only the resolutions of other men to whom they had delegated their freedom.[1]

The philosophical theory of the constitutive subject began as a response to these historical developments. It has aimed to describe how, in general, the items of experience appear as they do only in virtue of the constitutive role of the subject in shaping that content. It is important to note that the theory of the constitutive subject is not a psychological idealism that claims that experience takes place independently of the world. Kant, for example, never denied the necessary role of sensation through which the world impinges upon us; but he maintained that what we receive through the senses can only belong to our *experience* (to what we can be aware of) by virtue of being formed by the conditions of experience laid down by the subject. In Kant's idea that there are necessary and universal *a priori* conditions of experience lay his response to Hume's doubts about causality, substance, and the like. But it does not form a required feature of a theory of the constitutive subject. For the role of such necessary and universal conditions in Kant's theory was to provide the rules according to which the subject structures his experience by bringing the data of sensation under empirical concepts. The feature essential to the idea of a constitutive subject is that whatever appears in experience the subject must have shaped through such conceptualisation. It is possible to accord the subject this formative role even if the rules with which he operates vary historically or from person to person. In this way the concept of a constitutive subject has continued to thrive even after Kant's list of categories turned out to be less than inevitable after all. Witness the neo-Kantian movement beginning at the end of the last century and the various 'returns to Kant' proclaimed since then.

In an account of the constitutive subject, therefore, the *a priori* conditions of experience (be they necessary and universal or historically and psychologically variable) make possible the conceptualisation that underlies all contingent judgements of experience. The constitutive activity of the subject does not generate what the contingent features of experience are. But it does, according to the theory, lay down the conditions under which such features can be understood, under which they can come to be seen as part of experience. Essential to the concept of a constitutive subject, as Kant understood it (and, with some minor differences, as those after him, like Husserl, used the concept) is the thesis that the subject himself organises experience, by bringing together whatever material the external world gives him. The concept of a constitutive subject hangs together, therefore, with the concept of an organising activity that alone is responsible for the intelligibility of experience.

Since the philosophical theory of the constitutive subject was a response to historical developments, we should not be surprised to find elements of the theory at work implicitly and unsystematically in the thoughts of those engaged in different areas undergoing that development. Moreover, this historical movement has by no means now come to an end. Later in this article I will discuss another example of a stream of thought whose idea of the subject gets its systematic exposition in the philosophical theory: the ego-psychology that has arisen out of psychoanalysis in the last forty years.

Nevertheless, historical research during the past two hundred years has revealed that the scientific, political, and economic achievements of the autonomous individual did not stem purely from the decision to cast off the weight of tradition and to lay down freely the conditions that experience must meet. We now know that the early modern scientists and political thinkers were indebted to their medieval predecessors in ways beyond their awareness. Centuries of capital accumulation had to precede the growth of the bourgeois market-economy. Even the philosophers who concerned themselves most with a theory of the subject, Descartes and Kant, were beholden to the philosophical tradition in ways they little suspected (Cartesian doubt makes sense only against the background of late medieval nominalism; Kant's theory of the faculties belongs to the traditional psychology of his time). From a logical point of view there can be no argument from the historical relativity of an idea to its truth or falsity. But in the case of the theory of the constitutive subject, the historical embeddedness of its implicit and explicit forms does prove embarrassing. For the fact that experience depends, not simply upon the free organisation of the ways the world impinges upon us, but also upon our belonging to a tradition that shapes our experiences in advance of our free choices is what the theory deemed a mere contingency, an expression of man's immaturity. It is to this new awareness of the formative role of tradition, of what has been called the 'historicity' of experience, that Heidegger's critique of the notion of a constitutive subject responds. In the next section I shall examine the nature of his critique as well as the dangers to which it succumbs. In the subsequent section I shall discuss, in a similar manner, the critique of the concept of a constitutive subject that Jacques Lacan has presented on the basis of psychoanalytic theory. Through these discussions there will emerge the elements of a theory of the subject that does greater justice to the nature of experience than either the idea of a constitutive subject or the opposing concepts that Heidegger and Lacan have offered in their critiques of that idea.

II

From the appearance of *Sein und Zeit* (1927) onward, the concern of Heidegger's writings has lain with the question of 'the meaning of Being'. The aim of *Sein und Zeit* was to provide the groundwork for the solution to this question by examining the structure of human understanding (or *Dasein*), within which anything like the meaning of Being can first arise. The strategy has the air of Kant's 'Copernican turn', of his insistence upon the role of the subject in structuring experience. However, the brunt of Heidegger's analysis of *Dasein* fell precisely upon the theory of the constitutive subject.[2] I shall offer a reconstruction of Heidegger's analysis that stresses his critique of that theory.

According to Heidegger, the *meaning* of something consists in the way it points beyond itself toward something else (1967: 83–8/1962: 114–22). One initial advantage of this thesis is its generality. As far as linguistic meaning is concerned, it touches not only the sort of meaning that is relevant for ascertaining the conditions under which a proposition can be asserted as true, but also those other dimensions of meaning that always play some role in scientific discourse and a more important role in everyday language and in literature: traditional resonances, associations, and the evocation of images. Moreover, this concept of meaning also applies to other items of experience besides words and sentences: to natural and conventional signs, to human actions (when we ask about the meaning of someone's action, we may want to know what he was after or what he wanted to prove by it), and so forth. Of course, the generality of this concept of meaning gives us only the most rudimentary of hints about how to describe meaning in any particular case.[3] Still, Heidegger has a special reason for advancing a very general account of what meaning is. For he argues that understanding (*Verstehen*) is the fundamental characteristic of human existence, and thus he needs a theory of meaning broad enough to fit such a claim (1967: 142–3/1962: 182–4). In virtue of the general theory that meaning is the pointing of one thing beyond itself toward another, understanding is always understanding something *as* such-and-such. Heidegger's theory of meaning may perhaps appear trivial, but in thinking through its ramifications Heidegger shows that the structure of understanding belies any thought that the subject is constitutive of experience.

Heidegger points out that in order to understand something a person must participate in an established form of life, in a whole context of significations (*Bewandtnis-* or *Verweisungszusammenhang*) that governs the way that thing points meaningfully toward other things (1967: 84/1962: 115–16). The person must take for granted sizeable tracts of background knowledge in order to understand what to do with the thing or what to say about it. There are, therefore, no isolated acts of understanding, that could take place apart from the prior understanding or acceptance of a context.

To characterise this structure of understanding, Heidegger speaks of an '*a priori* perfect' (1967: 85/1962: 115–16). What makes possible the act of understanding some thing or situation is that an understanding of other things must *already* be taken for granted. Between the concept of the *a priori* that has to do with the constitutive subject's structuring of experience and this '*a priori* perfect' lies all the difference between the concept of the constitutive subject and its critique. For the condition of possibility of the experience to which the act of understanding is oriented lies, not simply in the conceptualisation that act brings about, but initially in the background of accepted beliefs that make that act possible. The subject can never put himself into the position where he might make sense of something without having to rely upon other beliefs. Even if he were also to rehearse the grounds for those beliefs, he would still have to appeal to those other beliefs that make possible his understanding of the grounds for the first set.

Thus the activity of the subject, that is involved in making experience intelligible, depends upon a passivity of the subject, upon his taking for granted that other things are true. This dialectic of activity and passivity differs altogether from the sort we find in a theory of the constitutive subject. There it is sensation that is passive, through which the world impinges upon us; for anything to appear as a part of experience, it must submit to the organising activity of the subject. But Heidegger's insight is that to understand some part of experience is to accept passively, not non-experiential sense-data, but large segments of experience itself. This critique of the concept of a constitutive subject underlies Heidegger's figurative description of human existence as 'thrown' or 'always already under way' (1967: 134–5/1962: 172–4). There can be no 'transcendental apperception' where the subject may encounter himself independently and in advance of experience.[4] There is no vantage-point from which he can settle alone what his experience will be like.

One obvious objection to this account might be that, although at any one time certain things must be accepted as understood in order for an act of understanding to be possible, those accepted beliefs themselves arose from previous acts of understanding in which the subject did organise the experience that they express. In other words, the objection would claim that while the subject may not be able to establish at one stroke the intelligibility of experience, everything that figures as part of his experience derives, in the last analysis, from the structuring activity of the subject.

Nowhere in Heidegger's work can we find anything like a clear response to such an objection. It seems to me, however, that the objection fails for at least three reasons. I do not mean to deny that often the accepted background-beliefs are the result of the subject having organised his experience in a certain manner. But I shall claim that far less than the sum of such beliefs can be so explained. First of all, the objection, if thought through to the end, must pose as a theory of childhood learning. Yet much of what an infant learns, that goes into his later background-beliefs, he acquires not through his own conceptualisation of the material his senses give him, but through training that conditions him by means of rewards geared to his more immediate needs to imitate the knowledge-embodying behaviour of those around him (speech, postures, expressions, techniques). In this way the infant does not form his experience himself, but absorbs ready-made experience from the outside.[5] A second weakness in the objection lies in its underestimation of the role of trust in experience. Some of the background-beliefs may be beliefs a person has taken over from others on trust, without having had the opportunity or the desire or the time to get first-hand knowledge of what they are about. Such beliefs do not come about through a person's organisation, at any time, of the experience they have to do with. And while the person's structuring capacities may be involved in his accepting the belief on someone else's word (he has to understand what the other person is saying, and he may have reasons for believing him), the belief he acquires on trust is not that someone else gave him that information or that that person is probably reliable in this case (for that he need not rely upon trust), but that that information is true. Trust makes possible, among other things, the cumulative character of modern scientific inquiry, the ability of the scientist to use the results of others without having to spend time in repeating them. In this regard, the concept of a constitutive subject turns on an older, pre-modern ideal of theory, in which the theoretician would be engaged in self-sufficient contemplation and not in a form of inquiry that is trans-generational— an ideal of theory that we have found no longer fruitful or tolerable.

Another weakness of the objection is that it runs counter to the results of historical research that, as I have mentioned, interested Heidegger so much. It appears that people have always worked on the basis of background-beliefs that they little suspected they had, assumptions that it is quite unlikely they ever made explicitly but that had a formative influence upon the way they dealt with particular problems. But there is a further defect of the objection that has to do with the case of background-beliefs that at a previous time the person did in fact arrive at through his own efforts at making his experience intelligible. Even if certain background-beliefs can be traced back to the subject at an earlier date, it does not follow that the subject at present could repeat or recreate the steps that led him to them. For if the person now thought of the reasons he had then for those beliefs, he might find them less cogent than he used to or even false. Or he may have even forgotten those previous reasons. So if the objection hoped to establish that, with such beliefs, the subject remained in possession of the means for structuring the experience they express and could rehearse his reasons for them at will, it failed.

Let us now return to Heidegger's account of the subject (*Dasein*), to see what consequences he draws from it. As I mentioned at the beginning of this section, Heidegger began with an analysis of human understanding because he thought that only in terms of the structure of understanding could we grasp what is the meaning of that term 'Being'. Now the word 'meaning' in Heidegger's phrase 'the meaning of Being' signifies nothing more than the sort of thing he described in his general theory of meaning. That, of course, does not tell us what Heidegger was looking for when he set out to investigate Being. But Heidegger believed that his account of the structure of understanding points toward that feature of experience with which the philosophical tradition was concerned when it brought forth its two chief definitions of Being. First there was the idea that Being, as opposed to particular entities, is something whose essence is to exist and which, in some way, is responsible for the existence of particular things (Aquinas's definition of God as *esse* is one example of this theme). Secondly, there was the idea that Being is that most universal property that belongs to all things in so far as they exist.[6] Heidegger is far from believing that these traditional notions are immune to question, but he thinks that they were on the track of something important. In this essay I shall not discuss the correctness of Heidegger's interpretation of the philosophical tradition nor try to illuminate the obscure communications about Being that fill his later writings. For Heidegger's claim is that the concept of Being forms the response to a problem that arises as a result of his analysis of the structure of understanding (1967: 85–6, 437/1962: 118, 276). And I shall show that this problem does not ensue at all and that there is no 'problem of Being', at least as Heidegger conceived it.

As we have seen, in *Sein und Zeit* Heidegger argues that all acts of understanding must take place against the background of previously accepted beliefs. He also supposed (as I mentioned, without much argument) that not all of these background-beliefs can be of the subject's own making; I indicated a number of lines along which this point can be defended. Now in the period of *Sein und Zeit* Heidegger recognised that although all particular acts of understanding—which he terms 'Interpretation' (*Auslegung*) or explicit understanding—takes place against a background of accepted beliefs that give a prior understanding (*Verstehen*) of the situation, these background-beliefs do not settle in advance what the subject will make of the situation. They consist only in the guidelines that make his individual choices *relevant* to what is at hand.[7] However, in his later writings this leeway left to the subject disappears. Heidegger comes to think of particular acts of understanding as simply implementations of the already accepted background-beliefs. In order to see the weight that Heidegger attaches to this idea we must look at a second feature that Heidegger always attributed to the background-beliefs that shape understanding. Throughout all of his writings we find the assumption that all of a person's background-beliefs are related to one another in such a way. that they form a single coherent system of beliefs—what Heidegger calls a 'world'.[8] Because these beliefs form a unified structure, the subject who maintains an understanding of how they serve to disclose a world and to make his experience possible can be the 'authentic' subject who has remained aware of his wholeness, in face of the threat of being scattered among particular concerns.[9]

It is Heidegger's continuing assumption that a subject's background-beliefs cohere in a unity that allows him to claim that the subject's world expresses a single, over-arching understanding of things—what he calls an 'understanding of Being'. In this lies his reworking of the second traditional conception of Being mentioned above (Being as the most universal concept, the *summum genus*); since he wishes to stress the background-beliefs that shape how we experience particular things, Heidegger understands by Being, not simply what each entity has in so far as it exists, but rather the way in which, in virtue of a system of beliefs, each entity appears as it does. When in his later writings Heidegger cancels all spontaneity of the subject, Being becomes what is responsible for establishing such a 'world' or system of beliefs (this is Heidegger's reworking of the first traditional idea of Being). Freedom then comes to consist in welcoming this thorough structuration imposed from the outside. Truly new possibilities become accessible, not because of anything the subject might do, but only when the subject—in this attitude of 'freedom'—welcomes the disclosure of a new world that does not depend upon his own initiative.[10] The thought that background-beliefs form a unity lies behind Heidegger's trust that in Being we have something to talk about. The theme of the later writings, that the subject can only implement the system of background-beliefs, is responsible for Heidegger's exaltation of man's radical dependence upon Being. Thus arises Heidegger's 'problem of Being'.

Let us first examine Heidegger's assumption that the background-beliefs that shape a person's experience cohere in a single system. Now although our various background-beliefs do hang together (or can be made to hang together) in one way or another, it is the variety of different ways they are interconnected that is of importance. Contrary to what Heidegger supposes, logical compatibility (much less an articulated systematicity) is not even a minimal property of the ways beliefs may interconnect. To be sure, some beliefs do hang together coherently in virtue of psychological associations or inferential connections. But it is not at all true that principles connecting all our beliefs have been given in advance. Often it takes some time to develop such principles, and the sense of discovery does not then amount to recollecting what we had understood all along. It is, after all, a common experience to discover that some of our background-beliefs are in outright conflict or, at least, that they are such as to weaken or impugn each other's justification. Many times, far from trying to determine how these beliefs might be modified for the sake of consistency or mutual support, we work out compromises in particular cases or follow sometimes the one belief and sometimes the other. Thus, it is never clear that all of our background-beliefs form a single coherent system, nor do we have any guarantee that we shall find some principle that will establish any coherency. Moreover, we sometimes do not find it *desirable* to systematise our background-beliefs in this way.

Behind Heidegger's notion that all our background-beliefs hang together systematically according to principles understood (however implicitly) in advance, stands the old Hegelian idea that history divides into epochs, each epoch putting into practice a single basic conception of man and the world. The Hegelian influence becomes manifest in the later writings, where Heidegger speaks of *Seinsepochen*, delimitable historical periods guided by a single thought (that he claims to find expressed in the period's representative philosopher!). Heidegger's point that all our background-beliefs have (or can be made to have) some sort of relevance for each other, with which there should be no disagreement, does not justify the quite erroneous conclusions he draws about their unity.

In virtue of the pluralism of the background-beliefs that shape an individual's experience, it no longer appears practical to trust that by gathering together all of his possibilities each of us will discover the one thing he really or 'authentically' is, or even desirable to strive single-mindedly for that kind of consistency. Much of the motivation for assuming that an individual's background-beliefs do or ought to form a single coherent system has lain in the idea that, since consistency supposedly is intrinsically rational, a subject that is constitutive of his experience would have that sort of belief-system. Once we have recognised the inadequacy of the concept of a constitutive subject, we should no longer expect to find an individual's background-beliefs to be mutually consistent. Heidegger's error thus turned on his having taken over an assumption from the theory that he was criticising. It is a further question whether consistency is a necessary feature of rationality at which, under all circumstances, we should aim. Just because we can know nothing with certainty, our beliefs tend to be more adaptive to experience, the less they are strait-jacketed by an obsession with consistency. But a defence of this thesis would lead us beyond the scope of this essay.

Let us turn now to the claim that looms so prevalently in Heidegger's later writings, the claim that the set of beliefs forming the background to an act of understanding delimits in advance the possible forms that act can take. Now compulsive behaviour occurs when a person can see only one alternative in a given situation; unimaginative behaviour takes place when he can see only the range of alternatives commonly seen to be available, the alternatives that people in general (or this person in particular) believe such situations afford. But very often, in varying degree, and with varying importance for our future behaviour, we elaborate responses different from those that were established in advance by what the background-beliefs commonly lead one to expect. Indeed, however much people themselves tend to typify their actions, thinking of them merely as instances of pre-set roles, the beliefs and expectations in which those roles consist are always to some extent open-ended and under-determining. Role-guided behaviour relies upon both general rules and a knowledge of paradigmatic exemplars of such behaviour, and these a person can apply only by making sense on his own of at least some of the contingent features of the particular situation.[11] But, furthermore, there are often possible responses alternative to the type that set beliefs lead us to expect, and accessible even without our recasting any of our background-beliefs. For the network of such beliefs always contains points of vagueness or inconsistency, as well as points where there is no settled opinion, but rather the ferment of conjectures and discoveries. After all, any set of background-beliefs is built up over time, and for that very reason we revise our background-beliefs not holistically but piecemeal. Only an exaggerated idea of the systematicity of our background-beliefs, only the holistic assumption that to change one requires the simultaneous revision of them all, would make it appear impossible to alter some on the basis of others held constant. Only that could suggest Heidegger's thesis that, to gain access to fundamentally new perspectives we must *wait upon* the disclose of a new world.

There is, then, no genuine problem to which Being or the understanding of Being would form a response. The fundamental mistake underlying Heidegger's insistence that the subject is radically dependent upon Being should be clear. He came to think that if the subject is not constitutive of experience, then there must be something else that is, something else that sets up in advance the way the subject understands himself and the things around him. But, first, there is nothing so unitary as 'an understanding of Being' that permeates and structures the background-beliefs that do shape our experience. And secondly, these beliefs organise our experience only somewhat; the subject, too, shapes his experience, somewhat, even if that is possible only against the background of those beliefs. The failures of Heidegger's critique of the constitutive subject can thus teach us two important lessons about how such a critique should proceed: (1) it should not enthrone any other single instance (like 'Being') as constitutive of experience. (2) In devising a better theory of the subject, we must be wary of carrying over assumptions that the concept of a constitutive subject made plausible: we saw that there is now little reason to skirt the fact that a subject's belief-system tends not to form a consistent and fully articulated whole.

I shall now move on to a discussion of Lacan's critique of the concept of a constitutive subject. There we shall encounter once again the temptation to which such critiques are so liable, the temptation to conclude that something else must be constitutive of the subject's experience. I shall then develop further some of the ideas just discussed.

III

Lacan agrees with Heidegger that the subject is never in the position to shape in advance on his own what his experience will be like. For Lacan, the essence of psychoanalysis best finds expression in Freud's comparison of his discoveries to the change Copernicus brought about in our world-picture: once again man has been displaced from the centre of a domain of experience to which (here as a subject) he had assigned himself (*E* 516–17/165). Lacan's writings are notoriously obscure, most of all because he has intended his mode of exposition to exhibit the role of the unconscious that his theory is supposed to be about. It is difficult to avoid the impression that his stylistic mannerisms are also aimed at covering over difficult theoretical problems by making it hard to pin down just what he is saying. Nonetheless, I believe that a reconstruction of his position is not altogether impossible or uninteresting.

Like Heidegger, Lacan wishes to stress the fact that the subject can act and think only against the background of previously accepted beliefs. This background includes some beliefs about the person himself, general conceptions he has of himself and particular self-images geared to the sort of situation at hand. It is through these beliefs that the person orients the actions that make up his behaviour. There can be no self-encounter at the transcendental limits of experience, therefore, not only because the subject always has previous beliefs about the world, but also because he already has some beliefs about himself. Where Lacan moves into topics untouched by Heidegger is in his investigation of the relation between the subject and these various self-conceptions. Lacan's central thesis is that the tendency of the subject to identify himself with what he perceives himself as amounts to a fundamental mistake (*méconnaissance*) that leads the subject astray from his actual nature.

The sort of person someone perceives himself to be consists in a particular way of behaving (what he does and to what end, the way he goes about it, what other objects and people are involved). For Lacan these self-conceptions, the ways a person appears to himself and understands himself, make up the person's ego, or *moi* (in this he means to follow Freud, for whom the ego is the system of beliefs that orient a person's dealings with the real world). But the experience of agency, of actually carrying out some mode of behaviour, can be distinguished from the mode of behaviour itself, from however a person may appear to himself. Of course, they do not form two different, temporally distinct events, but rather distinct aspects of the same event; the basis for the distinction lies in the fact that the subject could always have done otherwise than he did. This principle of agency Lacan calls the subject, the *je* (there is nothing arbitrary about connecting the concept of the subject with the concept of agency, for the tradition has always thought of the subject as the source of activity in behaviour; this idea must, however, be overhauled in the critique of the concept of a constitutive subject). Lacan tends to identify the subject with the Cartesian *cogito*, inasmuch as the *cogito* can be said to comprise, not any particular image a person may have of himself, but the very act of questioning (among other things) the truth of such images. Now while pointing to this distinction between the subject and the ego, Lacan insists upon the dependence of the subject on the web of self-understandings that make up the ego. Far from being constitutive of experience, the subject can act and grasp things only in virtue of the beliefs that yield him a prior understanding of his situation and of the relevant alternatives of thought and action. Before we examine in some detail what Lacan proposes to put in place of the theory of the constitutive subject, it will be best to look first at several further aspects of his distinction between subject and ego.[12]

First of all, Lacan has developed his psychoanalytic understanding of this distinction with constant appeal to the science of linguistics. Lacan believes that this attention to the phenomenon of language is justified by the nature of psychoanalytic therapy as a 'talking cure'. Now what is gradually becoming clear, after the vogue of the 'linguistic turn' in Anglo-American philosophy, is that (outside the special disciplines of phonology and perhaps syntax) there can be no *intrinsic* study of language apart from the other dimensions of human behaviour (intersubjectivity, belief-systems, action) and that no philosophical problems will yield to solution simply by appeal to the nature of language. What is important about language is not language itself but its role as a medium for these other dimensions. Lacan's interest in language lies chiefly in de Saussure's thesis of the systematicity of language, the way that the use of linguistic signs depends upon the backdrop of a web of other such signs with which they are intertwined (*E*: 497–8/149–50). Yet this systematicity of language is nothing else but an expression of the interconnection of beliefs that make up a subject's understanding of his world. For this reason, I do not think it misleading to continue to speak of *belief-systems* or *background-beliefs* when discussing Lacan's work. Of course, it is important not to take this talk of 'beliefs' as implying that they must have been elaborated by a person on his own. Furthermore, Freud's great discovery was that many of the beliefs shaping our experience, the ways we understand and respond to certain situations, lie deeply intertwined with the vicissitudes and frustrations of our desires and may resist being brought to conscious awareness. Background-beliefs may be not only prior to what the subject understands on his own, but even inaccessible to his explicit self-understanding. Thus, I shall be using the term 'belief' to mean a way of understanding certain situations (often with built-in expectations of how to act in them), but I shall not be assuming even that a person is aware of every belief that he has.

Let us next look at an example of how fruitful a tool of analysis Lacan's distinction between subject and ego can be. All desire for another person includes a desire to be recognised by that person and desired in turn. Thus, the projection of some particular way we have of understanding ourselves, some facet of our 'ego', belongs to our desire for another. But, Lacan points out, some awareness of the difference between ourselves as subjects and the self-conception we thus pursue must inhabit this desire, even if this awareness consists only in the fact that how we present ourselves is something *we* (as subjects) must *do*, continually renegotiating it in accord with how we perceive the other person to be reacting toward us. This difference or *Spaltung* (as Lacan puts it) between the subject and how he wishes to be recognised is responsible for the subject's inability ever to be altogether sure that he has won the other's recognition. In this phenomenon Lacan finds the reason for why desire always falls short of any definitive satisfaction (*E*: 627–8/263–4). This account of the unendingness of desire is quite powerful, although it is interesting that Lacan has not exploited its power fully. For the infinity of desire also thrives upon the recognition that the other person is a subject in a similar position, and that however we might come to characterise the other person must fail to capture him as a subject. Or, at least, here is where desire turns into love.

One last point about Lacan's distinction between subject and ego deserves mention, before we go on to examine his critique of the constitutive subject. Lacan claims that the subject eludes all self-perception. Anything like an orderly argument for this thesis is not to be found in Lacan's published writings. But what he has in mind seems to be this. When a person reflects upon his behaviour, he can find all the elements that go into a self-conception, he can make out the component actions, he can feel himself in the attitude of trying to attain some end, but he cannot find, in such reflection, the experience of actually carrying out the actions. For whatever he might have then before his mind, in trying to grasp that experience (some sequential way of doing the actions, the particular attitude in which he does them, the movements of his body) is something that he can imagine carrying out and hence is not the very activity of performing the actions. This argument stands behind Lacan's frequent statement that the subject is what one signifier represents to another signifier.[13] The definition is expressed in linguistic terms, but what it comes down to is this: when a person perceives what he is doing, the perceived self 'represents' or *stands for* the subject in the eyes of the person who perceives, but it is not identical with the subject, which thus is not open to self-perception. The perceived self stands for the subject in a positive sense by permitting the inference to the existence of the subject, but also in a negative sense by luring the person to take it for what it only represents (this would be, in effect, to identify the subject with some aspect of the ego). Now during a person's perception of himself the act of self-perception is itself one in which the subject is engaged. Lacan refers to this act as the 'other signifier' because he wishes to point out that the fate of that act, too, when it comes to be reflected upon, is to become a 'signifier' that can only stand for the subject. According to Lacan, therefore, there is no level of self-reflection where the subject becomes open to self-perception.

This thesis of Lacan is untenable. But I shall defer criticism of it until I have discussed his attack upon the constitutive subject. For the mistake underlying this thesis illuminates the way that Lacan's critique of the constitutive subject, to which we now turn, goes awry.

It should be plain that, although the ego consists in an apparatus of self-conceptions that orient behaviour, these cannot be constitutive of experience in the strong sense that a person possesses them in advance of experience. For these beliefs a person has elaborated or absorbed from others in virtue of other, already accepted beliefs about himself or the world. A theory of the constitutive subject would not claim that these various self-conceptions, or 'selves', are in their own right constitutive of experience, but it would assert that there is a subject that orders

them in varous relations and determines when any particular 'self'
is to come into play. This sort of distinction between subject and ego
would be similar to the Kantian distinction between the transcendental and the phenomenal 'subjects'. On this account, the subject
would be constitutive of experience in that it determines what self-
conception is called for by a particular situation, in advance of the
eventual response that embodies that self-conception. Such a
distinction is not Lacan's, but it does belong to contemporary ego-
psychology, which in the past forty years has grown out of
psychoanalysis, and which has been Lacan's *bête noire*. There is no
better example of recent ego-psychology than the works of Erik
Erikson. Erikson accepts the fact that no self-conception can be
constitutive (in the strong sense mentioned above) of the behaviour
it orients, since it developed out of particular situations (e.g.
childhood-identifications) and gets it significance through the
background-beliefs that shaped those situations as well as the
situations that the person now believes to call for it. But he does
claim that there is a subject (which he calls the 'ego', as opposed to
the 'selves') that orders the various self-conceptions, moulds them
into a 'personal identity', and thereby sets down the conditions
under which any particular self can come to the fore and orient
behaviour. Or, at least this is what happens, he believes, when a
person has developed a 'strong ego'. Erikson describes the ego (in his
sense) as

> The domain of an inner 'agency' safeguarding our coherent
> existence by screening and synthesizing, in any series of moments,
> all the impressions, emotions, memories, and impulses which try
> to enter our thought and demand our action and which would
> tear us apart if unsorted and unmanaged by a slowly grown and
> reliably watchful screening system. (1968: 218)

According to Lacan, ego-psychology is but a recent and rather
unsophisticated variant of the assumption that stands at the origin
of modern subjectivity: the equation of the ego (in his sense) with the
subject.[14] I have sought to show, in my attempted reconstruction of
Lacan's argument, why an equation of whatever a person may
believe himself to be with what it is for him to be a subject (namely,
the activity of carrying out the behaviour that embodies that self-
conception) is mistaken. Nowhere does Lacan draw out anything
like an orderly argument against ego-psychology. Still, I believe

that we can locate the basic weakness in Erikson's position by drawing upon what we have seen Lacan's distinction between subject and ego to consist in. This argument must be what Lacan has in mind, since he seems to be relying upon it when he contrasts the actual nature of the subject with its supposedly constitutive character.

Certainly we must agree with Erikson that each of us has ways of 'screening and synthesizing' the flow of his mental life, within which figure his various conceptions of himself. But the problem is whether any of us has the means for ordering, not just local areas of that flow, but *all* of that flow, *all* of his different self-conceptions. For, first of all, does not the way we organise a set of self-conceptions and determine which ones are to come into play in which situations proceed according to fairly specific rules? And does it not therefore itself embody a particular conception that we have of ourselves? The organising activity thus cannot be constitutive of experience overall, for the self-conception it expresses depends upon past identifications, background-beliefs, and even other beliefs that we have about ourselves, just like any other self-conception. Furthermore, because we organise a range of self-conceptions always with specific considerations and expectations in mind, the chances are that we also have other self-conceptions that are not relevant to the particular task at hand. Of course, the activity of the subject sustains all of a person's behaviour, even his attempts to arrange his various beliefs about himself, just because these are things that he does. But this carrying out of some behaviour, the activity in which being a subject consists, is not the same as *what* precisely he does. Erikson's concept of the ego, as what synthesises self-conceptions, confuses the subject and the ego (in Lacan's sense). For Erikson's 'ego' is universal as only the subject can be; but its function is specific as only a particular self-conception (belonging to the ego) can be.

The upshot of this reconstruction of Lacan's argument is that, not only particular self-conceptions, but also the ways a person has of organising them fail to be constitutive of experience. The modes of organisation themselves turn on beliefs that the person has about himself. Hence, far from settling in advance when each of a person's self-conceptions is called for and is to be allowed to orient his response to given situations, each such mode of organisation will hinge upon the prior acceptance of various beliefs and will be prompted by the sorts of situations those beliefs shape. While it attempts to regulate that dependence for those self-conceptions it orders, its own similar dependence will elude its grasp.[15] I also mentioned that the 'ego-activity' of which Erikson is so fond, usually leaves aside other self-conceptions as barely relevant. These two facts go some of the way toward explaining why, as we noticed in the earlier critique of Heidegger, our web of background-beliefs generally proves to be inconsistent.

The temptation of the subject to identify himself with the ego, with the hope thereby to master his experience, makes up what Lacan calls 'the imaginary order'. A proper recognition of the distinction between subject and ego, on the other hand, lets us see our system of beliefs (including our self-conceptions and our ways of organising them) as something radically 'Other' (*l'Autre*, in Lacan's terminology) to ourselves as subjects, though of course we are intrinsically dependent upon it. The fact that thus *all* of our beliefs are distinct from our position as subjects comprises what Lacan calls 'the Symbolic Order'.[16] Lacan's important insight has been that theories of the constitutive subject fail through not having distinguished between subject and ego. As we have seen, neither ego nor subject can be constitutive of experience.

But from this insight Lacan draws a consequence not unreminiscent of what the later Heidegger thought his critique of the constitutive subject implied. Lacan infers that, since the subject is not the sort of thing to synthesise beliefs, the system of a person's beliefs about himself and the world determines what a person's behaviour may be, and the agency of the subject consists but in carrying out what has been settled in advance. Thus, Lacan claims that 'the subject is determined by the chain of signifiers' (that is, by the person's web of beliefs), that 'the chain of the signifier commands whatever may be made present of the subject', etc. (1973: 65, 115, 137, 185, 188/67, 125–26, 149, 203, 206–7). The web of beliefs, or 'signifying chain', thus shapes the experience of the subject because, Lacan believes, the structure of the chain is *none other than* the structure of the unconscious (1973: 116; also E: 514, 719). Since the unconscious is thus constitutive of experience, of why the subject acts this way or that or construes things as he does, Lacan claims that the job of the analyst is not to interpret the utterances of his patient, not to try to put himself in the position of the patient, but to reconstruct the 'signifying chain' that governs those utterances. The effort of the analyst should lie in relocating the utterances on the 'other scene' where the patient can recognise them, no longer as products of his own doing, but as the system that shapes him. This Lacan takes to be the sense of Freud's adage, *Wo Es war, soll Ich werden.*[17]

It is plain that Lacan has fallen prey to the same mistake that we picked out in Heidegger's theory. He has misunderstood the relation between background-beliefs and the behaviour they shape. Background-beliefs somewhat determine behaviour, but the range of possibilities far outstrips any set of responses that may commonly be associated with those beliefs beforehand. To be sure, Freud's discovery was that many such associations work unbeknownst to a person, that much of his behaviour turns on unconscious associations between types of situation and sorts of response. But it is because even those associations do not express necessary connections, but when brought to light can be put aside or at least held at some distance, that there is any point to a psychoanalytic cure.

I stated before that there is something amiss with Lacan's idea that the subject resists self-perception. The error is what makes his notion of the subject incompatible with the existence of leeway between background-beliefs and the behaviour they (somewhat) determine. According to Lacan, the subject, in contrast to the ego, is not something that a person can grasp when he reflects upon his behaviour. When he reflects upon his behaviour, every attempt to focus upon the agency involved ends up only with another aspect of the mode of behaviour. For this reason, Lacan maintains that the subject is nothing more than this elusiveness, nothing more than a 'fading' or a 'vanishing point' (*Le Séminaire* XI: chs. XVI, XVII). If that is so, if there are no qualities that we can ascribe to the subject, then no wonder it has no role in determining behaviour, but is only the medium for the complete determination from the outside! But it is rather questionable to equate the actual nature of an experience with what explicit reflection, aiming to hold it like an object before the mind, can make of it (for example, that equation underlies erroneous theories which claim that the experienced present is but a fleeting instant, always already over). There is good reason to insist that the subject amounts to more than this 'fading'. For the sort of reflection that Lacan appeals to is not the only way we can be aware, or try to be aware, of the experience of agency. It is a basic, though sadly prevalent mistake to believe that the self-reflexivity of experience consists solely in our ability to distance ourselves from experience and reflect explicitly upon it.[18] Instead, what we then reflect upon is itself inherently reflexive in a variety of ways: in acting, in the action itself, a person sees what he is doing as leading to some end, and (of concern to us here) in acting a person is aware of his agency, of being a subject. Indeed, if we did not have that experience of agency in our actions themselves, we would not know what it is that we are looking for when we find, in *explicitly* reflecting upon behaviour, that it always eludes us. So, in our very actions, we are aware of ourselves as subjects carrying them out. There is no 'fading' of what we then are aware of; we are aware of our agency just so long as we are doing whatever we are doing, so that the experience really never ends at all, though it varies in intensity according to our alertness or to our interest in what we are doing. Even when we perform the experiment of trying to reflect explicitly upon this experience, we remain aware of ourselves carrying out the experiment (it is not just the experiment we are aware of). Furthermore, this experience of agency comprises, again in varying intensity, an awareness of our flexibility, of the fact that we could be acting otherwise than we are. What the other alternatives are will depend, of course, upon various prior beliefs (including self-conceptions belonging to the ego). The experience of flexibility, in which being a subject consists, covers only the fact that other alternatives may be available.

It is this flexibility that fills the space left over by the background-beliefs that determine behaviour only somewhat. In virtue of a recognition that he could always do otherwise, a person may range among the variety of commonly expected responses to a given situation or he can elaborate responses of his own; or, of course, he can revise the beliefs that shape the way he sees the situation, where again the other background-beliefs held constant determine only somewhat the revisions he can make—it depends upon his creativity. I am not claiming that one might deduce a creative response from the flexibility that belongs to the subject. On the contrary, it is the flexibility that rules out the possibility of any deduction. Creativity always outstrips the context in which it arises. Of course, this flexibility of the subject does not take place in a vacuum. There are always background-beliefs that determine (somewhat) what he does, that shape the situation he is responding to and the ends he may be seeking, that provide the standard of relevancy for what he does and structure the felt need he has to do something at all. Context and originality we must learn to see as intertwined instead of as mutually exclusive. We should now be able to recognise that, contrary to Lacan's theory, a recognition of the difference between the subject and the ego does not force upon us the idea that the subject has no role in determining behaviour. *Wo Es war, soll Ich werden*—that means, not that we should resign ourselves to what thoroughly structures our behaviour from without, but that where we acted compulsively or unimaginatively there is always room for a greater suppleness.[19] (It should be clear that by flexibility I mean an openness to new experience and not a routinised nonchalance where nothing matters very deeply—that is itself only another and tiresome self-conception.)

The two critiques of the concept of a constitutive subject that I have considered went wrong because they did not break with the old Kantian opposition between autonomy and heteronomy. That opposition is far too simplistic to apply to the complexity of experience. The subject does not lay down the conditions for experience as such; nor does anything else. Background-beliefs determine, somewhat, what the subject can understand and do; and so does the subject, somewhat. The merit of Lacan's distinction between subject and ego lies in showing that to the subject himself we cannot assign any particular beliefs about himself as a person or about the world. So the role of the flexibility of the subject does not consist in providing the extra beliefs that, along with the background-beliefs, would demonstrate why he necessarily acted or understood something as he did and not possibly otherwise. No set of beliefs, however, detailed, can yield such a deduction. My claim has been that in the flexibility of the subject explanations come to an end and we face the inherent contingency and open-endedness of experience.[20] It is important to spot the chief error to which critiques of the constitutive subject seem prone just because the concept of the constitutive subject continually reappears in contemporary thought. One recent example is Grice's proposal to explicate linguistic meaning in terms of communicative intent. As if the intention to impart something to someone else were possible except against the background of meanings previously understood (Grice 1969)!

Many may agree that the theory I have put forth is more faithful to our sense of experience than the idea of a constitutive subject and the theories of the subject that Heidegger and Lacan put in its place and yet still find this theory unsatisfactory and evasive. For them the problem will still remain why, within the leeway open to the subject, he acted as he did and not otherwise. They would then maintain that this outstanding problem will just have to force us to discard as inadequate any phenomenological account of experience. No explanation, they would claim, can be satisfactory until it shows why something had to be the way it is and not otherwise.[21] Yet problems do not stand outside of a theoretical context; something can be seen to be a problem only upon the acceptance of certain beliefs. And in this case, in order to see the outstanding problem as a problem at all, one must presuppose that our experiential sense of behaviour is wrong, and that, if we have not yet found a theory that can adduce the factors that necessarily led someone to do as he did, it is solely a matter of our ignorance and not an objective property of behaviour. There is, therefore, no non-circular argument from 'the existence of the problem' to the inadequacy of the account of behaviour that I have given here. Since there is now no adequate theory in existence that can explain away the felt contingency of behaviour, there is no reason we should give up our sense of experience by believing that there must be such a theory in the offing.

NOTES

1. See Kant's essay 'An Answer to the Question: What Is Enlightenment?' (1970: 54–60).

2. I shall call Heidegger's notion of *Dasein* his concept of the subject, since he discards the word subject only because of its past associations with the theory of the constitutive subject and with the dependent problem of how the subject can ever prove the existence of an external object (cf. 1967: 60/1962: 87).

3. But, significantly, the concept does capture just what is wrong with the old idea that the meaning of a sentence can be traced back to the indubitable and self-evidencing sense-data that would verify it. If the sense-data are not to be occult but discriminable, if they are going to be meaningful items of experience, then there must be grounds we can have for saying when they occur and which ones occur, grounds to which they 'point'; and in that case it cannot be self-evidently true that such a sense-datum has occurred, but true only in virtue of the obtaining of those grounds.

4. Kant, of course, maintained that in self-apperception we can meet ourselves only as phenomenal subjects existing in time and not as (transcendental) subjects constitutive of experience. But this thesis expresses just how careful Kant was to locate the self-identity of the constitutive subject as in advance of *all* experience (even of our experience of ourselves).

5. Conditioning theories of human learning would appear more plausible if they took this area as their proper domain.

6. See Heidegger, *Sein und Zeit* (1967): 3; *Being and Time* (1962): 22; and *Identität und Differenz* (1957) *Identity and Difference* (1969): 65–66.

7. See *Sein und Zeit*: 148–9; *Being and Time*: 188–90 and especially *Die Grundprobleme der Phänomenologie* (lectures Heidegger gave in 1927, now vol. 24 of the *Gesamtausgabe* (1975): 233).

8. *Sein und Zeit*: 83–88, 235–7; *Being and Time*: 114–22, 279–81. See also his *The Essence of Reasons* (1969b): 81–91. Heidegger expresses this point by stating that a 'world' is an *Entwurf des Seienden im Ganzen*.

9. *Sein und Zeit*: 167–84, 233; *Being and Time*: 210–28, 276. Death acquires ontological significance in Heidegger's thought because, as the extreme negation of all possibilities, it is supposed to point to how they all cohere in a whole.

10. See, for example, his *Über den Humanismus* (1949) (*On Humanism*) in *Martin Heidegger: Basic Writings* (1978): 193–242.

11. For a recent statement of this point, which goes back of course to Aristotle's concept of *phronesis*, see P. Bourdieu, *Esquisse d'une théorie de la pratique* (1972) (*Outline of a Theory of Practice* (1977)).

12. For Lacan's distinction between subject and ego, see *E* 299–300, 304, 517, 520/86, 90, 165, 168 and *Le Séminaire* XI: 127, 138–9. There is a similar distinction between the 'I' and the 'me' in George Herbert Mead's *Mind, Self and Society* (1934): 173–4.

13. See, for example, *Le Séminaire* XI: 188, 207.

14. *E* 281, 421–2, 517/70, 131–3, 165. Lacan's conception of modern subjectivity is rather questionable. To be sure, identification of the ego with the subject, often in the hope of knowing who one 'really' is, is a pervasive feature of our culture. But it is doubtful whether there is anything specifically modern about this phenomenon. Indeed, it is more likely that the *distinction* between subject and ego, an increased awareness of the contingency of whatever we might believe ourselves to be, is a modern achievement.

15. Furthermore, since among the background-beliefs upon which the mode of organisation depends will often figure beliefs upon which the self-conception being organised turns, the organisation generally does not yield anything like a full mastery of what it is dealing with.

16. This should clarify the sense of Lacan's formula that *l'inconscient, c'est le discours de l'Autre* (the unconscious associations belonging to a system of beliefs leave their traces in what the subject says). Cf. *E* 549/193–4.

17. *E*: 416–17, 864–5/128–9. Cf. *Le Séminaire* XI: 192/212. 'Interpretation is directed not so much at the meaning as towards the reduction of the signifiers in their non-meaning so that we may rediscover the determinants of the subject's entire behaviour.'

18. The classical theory of self-reflexivity made it a second-order attitude toward experience itself which was directed solely toward the world. Cf. Locke, *Essay on Human Understanding*, bk II, ch. 1, s. 24; Hume, *Treatise of Human Nature*, bk I, pt I, s. 2. It is of interest to note that in another passage Locke (whose chief virtue as a philosopher was to think instead of trying to remain consistent) writes of 'it being impossible for anyone to perceive without perceiving that he does perceive' (*Essay*, bk II, ch. 27, s. 9). Leibniz criticises this remark on the basis of the classical theory (*Nouveaux Essais*, bk II, ch. 1, s. 19).

19. Isn't the thought that our behaviour is but an instantiation of forms given in advance itself a particular self-conception? No doubt many find that it gives them a sense of destiny. Might not Freud's idea be relevant here, that the ego-instincts are tied to repetition-compulsion, especially if we think of the ego-'instincts' as a denial of the subject?

20. For a suggestive account of this idea see the final chapter of Merleau-Ponty's *Phénoménologie de la perception* (1945).

21. This idea has a long tradition. Cf. Aristotle, *Posterior Analytics*, 71b 10f.

7 The Imaginary

JACQUELINE ROSE

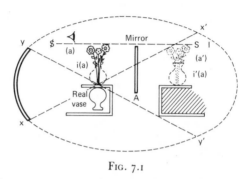

FIG. 7.1

I cannot urge you too strongly to meditate on the science of optics
. . . peculiar in that it attempts by means of instruments to produce that
strange phenomenon known as *images*, unlike the other sciences which
carry out on nature a division, a dissection, or anatomical breakdown. (*Le
Séminaire* 1 : 90)

. . . in so far as it is an optical schema, the model is precisely unable to
indicate that the look, as a partial object *a*, is deeply hidden and unattain-
able to the same extent as I am unable to see myself from the place where the
Other is looking at me. *Scilicet* no. 2/3: 120

This article attempts to do three things: (1) to place the concept of
the Imaginary as used in recent papers on film theory back in its
psychoanalytic context; (2) to show how the psychoanalytic
literature from which it has been drawn has itself undermined the
concept as an original reference to an autonomous psychic instance;
(3) to suggest that this partial collapsing of the Imaginary throws
into question the use of the concept to delineate or explain some
assumed position of plenitude on the part of the spectator in the
cinema.[1]

The proliferation of references to psychoanalysis in recent
literature on the cinema is probably exceeded only by the number of

references to the camera and geometrical optics in the literature of psychoanalysis itself. These references could be said to fall broadly into two main categories:

1. The relationship between the observer and the camera/mirror/screen/microscope, taken as the model for the psychic apparatus; in which case the stress is on 'virtuality', referring either:

(a) to positions within the apparatus:

we should picture the instrument which carries out our mental functions as resembling a compound microscope or a photographic apparatus, or something of the kind. On that basis, psychical locality will correspond to a point inside the apparatus at which one of the preliminary stages of an image comes into being. In the microscope and telescope, as we know, these occur in part at ideal points, regions in which no tangible component of the apparatus is situated. (*SE* v: 536)

(b) to the status of the object to be recorded in relation to that of the apparatus:

When you see a rainbow, you are seeing something purely subjective. You can see it at a certain distance where it joins the surrounding scenery. It is not there. It is a subjective phenomenon. And yet, thanks to a photographic apparatus, you will be able to record it quite objectively . . . Is it not true to say that the photographic apparatus is a subjective apparatus constructed entirely through the assistance of an x and y which inhabit the domain in which the subject lives, that is the domain of language? (*Le Séminaire* 1: 91)

(c) or to the status of the image itself:

The interest of what I have called *the mirror stage* is in its manifestation of the affective dynamism whereby the subject primordially identifies with the visual *Gestalt* of its own body . . . an ideal unity, or salutary *imago*. (*E* 113, 18–19)

In each of these cases, the virtual nature of image, object, or apparatus seems to be displaceable; the experiment of the 'inverted vase' can be used to produce a virtual image of an upright real image of a real object, which is in fact upside down and out of sight (cf. p. 142 for explanation of the stages of the experiment).

2. The subject as producer of symptoms, taken as the metaphors for a repressed signifier, where the emphasis on the visual image can refer to:

(*a*) complete foreclosure of symbolic or verbal representation, as in the case of hallucination;

(*b*) scenic substitution, as in the case of the screen memory;

(*c*) regression through the mental apparatus during sleep to the visual cathexis of mnemic traces as immediate perceptions. (In this last case, the comparison with the symptom only becomes legitimate if the visual cathexis of the image is related to its latent content, and hence to the dream as compromise-formation).

Any appeal to these references by film theory has to ask whether they are simply generalisable as references to the subject's constitutional drive towards fabrication, or whether they can act as the point of a more precise dialogue between psychoanalysis and analysis of the cinema, in which the relationship of spectator to film could be seen as the formal microcosm, and reiteration, of this fictional insertion of the subject into its world. The conflation of the optical language of projection and identification as specified in Lacan's concept of the Imaginary with the looser connotation of the term as some form of fictional narrative has made this concept the nodal point of such an encounter; 'identification' again often being used loosely to refer to the assumed compliance of the film with the desire of the spectator (also assumed).

The foundations of Lacan's concept of the Imaginary first appear in his paper 'The Mirror Stage' (*E* 93–100/1–7), which takes as its major reference point Freud's 1914 paper 'On Narcissism–an Introduction' (*SE* XIV : 73–102). 'On Narcissism' will therefore form the (belated) starting-point of this discussion, the myth of Narcissus being especially apt to delineate that moment in which an apparent reciprocity reveals itself as no more than the return of an image to itself.

I

In 1914, Freud's original postulate of an opposition between sexual libido and ego or self-preservative interest had been challenged by a body of psychic disorders, loosely called schizophrenia or daementia praecox, and which Freud preferred to call paraphrenia to cover both daementia praecox and paranoia, in which the sexual libido withdrawn from objects of the external world and redirected on to objects of phantasy in neurosis, was simply displaced on to the subject's ego with no intermediary substitutes. The presence of what appeared to be purely ego-directed libido, with the corresponding shift of emphasis to this question of direction, veered dangerously close to the Jungian concept of libido as a pure energic reservoir distinguishable only according to the direction of its moments. It was in order to anticipate and forestall this interpretation of ego-libido that Freud makes his crucial distinction, in the paper on narcissism, between auto-erotic instincts (the child derives its first sexual satisfaction auto-erotically, that is, from its own body) and the ego as a separate function:

> The auto-erotic instincts, however, are there from the very first; so there must be something added to auto-eroticism—a new psychical action—in order to bring about narcissism. (*SE* XIV: 77)

For Lacan, it is this moment which sets up the ego as an imaginary instance:

> The *Urbild*, which is a unit comparable to the ego, is constituted at a specific moment in the subject's history, from which the ego begins to take up its functions. In other words the human ego is constituted on the foundations of the imaginary relation The function of the ego, Freud writes, must have *eine neue psychiche . . . Gestalt*. In the development of the psychic organism, some thing new appears whose function it is to give shape to narcissism. Surely this marks the imaginary origin of the ego-function? (*Le Séminaire* I: 133)

—a specific Urbild or construct, therefore, which from then on functions as the instance of the Imaginary, commanding both the illusory nature of the relationship between the subject and the real world, and the relationship between the subject and the identifications which form it as 'I'. The confusion at the basis of an 'ego-psychology' would be to emphasise the relationship of the ego to the perception-consciousness system over and against its role as fabricator and fabrication, designed to preserve the subject's precarious pleasure from an impossible and non-compliant real. The various shifts in Freud's own use of the concept from *Studies on Hysteria* (*SE* II)

(1893–5) where it is presented as an ideational mass, to its complete delineation as a separate function in the final topography (*The Ego and the Id*, 1923) (*SE* XIX: 12–66) partially lend themselves to such a confusion. Lacan grafts his concept of the Imaginary on to the moment at which the fortification of the ego is conjoined with the possibility of deceptive self-reference in the concept of narcissism. In the 1936 paper 'The Mirror Stage', the relationship between narcissism and ego-formation 'reverses': the ego itself becomes the reflection of a narcissistic structure grounded on the return of the infant's image to itself in a moment of pseudo-totalisation. In Section II of the *Ecrits*, narcissism will be taken as the starting-point for three constitutive moments—that of the ego, of the function of recognition in its capacity to engender a potentially infinite number of objects in the world, and of the correlative functions of aggressivity and libidinal object-choice.

What does Lacan mean, therefore, when he states that the ego is an imaginary function? In what way is his concept of the Imaginary distinct from the point, stressed as early as 1895 by Freud in his *Project for a Scientific Psychology* (*SE* I: 295–397), that the establishment of perceptual identity by the ego allows reality to be set up only to the satisfaction of the pleasure principle?

In his seminar of 1954, Lacan introduces the case-history of a six-year-old boy, named as Robert, as relevant to the psychoanalytic distinction between neurosis and psychosis. The case is presented by Rosine Lefort, who describes her patient as he first appeared to her at the age of three years and nine months in a state of hyper-agitation aggravated by complete motor and linguistic inco-ordination. I will not go into the details of the child's development through analytic treatment, but will stop at one of the first behavioural manifestations of the patient to be presented by the analyst: 'Unco-ordinated prehension—the child would throw out his arm to grasp an object and if he missed it, he would not be able to rectify his movement, but had to start it again from scratch' (*Le Séminaire* I: 108). Lacan seizes on this factor as revealing that the subject's control of objects is not dependent on its visual capacity, but on the *synthesis* of this with the sense of distance, their co-ordination dependent on its ability to conceptualise its body as total; the rectification of the child's motor inco-ordination during analysis is taken to demonstrate the relation 'between strictly sensori-motor maturation and the subject's functions of imaginary control' (*Le Séminaire* I: 122). The early emphasis by Lacan on *Gestalt*, on the child's ability to represent its body to itself, is, therefore, not simply a notion of some comforting if illusory poise, but is directly linked at this stage in his theory to its ability to control its world in a physical sense. In fact, one of the key factors of the mirror-stage is that the child is in a state of nursling dependency and relative motor inco-ordination and yet the image returned to the child is fixed and stable, thereby anticipating along the axis of maturation. Robert's incapacity is therefore a type of regressive paradigm of the mirror-stage where the absence of image leads to a failure in the function of bodily co-ordination. What is important here is the relationship between control, and an auto-synthesis based on a projected image of the subject, a relationship confirmed by the behavioural phenomenon of transitivism, in which the child imitates and completes the action of the other child in play:

> those gestures made up of fictive actions whereby a subject redirects the imperfect effort of the other's gestures by confusing their distinct application, those synchronies of specular cap-tation, all the more remarkable in that they anticipate the complete co-ordination of the motor apparatuses which they bring into play. (*E* 112/18)

Taking off from the behavioural confirmations of the mirror-stage, Lacan then reads it back into a structure of subjectivity, whose basic relation is that between a fragmented or inco-ordinate subject and its totalising image (the structural equivalent of the metonymic relation part for whole). In order to vehicule the image, the subject's own position must be fixed (in the first stage of the inverted vase experiment—cf. Fig. 7.1.—the eye must be inside the cone formed by a generating line joining each point of the image i(a) to the surface of the spheric mirror). It is from this fixity, and the images that are thus produced, that the subject is able to postulate objects of permanence and identity in the world.[2]

The mirror stage is, therefore, the focus for the interdependency of image, identity and identification: 'We have only to understand the mirror stage *as an identification*, in the full sense that analysis gives to the term: namely, the transformation that takes place in the subject when it assumes an image' (*E* 94/2). As a result of identifying itself with a discrete image, the child will be able to postulate a series of equivalencies between the objects of the surrounding world, based on the conviction that each has a recognisable permanence. Identification of an object world is therefore grounded in the moment when the child's image was alienated from itself as an imaginary object and sent back to it the message of its own subjecthood. It is the process of enumeration and exchange which sets off from this point that will inform Lacan's later concept of linguistic insistence, defined as a process which starts off from this position of a signifier which was primarily evicted from its own place.

The narcissistic mode of identification has as its corollary both the libidinal object-tie and the function of aggressivity. Lacan refers to Weissman's theory of the germ-plasm as confirmation of Freud's distinction between the subject as individual ego and the subject as the member of a species whose sexual function it is to privilege the type, and stresses that sexual drive depends on a recognition of appropriateness or typicality (rarely is sexual drive aroused by.a member of another species).

In Freud's 1914 paper, narcissism became the prototype of a form of object choice based on the subject's own image(s) and was opposed to the anaclitic, where sexual desire was attached to self-preservative interest and hence selected its object according to the image of provider or protector. Lacan's emphasis places narcissism not only in opposition to the anaclitic form of object choice, but actually at the root of the miminal recognition necessary to ensure the subject's sexual engagement. Thus libido, far from being an energic or substantialist concept, is constitutionally bound to the Imaginary: 'We call libidinal investment that which makes an object desirable, that is, what leads to its confusion with the image we carry within us, diversely, and more or less, structured' (*Le Séminaire* I: 162). What this means simply is that access to the object is only ever possible through an act of (self-)identification.[3] At the same time this relation of the libidinal object-tie to identification reveals perhaps at its clearest the paradox that the subject finds or recognises itself through an image which simultaneously alienates it, and hence, potentially, *confronts* it. This is the basis of the close relationship between narcissism and aggressivity, and Lacan turns to Klein for confirmation of the aggressive component of the original imaginary operation. The child expels objects which it fears as dangerous: 'Why dangerous? For exactly the same reason as it is dangerous for them. Precisely *en miroir*, the child reflects onto them the same destructive capacities which it feels itself to contain' (*Le*

Séminaire I: 96). It then turns to other objects, distinguished from and related to the first by means of an imaginary equation:

Different objects from the external world, more neutralised, will be posed as the equivalents of the first, will be related to them by an equation which, note, is imaginary. Thus the symbolic equation [faeces—urine] which we rediscover between these objects arises from an alternating mechanism of expulsion and introjection, of projection and absorption, that is to say, from an imaginary game. (*Le Séminaire* I: 96)

Lacan goes on to make a distinction between projection and introjection, which will be discussed later. The point here is that the expulsion and absorption of objects in a Kleinian sense acts as the aggressive counterpart of the subject's discovery of itself in an alienated and alienating image which presents itself as dangerous and hence potentially as a rival. The final Oedipal identification of the subject with his or her rival (the parent of the same sex) is only made feasible by this primary identification which places the subject in a position of auto-rivalisation. The death instinct can be reformulated at this stage by Lacan as stemming not only from the submission of the individual to factor x of 'eternal life', but also from the libido's obligatory passage through the Imaginary, where it is subjected to a master image, and ultimately to the image of the master (the Oedipus complex).

Two factors emerge from this preliminary delineation of the Imaginary—the factor of aggression, rivalry, the image as alienating on the one hand, and the more structurally oriented notion of a fundamental mis-recognition as the foundation of subjectivity, with the image as salutary fiction, on the other. The division is in a sense arbitrary, and the two are bound by the concept of the ego as the instance of negation, presented by Freud in his 1925 paper of that title (*SE* XIX: 235–9) as the symbolic equivalent of the original expulsion mechanism whereby the subject builds itself and its world. The mirror-phase demonstrates this process whereby the subject negates itself and burdens/accuses/attacks (*charger*) the other, and this has its corollary in the analytic setting where inclination towards the imaginary relation between analyst and analysand is always the sign of a resistance to signification:

it is to the extent that the being's admission fails to reach its

destination that the utterance carries over to the axis where it
latches onto the other . . . The subject latches onto the other
because what is struggling for utterance fails. The blocking of the
utterance, in so far as something perhaps makes it fundamentally impossible, is the pivot where, in analysis, speech tips
over entirely onto its original aspect and is reduced to its function
of relating to the other. (*Le Séminaire* 1: 59–60)

The emphasis on verbal communication[4] belongs here to Lacan's
distinction between the Imaginary and the Symbolic, in their
relationship to the third category, the Real. Before discussing these
categories, it is necessary to show how the concepts which have so far
emerged from that of narcissism can be further broken down into
ideal ego and ego ideal on the one hand, and into the three types of
identification put forward by Freud in Chapter 7 of *Group Psychology
and the Analysis of the Ego* (*SE* XVIII: 105–10) on the other, since it is on
to these further distinctions that the Lacanian triptych will be
charted.

In his paper on narcissism, Freud goes on to discuss the relationship of the ego to repression, in that the ego becomes the
guardian of that narcissistic self-regard lost with the insertion of the
infant into a social world, and hence only retrievable by the setting-
up of an image on which the subject will model itself. It is in the
paragraph which describes this process, through which the subject
conforms to an image which is, and can make it, the centre of its
world, that the distinction between ideal ego and ego ideal appears:

The subject's narcissism, makes its appearance displaced on to this
new ideal ego, which, like the infantile ego, finds itself possessed of
every perfection that is of value . . . He is not willing to forego
the narcissistic perfection of his childhood . . . he seeks to recover
it in the new form of an ego ideal. (*SE* XIV: 94)

The distinction would seem to correspond to choice (*b*) and (*c*) of
the four alternative narcissistic object choices:

(*a*) what he himself is (i.e. himself);
(*b*) what he himself was;
(*c*) what he himself would like to be;
(*d*) someone who was once part of himself (*SE* XIV: 90)

—the ideal ego corresponding to what 'he himself was', and the ego ideal to what 'he himself would like to be', at the moment at which they can be identified as disjunct. The ideal ego would therefore be a projected image with which the subject identifies, and comparable to the imaginary captation of the mirror-phase; the ego ideal would be a secondary introjection whereby the image returns to the subject invested with those new properties which, after the 'admonitions of others' and the 'awakening of his own critical judgement' (*SE* XIV: 94) are necessary for the subject to be able to retain its narcissism while shifting its 'perspective'.

The distinction here is that between projection as related to *Gestalt*, and introjection as invariably accompanied by the speech of the Other,[5] that is, to introjection as a symbolic moment, and the basis on which the further social investment necessary for the formation of the super ego will intervene. Significantly, when Freud introduces category (*c*), he adds the proviso that it will not be justified until a later stage in the discussion, the point at which he introduces the concept of the super ego.

The ideal ego will therefore be what the subject once was, the ego ideal what it would like to be in order to retrieve what it was, this being achieved by the introjection of someone who was once part of itself, the movement between them being the attempt to present-ify (make present or actual) their relation (what the subject is (*a*)). What Freud is describing is the impossible and continually re-asserted attempts of the subject to maintain the imaginary fiction of its own totality through which it was primordially constituted. The problem of a clash between an existential and formal ego ideal is raised, during the March 1954 seminar on this topic, by Leclaire:

> either displacement of the libido takes place once more onto an image, an image of the ego, that is, onto a form of the ego, which we call ideal, since it is not like that of the ego as it is now, or as it once was—or else we call the ego ideal something which is beyond any one form of the ego, something which is strictly speaking an ideal, and which approximates more to the notion of idea or form. (*Le Séminaire* I: 156)

The formal moment of the ideal ego is its structuration at the primary point of the mirror-phase, and the distinction between ideal ego and ego ideal resolves itself into the two moments of that phase, that of the corporeal image, prior and resistant to symbolisation, and that of the relation to the other, ultimately dependent on such symbolisation (the Other).

The experiment of the inverted vase is Lacan's illustration of these distinctions. It falls into two stages, the first of which is a fairly well-known experiment of geometrical optics:

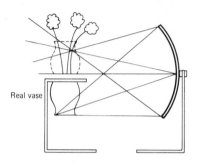

Real vase

FIG. 7.2

By means of a spheric mirror, a real and inverse image can be produced of a vase which is upside down and concealed from sight. The image does not require an interposed screen for its observation but merely that the observing subject be situated in line with the point where the rays of light reflected off the mirror converge. This is the corporeal image of the subject and Lacan describes it as primary narcissism: 'This first narcissism is situated, if you like, on the level of the real image of my schema, in so far as that image makes it possible to organise the whole of reality within a certain number of pre-formed frames' (*Le Séminaire* 1: 144).

The corporeal image is identical for all mechanisms of the subject, and gives form to its *Umwelt*, in so far as it is a man or woman (and not, say, a horse). The unity of the subject depends on that image, and it becomes the basis for all future projection. The image of the upside down vase reversing itself into a position where it contains the diversity of the separate flowers (the original experiment is in fact the other way round) makes the experiment especially apt to demonstrate the slight access which the subject has to its own body.

In the second part of the experiment (Fig. 7.1), a virtual image is produced by means of a second mirror placed in front of the real image; the observer is now placed in such a position that he or she can see this virtual image without being able to see the real image of which it is the reflection; at each point it is the subject's necessary remove from the source of its own 'imagery' that is stressed. The virtual image is the place of secondary narcissism which enables the subject to situate its imaginary and libidinal relation to the world: 'to *see* in its place, and to structure as a function of that place and its world (. . .) its *libidinal being*. The subject sees its being in a reflection in relation to the other, that is to say, in relation to the ego ideal' (*Le Séminaire* 1: 144–5).[6]

The relationship posited here is given striking corroboration by Freud's own comment in a footnote to *Group Psychology and the Analysis of the Ego*: 'A path leads from identification by way of imitation to empathy, that is, to the comprehension of the mechanism by means of which we are enabled to take any attitude at all towards another mental life' (*SE* xviii: 110n2)—especially when taken in conjunction with his separate observation on the 'narcissistic origin of compassion (which is confirmed by the word itself)' (*Mitleid*) (*SE* xvii: 88).

How then does this place and structure inform the subject's future identifications? In *Group Psychology and the Analysis of the Ego*, Freud sets out to explain the relationship between this introjected ego ideal and the socialisation of the subject in a further group identification between egos. Taking the group phenomenon as the culmination of the deceptive function of identification, Lacan reformulates the question:

> how an object reduced to its most stupid reality, and yet assigned by a certain number of subjects the function of common denominator, thereby confirming what we will call its function as token, is capable of precipitating the identification of the ideal ego straight into that idiotic power of mis-chief that it basically reveals itself to be. (*E* 677)

The power of the ego ideal to propel the subject into a position of dual submission to the master image introjected as ego ideal, and to those egos with which it posits itself as equivalent, becomes the starting-point for a second set of questions about the effective modes of identification, and their relationship to a demand which attempts to posit its own sufficiency, to retrieve or reconstitute a position of plenitude, and desire, the concept now introduced which gradually undermines this certitude.

Freud posits three types of identification:

(*a*) identification as the original form of emotional tie with an object;

(*b*) regressive identification as a substitute for a libidinal object-tie by means of introjection of the object on to the ego;

(*c*) identification which arises with a new perception of a (repressed) common quality shared with some other person who is not the object of the sexual instinct.[7]

I will start with the first form of identification to illustrate the problems which emerge from this new breakdown in relation to what has been presented so far, before going on to discuss them separately in terms of the Lacanian categories.

Freud first makes a distinction between identification and desire (object choice), giving the former precedence over the latter:

> In the first case one's father is what one would like to *be*, and in the second he is what one would like to *have*. The distinction, that is, depends on whether the tie attaches to the subject or the object of the ego. The former kind of tie is therefore already possible before any sexual object choice has been made. (*SE* xviii: 106)

By making the small boy's pre-Oedipal identification with his father the model of primary identification, Freud clearly anticipates Lacan's stress on the alienating function of identification, and its close links with a potential rivalry which seeks to eliminate its object. Freud confirms the link by making this identification with the father, that is the primary socialisation of the subject, a derivative of the first, oral, phase of development:

> Identification, in fact, is ambivalent from the very first; it can turn into an expression of tenderness as easily as into a wish for someone's removal. It behaves like a derivative of the first, *oral* phase of the organisation of the libido, in which the object which we long for and prize is assimilated by eating and is in that way annihilated as such. (*SE* xviii: 105)

Introjection of the ego ideal has its purely libidinal equivalent in the mechanism of incorporation, which acts here as a double reference to the cannibalistic relationship between mother and child (later to be stressed by Klein), and to the totem meal, where absorption of the father's body leads to the appropriation of his status and name.

Only the first part of this dyad can strictly speaking be termed incorporation, since the second is its ritualised and social derivative, and is therefore related to the introjection of the ego ideal which had been defined as necessarily bound to language.

The totem meal now appears as a ritual symbolisation of the transcendence of those forms of rivalry (Oedipus as a secondary rivalisation) which only appear at the point where identification becomes contaminated with the question of desire. This question appears excluded from the unmitigated demand characteristic of the oral and anal phases of development which imply the possibility of the total incorporation or mastery of the object (the fiction of plenitude). Lacan reads the three types of identification posited by Freud in terms of the gradual intrusion of the axis of desire on to the axis of identification, an intrusion which can be measured against the shift from the drives of demand (oral, anal) to those of desire (scopic, invocatory) in which the physical distance of the object reveals the relation between subject and object to be necessarily disjunct. Note that it is precisely at the moment when those drives most relevant to the cinematic experience as such start to take precedence in the Lacanian topography that the notion of an imaginary plenitude, or of an identification with a demand sufficient to its object, begins to be undermined. The three forms of identification can tentatively be equated with three moments which correspond to the Lacanian division Real, Imaginary, Symbolic:

(a) privation (demand directed to a lost object);
(b) frustration (demand which cannot be given its object);
(c) castration (demand for which there is no object).

Each type of identification is thus taken as the model for a mode of relation (primary object-relation, regressive identification with libidinal object, identification between egos), a structure of insufficiency (privation, frustration, castration), and a tension between demand and desire with a corresponding set of alternative drives.

What is important here is that the demand of the subject is in each case directed outwards to an external object, and it is the relationship of this demand to the place of the object it claims that becomes the basis for identification. The earlier emphasis on ideal ego inevitably fades as both incorporation and introjection obscure the plane of a projected or objectifiable totality. The precedence of the Real in the Lacanian scheme, as the point of the subject's confrontation with an endlessly retreating reality, signals this definition of the subject in terms of an object which has been lost, rather than of a totality which it anticipates.

The reference for this can again be taken from Freud, in the path that leads from his early remarks on the loss of the object which characterises the infant's relation to the world (*The Project for a Scientific Psychology* (*SE* I: 366–7)) to the concept of repetition elaborated in the *Fort Da* game (*Beyond the Pleasure Principle*) (cf. *SE* XVIII: 14–17). Thus in the first instance Freud indicates that the child's first utterance (the cry) is predicated on the missing object which it thereby represents, and in the second that the infant only finds or constitutes itself through the articulation and the repetition of the loss of the object in play: '. . . the alternation presence/ absence only *makes sense* to the extent that the infant can identify itself with the reel of cotton as absent, which presupposes the logical foundation of its identification to a signifier which is missing' (*Scilicet* no. 2/3: 111). Taken together these instances point to what Lacan will call the constitution of the subject in the moment of its splitting (hence *Ichspaltung*), a moment which we can already discern in the fiction of self-representation—the subject sees itself as a whole only by being placed *elsewhere*—of the mirror-stage. It is the loss of the object and the relation of the subject to this loss—the knots which the subject gets into in its attempts to elide or re-place it—that Lacan terms the structure of desire.

II

At this point the two-dimensional optical schema is no longer adequate since the object is visible, or rather on the same dimension as the image which is its substitute. What is now needed is a means of representing the essential disjunction between the imaginary and the lost object as existing on a separate plane. The author of 'The Splitting of the Subject and Its Identification' (*Scilicet* no. 2/3: 103–36) takes the torus or solid ring to represent this disjunction, since operation or movement carried out on its surface circumscribes a central void which determines the limits of that movement while remaining essentially outside it. I will use these diagrams together with the first optical schema, as I think they most clearly illustrate the inadequacy of that schema and the need to reformulate the question of the subject in relation to the object of the scopic drive. The subject is now defined no longer in terms of reflection (the image) but in terms of differentiation (cuts, joining, disjunction).

The author of 'The Splitting of the Subject' quotes Freud to show how identification in itself depends on a repetition which can only be the mark of its own difference: 'The identification is a partial and extremely limited one and only borrows a single trait from the person who is its object' (*SE* xviii: 107). This single trait is the 'unique' trait since the whole series will depend on its pure repetition; the idea of unity is here rigorously dissociated from the idea of totality, at the basis of the earlier concept of *Gestalt*, and attached to the structural concept of a unit as a single element in an already functioning enumeration system. It is therefore called a unary rather than a unique trait, since it can only be articulated as that which is apparently identical. The example drawn on here is de Saussure's 8.45 Geneva–Paris express (de Saussure 1972: 151/1974: 108) which, although it can manifestly be a different train from that of the previous day, is yet identifiable as the same since it is different in function from the rest.

Thus Freud's remark, made in reference to the second form of identification, is extrapolated as the indication of a potentially structuralist concept of identity, where each element is distinct from its own origin, different at each new instance of its repetition, and identical only in its opposition to all the other elements in the signifying chain. This concept was obviously implicit in Lacan's stress on the determinate role of the 'other' image in the mirror-phase; here it represents a new emphasis on *coupure* or splitting, of which the compulsive repetition of trauma will be the clinical counterpart: '. . . we see here a point that the subject can approach only by dividing itself into a certain number of agencies' (*Le Séminaire* xi: 51). The movement away from a stress on illusory totality and identity, to identity as a function of repeated difference can thus be seen as representing a shift in Lacan's emphasis from the Imaginary, to the structure of linguistic insistence as already underpinning moments prior to its intervening symbolisation.

The first diagram (Fig. 7.3) shows the relationship of demand to privation, the circles repeating themselves in a helix around the ring representing demand in its repetitive function, while showing

(*a*) that demand cannot attain itself, but increases its distance

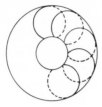

Fig. 7.3   Fig. 7.4

from its point of departure at each turn, thereby testifying to its incapacity to seize the object which supports its own movement;

(*b*) that the point at which demand does meet up with itself is the point at which it has outlined the central void, but *without knowing it*, since it has no point of contact outside its own surface.

Here the subject identifies with the all-powerful signifier of demand from which it is indistinguishable; but already unable to signify the lost unit except by repeating it as different, it fades before that signifier.

In the second drawing (Fig. 7.4), the subject thinks it has gone the round of its own space, but fails to distinguish between the space interior to its outer surface, and the central void which it has simultaneously circumscribed without realising it. The diagram illustrates the distinction between idealisation—a 'complete' rotation—and desire—a central void—of which there is no knowledge.

Turning next to Lacan's optical schema, the emphasis is now placed on the second mirror A, manipulate by the Other (*Autre*), so that whereas the first image depended on the fixity of the observing subject, the second virtual image is a function of the relationship between the rotation of mirror A and the field of space behind it. The distinction between projection and introjection, the image emitted and received, is now reinforced by the intervention of the Other as the locus of speech, which, investing the ego ideal with language, sets it up for subsequent identification with the Law. This role of the Other

(*a*) undermines the autonomy of the primary *Gestalt*;

(*b*) reveals its own position as exponent of desire, which means that it is seen to be determined by the same loss or void as that which underpins the demand of the subject itself.

The Imaginary can now be defined in terms of this intrusion of the Other, and the corresponding tension between the assumed plenitude of A and its gradual emergence as incomplete. Lacan criticises his first schema in these terms:

> we would be wrong to believe that the big Other of discourse can be absent from any distance taken up by the subject in its relation to the other, which is opposed to it as the small other, as belonging to the imaginary dyad. (*E* 678)

This Other is now even referred back to the primary moment of the mirror-stage:

> For the Other, the place of discourse, always latent to the triangulation that consecrates that distance, is not yet so as long as it has not spread right into the specular relation in its purest moment: in the gesture with which the child in front of the mirror, turning to the one who is holding it, appeals with its look to the witness who decants, verifying it, the recognition of the image, of the jubilant assumption, where indeed *it already was*. (*E* 678)

The permeation of the Other over the specular relation therefore reveals the necessity of *appeal*, and hence the structural incompleteness of that relation, and then, through that, the irreducible place of desire within the original model:

> The problem is that our model throws no light on the position of the *objet a*. For as an image for a play of images, it cannot describe the function which that object receives from the symbolic. . . . *a*, the object of desire, at the starting point at which our model situates it, is, as soon as it begins to function there . . . the object of desire. . . . Which is why, reflected in the mirror, it does not only provide a′ as the standard of exchange, the currency whereby the other's desire enters into the ideal ego's moments of transitivity. It is returned to the field of the Other as exponent of the desire in the Other. (*E* 682)

Thus the object is missing from the Other, while this still acts as the place wherein the subject alienates its own image and simultaneously grounds its desire.

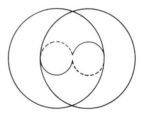

Fig. 7.5

In a next stage, the subject, having gone the round of its own impossibility, will simply displace on to the Other its conception of a full subjectivity or plenitude which it addresses to the Other as demand. Fig. 7.5 is the model of frustration, as that moment when, basing its desire in this alienating image, the subject finds that its own demand as subject is identifiable with the desire of the Other; and the demand of the Other identifiable with its own desire. The outer circle of repetition can be seen to coincide with the central void of the secondary torus to which the first makes its appeal. This can be taken as the new model for the imaginary structure, manifested most clearly in transference, when the neurotic directs its demand to the object of desire, the one object that cannot be demanded, and simultaneously submits its desire to the Other's demand; this latter expectation is recognisable as the basis for the impositions of the super ego. The author of 'The Splitting of the Subject' defines this relationship:

> It is this very moment that reveals what it is that binds the Other to the imaginary function, since it is through its identification to the specular image that the subject of privation now comes to differentiate, from those circles which can cancel each other out on the surface of the torus, those which are irreducible because they circumscribe a void. (*Scilicet* no. 2/3: 121)

In this way, the subject relies on the Other in the imaginary relation, not to constitute a full identity, but in order to circumscribe a void identified with the Other's demand; the object of desire at this point appears to be concealed within that demand, which acts as the metaphor for the unary trait. Specular identification replaces a previously undifferentiable series of repetitions with this new equivalence. The rigour of the subject's conformity is not due to the cancellation of a void, but to the simultaneous differentiation and displacement of that void which such identification permits. This mode of identification corresponds to the regressive mode of identification which is a substitute for the lost libidinal object tie; the subject identifies with the object of its demand for love.

In the final stage of the topography, the object of desire has been stamped as the effect of the impossibility for the Other to reply to demand. Henceforth 'the object is no longer an object of subsistence, but object of the ek-sistence of the subject: the subject there finds its place outside of itself, and it is to this function that the *objet a* of the first rivalry will ultimately be led' (*Scilicet* no. 2/3: 123). The moment of castration is that in which the Other reveals itself as exponent of desire or false witness, and it represents the final collapse of the Other as the guarantor of certitude. Desire is now the point of intersection between two demands, and is left over as that which simply cannot be signified. This form of identification could be defined as that which arises with a new perception of a common quality shared with someone who is not an object of sexual desire; it is identification now conditioned by its function as support of desire.

Having now demonstrated the distinction between the optical schema, as positing an autonomous Imaginary, and the torus as revealing the irreducible nature of the object of desire, the author of 'The Splitting of the Subject' points to the need for a diagram which could illustrate the possibility of grasping internally to the model

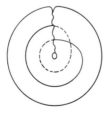

Fig. 7.6

this irreducible void, which is now defined as the object of the analytic process (the subject's advent to desire). The model used is the cross-cap or projective plane. By means of a cut the model can be split into two separate parts, one of which will seize its central point and the other of which will appear as a Moebius strip. The latter now represents specular identification, the former the subject in its relation to desire. The model is difficult, but two basic factors should be retained:

(*a*) the cut which constitutes the subject in its dependent relation to the object of desire also allows the subject to *detach* itself from the specular illusion;

(*b*) the cut which detaches this fragment also determines the topological properties of the fragment which remains; hence the specular illusion as apparently separate, but always the *effect* of the basic structure of desire:

the essential factor is that the *coupure* which detaches the object is that which simultaneously determines the topological properties of the fragment which remains and which does have an image in the mirror. (*Scilicet* no. 2/3: 132–3)

It is to the way in which this radical cut or *coupure* informs the structure of specularity itself, the subject's position in relation to the image rather than to the image it vehicles, that Lacan addresses himself in that part of his 1964 seminar entitled 'The Look as *objet petit a*' (*Le Séminaire* xi: 65–109/67–119). Projective geometry is now used to show the presence or insistence of desire inside those very forms which are designed to reproduce or guarantee the specular illusion itself (image, screen, spectator).

III

In the four seminars grouped under the heading 'The Look as *objet petit a*', Lacan uses a series of models and anecdotes to challenge what he calls the idealising presumption whereby the subject assumes it 'can see itself seeing itself', persistently referring back to its own subjectivity a 'look' which manifestly pre-exists its intervention as subject. The Imaginary itself, through which the subject sets itself up as subject and the other as object, can be seen to contain a potential reversal—the subject is constituted as object by the Other—for which the structure of specularity is now taken as the model.

The dual screen relationship of the spectator in the cinema, described by Metz (1975a; 1975b)—the screen on to which the film is projected and the internalised screen which introjects that imagery—is the exact counterpart of that process whereby the subject is endlessly 'pictured' or 'photographed' in the world:

> in the scopic field, the look is outside, I am looked at, that is to say, I am a picture.
>
> It is this function which lies at the heart of the subject's institution in the visible. What fundamentally determines me in the visible is the look which is outside. It is through the look that I enter into the light, and it is from the look that I receive its effect. From which it emerges that the look is the instrument through which the light is embodied, and through which—if you will allow me to use a word, as I often do, by breaking it up—I am *photo-graphed*. (*Le Séminaire* XI: 98/106)

Thus the subject of representation is not only the subject of that geometrical perspective whereby it reproduces objects as images:

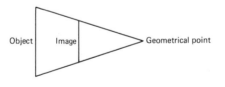

FIG. 7.7

it is also represent*ed* in that process, illuminated by the light emitted by the object of its own look, and thereby registered simultaneously as *object* of representation. Lacan relates the anecdote of the fisherman who pointed at a can of sardines floating on the water, and, turning to the young Lacan with a laugh, said: 'You see that can? Do you see it? Well, it doesn't see you!' (*Le Séminaire* XI: 89/95). Lacan attributes his discomfort at the 'joke' to his sudden realisation of the alien 'figure' he made within that community; but he goes on to use the anectode to illustrate the *schize* between the eye and the look, since if the can couldn't *see* him, yet, as the converging point of the light which it emitted back to the observer, it was in a sense *looking* at him:

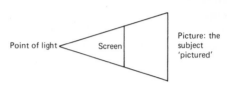

FIG. 7.8

The introduction of the screen demonstrates:

1. The subject's active intervention in the imaginary relationship, in which it is seized by the object of its look:

> Only the subject—the human subject, subject of desire which is man's essence—is not, unlike the animal, entirely taken in by this imaginary capture. He manages to locate himself within it. How? To the extent that he isolates the function of the screen and plays off it. Indeed man knows how to play with the mask as that beyond which there is the look. The screen acts here as the site of mediation. (*Le Séminaire* XI: 99/107)

2. The role of desire within that relationship; an object veiled from sight by an over-intense light can be discerned only if a screen is interposed which partially obscures that light and/or the observing subject; the screen thus blocks the subject from the light in order to expose its object, and the 'look' of that object is seen to emerge only in this moment of partial elision:

> As soon as the subject attempts to accommodate itself to this look, it becomes that punctiform object, that vanishing point of being with which the subject confuses its own failing. Thus, of all the objects through which the subject can recognise its dependency in the register of desire, the look specifies itself as that which cannot be grasped. (*Le Séminaire* XI: 79/83)

The screen therefore serves a dual function, as locus of the image off which the subject will play in an attempt to control its imaginary captation, and as a sign of the elusive relation between the object of desire—the look—and the observing subject: 'The subject presents itself as other than what it is, and what it is given to see is not what it wants to see. It is in this way that the eye can function as *objet a*, that is, on the level of lack' (*Le Séminaire* XI: 96/104). It is this look, as object of desire, which already functioned as a question mark over the asserted triumph of the mirror stage: 'What is manipulated in the triumph of the assumption of the image of the body in the mirror, is that object, all the more elusive in that it appears only marginally: the exchange of looks' (*E* 70). The super-imposition of Lacan's two triangles:

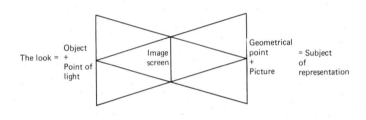

FIG. 7.9

illustrates the conjunction of screen and image which now reveals the elision both of the inaccessible object and of the subject as the guarantor of certitude: ' . . . in so far as the picture enters into a relation with desire, the place of a central screen is always marked, which is precisely the means whereby, in front of the picture, I am elided as subject of the geometrical plane' (*Le Séminaire* XI: 100/108). Even the first triangle which demonstrated the laws of perspective contains a potential reversal, since the lines drawn from the object on to a surface to produce an image of that object, can be redirected onto a further plane to produce a gross deformation or anamorphosis. Conveniently for Lacan's demonstration, the most famous pictorial illustration of anamorphosis—Hans Holbein's *The Ambassadors*[8] not only challenges the subject's fixed relation to the picture, since it is only as the subject withdraws that the object can be discerned, but also demonstrates this challenge on the level of its content, since the object perceived as the subject moves aside is a human skull.

This whole section of the seminar appears as a repeated

collapsing of the imaginary relation into desire, here related to death as the zero point of the subject. This central role of desire is read by Lacan into the passage in *Being and Nothingness* in which Sartre describes the observer at the keyhole, suddenly startled by the sound of approaching footsteps from his complacency as *voyeur* (1943: 317–19/1966: 347–50). The subject is not just caught by a look which subjects it and cancels its position as 'pure' observation; it is caught by a look which it cannot see but which it imagines in the field of the Other; and it is literally caught in the act, which is not an act, that is, in its role as *voyeur* or support of desire.

The *voyeur* is not, therefore, in a position of pure manipulation of an object, albeit distant, but is always threatened by the potential exteriorisation of his own function. That function is challenged three times over: first, by the fact that the subject cannot see what it wants to see (it is this which becomes the conditioning factor of voyeurism which deliberately distances its object); secondly, by the fact that it is not the only one looking; thirdly, that the reciprocity implied in this is immediately challenged, since the subject can never see its look from the point at which the other is looking at it. These three moments can be seen to correspond to the three moments of privation, frustration and castration: the subject is depossessed of its object, the subject posits a full equivalence between itself and another subject, the subject is led to realise that this apparent reciprocity is grounded on the impossibility of complete return.

IV

The gradual ascendancy of the question of desire over that of identification in Lacan's theory seems to raise several issues of potential importance for film theory. It is no coincidence that the late emergence of the concept of 'splitting' in Freud's own work (the 1927 paper on 'Fetishism' (*SE* xxi: 152–7) and the 1938 'The Splitting of the Ego in the Process of Defence' (*SE* xiii: 275–8)) is echoed in Lacanian theory by the movement from a concept of *Gestalt* to one of identity as a function of repeated difference. It does seem to me that certain propositions made by Christian Metz in his article 'The Imaginary Signifier' (1975a/1975b) could be questioned in terms of that movement, and I will conclude by tentatively suggesting where this article diverges from his position.

Metz's article sets itself the question 'What contribution can Freudian psychoanalysis make to the study of the cinematic signifier?' Its most important aspects for this discussion are the sections on the theoretician's relation to the film object (described in Kleinian/Lacanian terms as the imaginary restoration of the 'good' object which the critical activity endlessly destroys and repairs), and the spectator's relation to the image on the screen (described more specifically in terms of Lacan's concept of the mirror-stage).

Metz distinguishes identification in the cinema from the primary identification of the subject with its body in the mirror, since the spectator's own body is not seen on the screen and, as a subject, it has already passed through this primary identification; it can therefore recognise objects in the world without needing to see itself as such. The spectator's identification with the image and/or characters on screen is therefore described as secondary, the subject's identification being primarily with the camera itself. This is the phantasy of the all-perceiving subject (subject and centre of the look) which is thus seen to be inscribed within the very apparatus of cinema itself. This same phantasy can be recognised in an idealist ontology of film which sees the development of cinema as an increasingly realistic appropriation of the world. Metz rightly challenges this 'delusion' or 'idealising presumption' (Lacan) of the centred subject, but he remains largely within the terms of the theory he is criticising. Thus for Metz, what deludes the subject is the sense of a perceptual mastery of the world, whereas what the spectator is in fact seeing are mere images demanding to be recognised as real (verisimilitude). The subject is, therefore, deluded by the nature of the perceptual phenomena, rather than by its very position as origin or centre of vision.

This stress on the absence of the object seen has as its corollary a notion of a full non-imaginary relation to the object, and the assigning of the invocatory and scopic drives to the realm of the imaginary *because of* the distance which underpins their relation to the object. As we have seen above, however, the scopic and invocatory drives, which could be said to specify the spectator's relation to the cinema, simply reveal the absence of the object which underpins the drive *per se*, rather than being characterised by an absence which can be equated with the physical absence of the object from the cinematic screen. What follows are a number of differences with Metz's arguments which lead on from these remarks:

1. Inasmuch as the Imaginary becomes conditioned by the object of desire exposed in the field of the Other, the Imaginary cannot simply be equated with Klein's 'good' and 'bad' objects, even if the imaginary game she describes is at the basis of the first moments of that function.

2. The fact that the subject's own body is not on the screen does not necessarily distinguish its experience from that of the mirror stage; the subject never specularises its own body as such, and the phenomenon of transitivism demonstrates that the subject's mirror identification can be with another child.

3. The relationship of the mirror stage to the structure of the look is not a sequential one; the emergence of the latter in Lacan's theory throws into question the plenitude of the former in its very first moments, where the Other is not just the sign of an intervening symbolisation but also the exponent of desire; one cannot, therefore, refer to the mirror stage as primary identification, and to that of the look as secondary identification which is primary in the cinema; the question of secondary identification needs to be examined more closely in relation to Lacan's reading of the three modes of identification posited by Freud.

4. Since the structure of specularity undermines the Imaginary topic, certain aspects of that structure cannot be taken as marginal instances of the cinematic experience:

(*a*) The relationship of the scopic drive to the object of desire is not simply one of distance but of externalisation, which means that the observing subject can become object of the look, and hence elided as subject of its own representation (the *œil derrière la tête*[9] could therefore be the means whereby the subject's position as spectator in the cinema is continually threatened); the illusion at the basis of the subject 'seeing itself seeing itself' does not only appear in the meta-activity of critical analysis, but is raised and challenged by the operations of the specular illusion *per se*.

(*b*) The intervention of the specular relation in the imaginary plane demonstrates that the structure of subjectivity, grounded on a decisive *coupure*, is in itself fetishistic: (*i*) fetishism has virtually no connection with Klein's 'good' object (Metz 1975a: 52/1975b: 72), since the third term necessary to its formulation is completely excluded from her description of the child's paranoid-schizoid and then depressive relationship to the mother; (*ii*) fetishism cannot be placed as a marginal instance of the cinematic experience, manifested by a passion for technique (Metz 1975a: 51–2/1975b: 71–2), but must be re-centralised in relation to the subject's precarious control of that experience, precisely because that control is first affirmed by the subject's apparent centralisation in the cinema as subject of the geometrical plane; Metz's points about scopic perversion therefore need to be referred directly to those relating to the 'all-perceiving subject'; equally, the disavowal and affirmation which he ascribes to the reality status of the objects portrayed on the screen, and secondarily to the subject's critical posture in relation to the film, need also to be related to a query hanging persistently over the subject's position as centralised Ego.

5. All these points could perhaps be formulated in relation to the ambivalent function which Lacan ascribes to the screen itself, as the locus of a potentially ludic relationship between the subject and its imaginary captation, and the simultaneous sign of the barrier between the subject and the object of desire.

6. Finally, what Metz says of the 'presentified absence' of the object in the cinema, is, as he points out, equally applicable to any pictorial representation. Whether the density of the sensory register in the cinema makes this any more true of the cinema can perhaps best be queried by the story of Zeuxis and Parrhasios, used by Lacan to illustrate the distinction between lure or decoy and *trompe–l'œil* or illusion; Zeuxis draws grapes on to a wall which act as a bait for unsuspecting birds, but Parrhasios goes one further by painting a veil on to a wall so effectively that Zeuxis turns to him and asks what lies behind it; in order to dupe a human subject: '. . . what one presents to him or her is a painting of a veil, that is to say, something beyond which he or she demands to see' (*Le Séminaire* XI: 102/112).

NOTES

1. This article was written in 1975 in response to a specific demand—for some clarification of the concept of the Imaginary which was being fairly loosely imported into certain areas of literary, and specifically filmic, criticism, at a time when works by the French psychoanalyst Jacques Lacan, from which it had been taken, were relatively unavailable in this country.

The main body of the article is therefore a fairly straightforward exposition of the concept within psychoanalytic theory. At the same time as it was being written, Christian Metz wrote his seminal article 'The Imaginary Signifier' on the pertinence of the concept of the Imaginary for study of the cinematic signifier, his interest reflecting a shift within semiotic theory from the concept of code and film product to that of textual system and production, a move which signalled a new attention to the position of the subject in relation to the cinematic apparatus within film theory. Some of Metz's arguments are taken up in a final brief section of the article published here.

I have modified the text only slightly where necessary for sake of clarification; where some aspect of the article seemed to require more serious modification, the reader has been referred to a footnote. I would like to thank Ben Brewster and Juliet Mitchell for their comments on the original draft, which was presented as a British Film Institute educational seminar paper in November 1975.

2. Note that Janet (quoted by Lacan) compared the formal stagnation of the images thus produced to the frozen gestures of actors when a film is halted in mid-projection (i.e. when it is not a film).

3. Cf. Freud on identification in relation to love and hypnosis, *Group Psychology and the Analysis of the Ego*, Chapter 8, 'Being in Love and Hypnosis' (*SE* XVIII: 111–6).

4. *Le Séminaire* I: 159. Certain points should perhaps be clarified here. At this stage in Lacan's work the relation between the Imaginary and the Symbolic was often posed as a sequence—from the image (fixed, stable) to language or the word (the means of intersubjective communication). Since language is properly the domain of psychoanalysis, it is easy to see the relation between this and analytic practice. Resistance has two meanings here—as a reference to the stranglehold of the imaginary relation (hostility, rivalry, etc.) and as the refusal of the subject to relinquish that position and enter the domain of language. Language is therefore conceived of as a (potentially full) speech which breaks the impasse of the imaginary relation. However, this notion of language, which also informs the distinction between ideal ego and ego ideal (the speech of the Other) discussed below, undergoes a crucial alteration in Lacan's own work, which also affects that between the terms Imaginary and Symbolic. At the point where language ceases to be a potentially full speech and is seen as a structure or set of differences based on a primary absence, there can no longer be a simple progression from the Imaginary (mis-recognition) to the Symbolic (mediation, recognition), since the emphasis is now on the 'splitting' which is constitutive of language itself. It is this conceptual shift which the article goes on to describe in Part II.

5. Lacan seems to take his reference for this distinction from Freud's own comment that the 'admonitions of others' are 'conveyed to him by the medium of the voice' (*SE* XIV: 94–6), thus again on a concept of language as the medium of intersubjective communication (cf. note 4 above):

> What is my desire? What is my position in the imaginary structuration? This position can only be conceived in so far as a guide is found beyond the imaginary, on the level of the symbolic plane, of the legal exchange which can only be embodied through verbal exchange between human beings. This guide who governs the subject is the ego ideal. (*Le Séminaire* I: 162)

6. The use of the other (small o) here is problematic given the earlier definition of the ego ideal in its relation to language; the author of the *Scilicet* article (cf. Part II) uses Other throughout; certainly there is a shift in Lacan's own usage from the

small *a* as a reference to the imaginary other (*autre*) to its use as a reference to absence (the *objet petit a*). I take these shifts as indicative of the intrusion of the symbolic Other back over the imaginary relation. Cf. commentary by Jacques-Alain Miller, 'Table commentée des représentations graphiques', *Ecrits* (2nd edn): 903–8:

> the real image, henceforth designated as i(a), represents the specular image of the subject, whilst the real object *a* supports the function of the partial object, precipitating the formation of the body. We have here a phase prior to the mirror stage (according to an order of logical dependency)—*a phase which presupposes the presence of the real Other*. (p. 904, my emphasis)

7. The problem of sexual difference clearly informs the first two categories, since the second type of identification is obviously the prototype for the girl's identification with the lost primordial object (the mother), in fact one of the examples which Freud gives for category two is the male homosexual's identification with the mother. However, he also gives that of Dora's symptomatic identification with her father's cough (*SE* VII: 82–3), which shows that the second category is a pivotal point for identification based on sexual identity, and identification related to the repression of a secondary object of desire (the father). The third form of identification is illustrated by the 'smoked salmon' dream (*SE* IV: 147–51), in which the dreamer identifies with the woman she has unconsciously posited as her sexual rival. The relationship of this form of identification to a repressed object of desire, no longer an object of demand, is here clear (cf. Lacan's discussion of this dream in 'La direction de la cure et les principes de son pouvoir': 620–6/256–63); this form of identification could also be taken as the model for the post-Oedipal identification of both girl and boy with the parent of the same sex.

8. The picture forms the front cover of *Le Séminaire* XI.

9. This phase of André Green's is quoted in Metz (1975a: 35/1975b: 52).

8 Verneinung, Verwerfung, Ausstossung: A Problem in the Interpretation of Freud

MARTIN THOM

The first term in my title, *Verneinung*, is used at several points by Freud, but most crucially in 'Negation', a paper whose German title is 'Die Verneinung'.[1] I want to isolate the basic concepts in this and in various other (linked) writings in order to consider the problem, touched upon in the second part of my earlier article, of the specifically psychotic mechanism that Freud seeks to define. But why, in presenting the three key terms at the head of the page, have I left them in the original German? Theoretical work implies translation, whether it be literal transfer of terms from one language to another or transposition from original document to commentary, and if one leaves a term in another language it is as if one's attempt to translate has failed. If, however, a term has no adequate translation and if one can establish that it has been inexactly translated and therefore condemned to howl on desolate margins, it is reasonable to argue for a kind of 'transitional' usage of a term from the original language. But admixtures of Latin and of Norman French to an Anglo-Saxon core make of English a language well-suited to re-fashion any French or German term. Italicisations lead us into thinking that truth walks in some other gaudy meadow, and so they are at best temporary measures, spurring us on to further work.

It is nonetheless clear that Freud's article 'Die Verneinung' has been translated in so many different ways that it is worth arranging a parade of the original German terms in order to see what it is that was lost in the English and French translations. In doing this I am following the work done by Lacan in the 1950s, and, in addition, a line by line and word by word commentary by B. This and P. Thèves, two members of the *Ecole Freudienne* (1975). This latter article includes both a new French translation and the original German text, and I have therefore followed many of its principle assertions quite closely.

I am not insensible to the risks of this sort of activity. It was, after all, to England and not to France that the International Psychoanalytic movement had fled in the late 1930s, and it was therefore altogether to be expected that the English language—in the shape of the *Standard Edition*—should have become a filter for Freud's thought. A quick examination of the versions of 'Die Verneinung' that have been done in French—I do not claim to have read all ten, but This and Thèves give the variants for the crucial passages—shows clearly that James Strachey's version is superior. My own German is minimal, but I do not feel that by tying my argument to the three terms cited I have, like the fabled Baron Münchausen, tied my horse to a church steeple. I would emphasise that this work of cross-checking can be done in this way, since it concerns little more than the erasure of two or three key terms at critical points, and that it is valuable to do it. Otherwise it is extremely hard to assess the polemical assertions made by Lacan, and others, about the significance of Freud's 'Die Verneinung' article, and about the way in which mistranslations had obscured that significance.

Thus, both the English translations and the original French translation take *Verneinung* to mean 'negation'. Strachey, whose efforts to clarify these sorts of terminological problem are everywhere apparent, adds a note to the effect that, in the *Standard Edition*, *verneinen*, 'to negate', is consistently contrasted with *verleugnen*, 'to disavow'. Both verbs had in previous renderings been taken to mean 'to deny', whereas the mechanism of disavowal in fetishism should properly be distinguished from the sorts of negation that occur in an analytic session. Why is this terminological distinction not sufficient, and why does Jean Hippolyte, following Lacan, suggest that *Verneinung* should more properly be rendered *dénégation* (*E* 879).

This new translation has, in France, come to dominate the old one, and justifications for it have assumed a more and more sophisticated linguistic form.[2] An English speaker might well be tempted to argue that *dénégation* is more prominent in the French than in the English lexicon and that the debate is therefore restricted to a social context where the term already has some purchase. However, in terminological debate, we work as if we ourselves were language-makers, a little elemental in our capacity to prise loose an element from a conglomerate in which it had been embedded or to fuse several such elements together into a new conglomerate. The value of translating *Verneinung* as 'denegation' cannot be proved philologically, as This and Thèves run the risk of asserting, but theoretically. To over-estimate the philological aspect is to presume the paramount importance of Freud's actual intentions when choosing one term rather than another. It is simply that the translation of *Verneinung* as 'denegation' gives the concept more work to do, gathers together more strands in a necessarily dispersed argument. The work that the concept does is therefore reducible neither to the intentions of the now dead writer nor to a posited unconscious of the text. The point is that the negation that is described in the 'Die Verneinung' paper concerns the relation that links repression with the return of the repressed: the use of the word 'denegation' helps one to separate this usage from the more general operation whose absence in the workings of the primary process had long since been noted by Freud.

REPRESSION, THE RETURN OF THE REPRESSED

How then are repression and the return of the repressed linked? The lifting of the repression—which allows repressed material to return—occurs at the same moment as repression itself. This critical fact is hard to grasp if one has a too hydraulic conception of the way that repression works, a notion that carries with it an inaccurate narrative in which an actual father represents law and nips desire in the bud. Accounts of analyses are of some help here. [3] They suggest that repression entails the introjection of a particular signifier (the signifier representing the Name of the Father) and that it is this that permits the return of repressed material.

Analysis therefore works to introduce a particular signifier into the analysand's discourse and in this way to re-order his or her relation to the Other, a relation of subjection to the mother's demand. This re-ordering, which may also be described in terms of the symbolic castration it recapitulates, will release various imaginary figures. Symbolic castration, since it allows phantasy to return and assert itself as truth in human speech, is a splitting and a separation that is not therefore to be confused with Imaginary castration. Imaginary castration is constituted by all those mutilatory phantasies that are stored in the psychic apparatus—the phantasy of the fragmented body is one of them, but they also include the 'birth trauma', weaning, and any castration threat that may happen to have been uttered—and return as ferocious figures that strike out against the subject. If one does not grasp this critical distinction one is in no position to perceive why it is that symbolic castration should, in a certain sense, be desired, and that the separation from the demand for love that it entails could be achieved by a variety of symbolic practices, from curative rituals to psychoanalysis. Both symbolic castration and the phantasy of the fragmented body are universals of human experience, since they represent the fact of having been born, embodied, into a world where language is. It is simply their articulation, one with another, in a particular social formation, that will differ. It is clear, however, that symbolic castration both represses and permits the return of repressed material, that it is, in fact, *Verneinung*, denegation.

This is quite explicitly stated in Freud's article. He cites the analysands' utterances—utterances in which their professed negation is belied by the substance of the sentence smuggled in— in order to proceed with a metapsychological explanation:

> the content of a repressed image or idea can make its way into consciousness, on condition that it is *negated*. Negation is a way of taking cognizance of what is repressed; indeed it is already a lifting of the repression, though not, of course, an acceptance of what is repressed. We can see how in this the intellectual function is separated from the affective process. (*SE* xix: 235–6)

This paragraph states very clearly that the content of 'a repressed image or idea'—derived from what Freud in another context calls 'the storehouse of images'—can make its way into consciousness provided that it is negated. In the next sentence Freud proceeds to emphasise the affirmative aspect of the negation. Negation is stated to be 'a taking cognizance of what is repressed' and 'a lifting of

repression' and these aspects of the operation justify translating
Verneinung by denegation, for the negation of the storehouse of
images is at the same time a liberation of them. A commentary on
the myth of Pandora's box—in which the etymology of the name
would be taken to represent all the gifts that child and mother
exchange—would have it that the box and the imaginary contents
are constructed at the same moment, with the prohibition to open
constructing the desire to open. The point is that repression frees the
child from its infatuation with the container/contained dialectic so
characteristic of the narcissistic ego, and gives it the means of
symbolising its relations with others. The case of Little Dick, as
presented by Melanie Klein (1964), is a good example of what
happens to a child who has not achieved the distance that
symbolisation of parts of the body allows the human being. But
between the lifting of the repression and the acceptance of what is
represented there is a kind of gulf, and what Freud here calls the
intellectual function is irretrievably separated from the affective
function. This separation is represented in Lacan's writing by an
endless oscillation between the truth of the subject's desire and the
knowledge he or she has of that desire. Where there is *jouissance*
there is no subject to say 'I am . . . enjoying', and where there is
knowledge there is no *jouissance*. The human comedy therefore
touches on farce—there is, as Lacan stresses, no sexual relation—
and one figure leaves the room as another enters it. The phallic
mother is the element around which the scenes turn; she is there
until one enters the room or walks on to the stage—and the
phantasy is the support for one's *jouissance*—but as soon as one enters
the room and turns to speak of one's *jouissance* to an ideal audience
hidden by silence and darkness—she has disappeared. Human
sexuality is therefore founded upon an order of representation, and
it is this that Freud's 'Die Verneinung' paper shows.

Whilst Freud's paper opens and closes with a reference to details
of analytic practice, it has as its scope nothing less than a
consideration of 'the origin of an intellectual function from the
interplay of the primary instinctual impulses' (*SE* xix: 239). In
short, the paper deals with the origins of human thought and it does
so by reference to the raising of 'the primary instinctual impulses' to
the status of representations. It is this particular aspect of 'Die
Verneinung' that distinguishes it from the passages in 'Instincts and
Their Vicissitudes' (1915) and *Civilization and Its Discontents* (1930),
in which many of the same notions are considered. But how does it

happen that 'the intellectual function is separated from the affective process'? And what does Freud, in this paper, mean by affective process?

To answer these questions one has to bear in mind that the few lines quoted above do give an inexact impression of the sequence in which these operations unfold. For all the terms in use—repressed, image, idea, consciousness—derive their meaning from the same operation, and from their relation, each to each, within that operation. Negation, or denegation, is therefore the necessary *condition*—and Freud does use this word—for both the return of the repressed (the fact that the content of a repressed image or idea can make its way into consciousness) and for repression itself. The *negativism* of psychosis derives from a fault in primal repression and represents a negativity uncaptured by the fact of negation and unassimilable to the opposition between intellect and affect. If Freud uses a dualism such as this—one of which we are so philosophically suspicious—it is surely because he means to show that human thought, once beyond the Oedipus, will spontaneously construct it.

In 'Die Verneinung' Freud writes of 'a primary pleasure ego'.[4] He had first advanced this notion some fourteen years earlier in a paper that also included the first reference to the reality ego. The separation of the intellectual function from the affective may therefore, I think, be considered analogous to the separation between the primary pleasure ego and the reality ego; the 'Die Verneinung' paper thus elaborates—in terms of analysands' statements—on the earlier formulation. But the emphasis on analytic practice is critical, for, in concentrating on what the analysand *says*, it shifts our attention away from an empirical notion of the real. We enter the human order negatively and love someone—the phallic mother—for what they don't have. But what, prior to denegation, are the operations of the primary pleasure ego?

The basic operations of the primary pleasure ego are incorporation and expulsion: ' . . . the original pleasure ego wants to introject into itself everything that is good and to eject from itself everything that is bad. What is bad, what is alien to the ego and what is external are, to begin with, identical' (*SE* xix: 237). I give Strachey's translation here, for it differs in one important respect from that of J. Rivière. He translates *alles Schlechte von sich werfen*, 'to eject from itself everything that is bad', whereas Rivière translates *werfen* as 'reject'. This may seem a trifling difference, yet the discrepancy between the two English verbs 'eject' and 'reject' is quite apparent and corresponds better to the sense of the German text *as a whole* if one renders *werfen* here as 'eject'. For, in a subsequent paragraph, the operation of the primary pleasure ego in spitting things out is described as *Ausstossung* (the third German term that figures in this paper's title)—and the particle *e-* better translates the German *aus-*. This is borne out by the fact that Strachey, in the later passage, translates *Ausstossung* as 'expulsion'.

I would therefore argue that Strachey's translation of *werfen* as 'eject' represents an improvement on Rivière's rendering, for it preserves the necessary and logical link between this passage and the later one, in which the term *Ausstossung* is used. The two passages both refer to the primary pleasure ego: the first describes its most fundamental operations, the second its capture by other mechanisms and its significance in terms of the opposition between Eros and Thanatos. Yet *werfen*, when linked to the particle *ver-*, denotes the mechanism specific to psychosis, the foreclosure of the paternal signifier. What then is the relation between *Verwerfung* and *Ausstossung*?

This question is the pivot around which this article turns and I will try to return to it again and again, from different angles. The term *Verwerfung* is absent from Freud's '*Die Verneinung*' paper yet the interpretation of it that Lacan has proposed depends on the interpretation that one advances of the concept of denegation. Supplementary reference has also to be made to the passages in 'From the History of an Infantile Neurosis (the 'Wolf Man')' (*SE* XVII: 7–122) in which the term is employed. Here I want just to note that *Verwerfung*, given the equivalence between *werfen* and *Ausstossung* in the passage discussed above, is necessarily of a different logical order to the initial mechanism of expulsion linked to the primary pleasure ego. *Verwerfung* is linked to the signifier that it does not affirm, and this non-affirmation of the signifier is its most critical feature, whereas *Ausstossung* does not bear on the signifier at all.

THE PRIMARY PLEASURE EGO

In a footnote to 'Negation' Strachey cites both an earlier and a later discussion of the operations of introjection and expulsion of the primary pleasure ego. It is to the earlier account, in 'Instincts and Their Vicissitudes' (*SE* xiv: 111–40) that I will now turn. Close inspection of this article and of the 'Verneinung' article reveals a slight discrepancy between the different accounts they give of the primary pleasure ego.

In the 1915 paper, a series of three polarities, Subject (ego)–Object (external world), Pleasure-Pain, Active–Passive, are posited, and Freud then asserts that the first and second of these are, in a 'certain primal psychic situation', coincident. In this primal psychic situation, which precedes the formation of the primary pleasure ego (also called a 'purified' and a 'pure' pleasure ego) the ego is equivalent to pleasure and what is outside of the ego is indifferent to it. Here then is the first discrepancy between the 1915 and the 1925 paper: the 1915 paper suggests a more archaic ego than the 1925 one, and posits a zone of indifference, whereas for the 1925 paper the judgement of attribution integral to the primary pleasure ego already involves, *ab initio*, a taking in of what is good and a spitting out of what is bad: 'What is bad, what is alien to the ego and what is external are, to begin with, identical' (*SE* xix: 237). The 1915 paper therefore posits a prior stage. Such that, when objects present themselves, in so far as they are sources of pleasure they are 'introjected', 'while, on the other hand, the ego thrusts forth upon the external world whatever within itself gives rise to pain.' The primordially indifferent outside is therefore divided by the purified pleasure ego, which is under the sway of the pleasure principle, and through 'introjection' and expulsion is once more able to establish a coincidence between itself and pleasure. The two papers are therefore fundamentally consistent one with another, the first simply providing an account of the formation of the purified pleasure ego whereas the second states its basic modes of operation.

The opposition between a judgement of attribution and a judgement of existence is the pivot around which the 'Die Verneinung' paper turns. The judgement of attribution judges whether a thing is good or bad. Of a thing's existence it knows nothing, for the child's ego is englobed by the mother's desire that it fulfil her desire. There is therefore a sequence primal ego—narcissistic ego—denegation. It is the latter that installs the judgement of existence, whereas there had hitherto been merely a judgement of attribution. It is the judgement of a thing's existence that now counts and the real ego installed by repression is no longer concerned with the goodness or badness of a thing. The double bar in the formula of the metaphor (Lacan)

$$\frac{S}{\$'} \cdot \frac{\$'}{x} \rightarrow S\left(\frac{I}{s}\right)$$

therefore represents the catastrophic action of metaphor in so far as it institutes a splitting of the ego (between a primary pleasure ego and a real ego). The paternal metaphor is therefore the raising of the child's desire to a second degree, where it becomes desire working on the memory trace of a satisfaction rather than the shifting between incorporation and expulsion of the narcissistic ego. This splitting, in relation to symbolic castration (where castration can be conceived as a cut in the flow of introjected and expelled things, an intrusion into the specular domain) allows the child the ideal possibility of assuming the attributes of a sexed being in relation to the phallus. It also, in the same moment, installs the repetition compulsion in the unconscious that is then created, a repetition compulsion that contravenes the tendency towards homeostasis of the primary pleasure ego. Whereas the good was that which was introjected it now becomes the good lost, which, through the primal repression, may be found again as representation once it has been cast out as thing.

But how, in terms of the 'Die Verneinung' paper, does the primary pleasure ego become the real ego? When the real ego is in place, one is within the order of the signifier, or, as Freud puts it: 'It is now no longer a question of whether what has been perceived (a thing) shall be taken into the ego or not, but of whether something which is in the ego as a presentation can be rediscovered in perception (reality) as well' (*SE* XIX: 237).

A memory trace therefore stands attendance on human desire, and human desire (as the *Fort Da* game shows) is built on the compulsion to repeat. But the denegation that installs human desire presupposes a recognition, an affirmation (*Bejahung*): thus, when Freud's analysand says 'You ask who this person in the dream can be. It's *not* my mother,' Freud simply brackets out the ostensible negation—'So it *is* his mother.' This example is highly instructive, for it shows how the recognition implicit in the specular order is subsumed within the Symbolic denegation, within a misrecognition integral to human thought itself. But if that is, broadly speaking, the relation between the terms *Bejahung* and *Verneinung*, what is the status of that which is absolutely not affirmed, *Verwerfung*?

Verwerfung, a term not employed as such in the 'Verneinung' article, describes the mechanism specific to psychosis, the mechanism that may result in hallucination. If this result occurs it is because hallucination represents the return in the real of what was never symbolised. This formulation, which exegesis of the Wolf Man case-study will illuminate, does at least illustrate that *Bejahung* (affirmation) is a precondition for entrance into a symbolic order. It is thus on the prior affirmation that denegation works, whereas *Verwerfung* is not a registration, not an inscription, but an absolute repudiation of a perception. Of any perception? No, for at least in the Wolf Man case-study it is a specific perception that is repudiated, and it is the genital order that is non-affirmed. I will return to this point later. Its citation here was intended simply to link the series incorporation–expulsion (of the primary pleasure ego) and the series affirmation–denegation (of the real ego produced by repression) to the splitting of the ego and the symbolic function of the phallus. And this linkage enables one to ask again the central question: is the concept *Ausstossung* as presented in the 'Negation' paper identical to the concept *Verwerfung* as presented in the Wolf Man case-study? The apparently slight discrepancy between the two—where one bears on the signifier and the other does not—is, I believe, the lever by means of which one can show that the conditions for the human child's entrance into a symbolic order differs in different social formations, and that this in turn enables one to subvert the logocentric residue of psychoanalysis, not by philosophical decree, but by investigating the fissures that appear in the internal ordering of its concepts.

But what then is *Bejahung*? If the reader refers to the exegesis of the *Fort Da* game in the earlier paper, she or he will find that it is asserted there that the affirmation of the singularity of the mother coincides with the construction of a signifying order which, in bearing with it the concept of universality (anything whatever can be thrown by the child in the *Fort* game) denegates the mother as singularity, as face-now-all-of-a-sudden-loved, and raises her to the general category 'she' (a 'shifter'). This 'double inscription' is identical to the series affirmation-denegation and may be thought of as a splitting of the ego in which the real ego denegates the statement that is concurrently affirmed. Without a grasp of this fundamental complicity between affirmation and denegation it is impossible to understand how, paradoxically enough, it is denegation that permits the return of the repressed, and that repression and the 'lifting' of repression occur at once.

But denegation is not only founded on the affirmation that it subsumes. It is also—as Freud puts it—the 'successor' of *Ausstossung*, the operation of expulsion associated with the primary pleasure ego. Is the link between *Verneinung* and *Ausstossung* then equivalent to the link between *Vereinigung* (incorporation) and *Bejahung*?

To answer this question it is necessary to look closely at Freud's text, and at the passage in which all these different terms are used. In the penultimate paragraph of the article Freud writes:

> Die Bejahung—als Ersatz der Vereinigung—gehört dem Eros an, die Verneinung—Nachfolge der Ausstossung—dem Destruktionstrieb. (*GW* XIV: 15)

This sentence is translated by Joan Rivière as follows:

> Affirmation, as being a substitute for union, belongs to Eros; while negation, the derivative of expulsion belongs to the instinct of destruction. (*CP* V: 185)

And James Strachey gives it as:

> Affirmation—as a substitute for uniting—belongs to Eros; negation—the successor to expulsion—belongs to the instinct of destruction. (*SE* XIX: 239)

This latter version is closer to the original German but both of them are more accurate than the first French translations. In these the distinction between *Ersatz*, substitute, and *Nachfolge*, successor, is eliminated. Yet, as Hippolyte points out (*E* 885–6), if this dissymmetry between the two parts of the sentence is obscured, the following sentence loses its meaning. For Freud goes on to talk of the defusion of drives manifested in the 'negativism' of psychosis (*SE*

XIX: 239), and how is one to understand this defusion if the original fusion is not properly understood? For the discrepancy between *Ersatz* and *Nachfolge* allows the reader to perceive that, whilst affirmation may substitute for the incorporation of the primary pleasure ego, negation does not do more than follow on after *Ausstossung*. In short, the expulsion of the pleasure ego is less completely captured by denegation than the incorporation of Eros is by affirmation. This slight terminological point is of enormous importance for any theory of psychosis, for it raises the whole problem of symbolicity's purchase on the body. I will return to this point in the course of the discussion on the Wolf Man case-study.

VERWERFUNG; THE WOLF MAN CASE-STUDY

The missing concept, *Verwerfung*, may be traced back to the Wolf Man case-study and to the passage in which Freud describes the $5\frac{1}{2}$ year old child's hallucinatory episode. The child hallucinates the severing of his finger and there thus appears in the 'real' an event that the child had never properly acknowledged. This return in the real of a Symbolic element is therefore quite different from the return of the repressed. For the return of the repressed, whether one thinks of it as coincident with repression (as in primal repression) or whether one thinks of it as occurring in a subsequent moment (as in after-repression), occurs in discourse, in slips of the tongue and forgettings. Yet the child who hallucinates the severed finger is 'speechless with terror'. He cannot speak of the event that captures his whole attention, he cannot even tell of it to his nurse who is sitting close by him. There is therefore a flaw in love that the signifier neither expresses nor assuages, since the flaw stems from the very moment in which love and the signifying order were originally, for the child, installed.

This installation of a signifying order, of a signifying chain, presupposes a syntactical order in operation, and this syntactical order depends on the function of negation. For it is negation that permits the subject a degree of independence from the pleasure principle and allows judgements of existence to take the place of judgements of attribution. An analysis will therefore uncover 'primal' sentences that, by means of all their possible transformations, exhaust the sum of relations between a subject and its objects. Thus Freud, in his commentary on Judge Schreber's memoirs, isolates a central proposition 'I (a man) love him (a man)', and then considers the various delusions that derive from Schreber's concern to deny 'this homosexual wishful fantasy of loving a man'.

The variations on this basic proposition do clearly obey a syntactical order in which the singular (I, he) and the general (the category 'man') are coherently articulated, one with another, through the primal repression. And, even if these transformations entail nothing more than lexical substitutions ('I hate him', for instance, instead of 'I love him') they nevertheless presuppose the mastery of syntax.[5] The minimal subject/predicate relation is thus analogous to the relation between the ego and the object that is pushed out and represented at the same time. The copula presupposes a separation, a splitting, and syntax and the (genital) sexual relation are therefore linked not phylogenetically (as Bopp thought) but ontogenetically. To be Schreber is to be proof of this.

For, in paranoiac projection, the subject of the sentence is cast out, and the message does not merely come back to its speaker in an inverted form, it returns in the real. As if an exorcist were to cast out devils in the name of . . . only to perceive real swine rising slowly backwards out of the sea of his desire. The first and merely neurotic circle binds the subject of the proposition to an imaginary questioning in which the person questioned is postulated as the origin of the exchange: 'You ask me who this person is . . . ', the analysand asks, when the analyst, in the locus of the Other, has asked not a thing. But the mechanism of this first and merely neurotic circle is subsumed within denegation, in the sense that the analysand himself answers the question that was never asked with a negative answer that is still, nevertheless, affirmative: '. . . it is not my mother.' In denegation there is thus no obliteration, no abolition of the signifier. In paranoiac projection, however, there is a non-affirmation that makes for the unceasing transformation of propositions in a delusional form. There is a hole in discourse where the subject starts to speak of itself and this hole represents the point at which the juncture between Real, Symbolic and Imaginary dimensions is flawed, and where, consequently, an element that was not symbolised will return in the real.

There was a 'current' in the Wolf Man's psychic life that did not acknowledge the genital order's existence. It was to account for this non-affirmation that Freud coined the term *Verwerfung*. Coinage is perhaps too strong a word to describe Freud's use of *Verwerfung*, for, like a whole cluster of concepts that have been broken free from the conglomerate of Freud's prose, it is a little obscured, and has a propensity to glint only when glimpsed and then grasped. It is used to describe the manner in which castration is, in the child's life, rejected, and therefore returns, not as the repressed returns (in discourse), but in hallucination (in the real). The separation of a part of the child's body is envisaged in the form of a severed finger, as though access to the genital order would then be offered. In the somewhat confused passage immediately preceding the account of the hallucination Freud writes:

> We are already acquainted with the attitude our patient first adopted to the problem of castration. He rejected castration, and held to his theory of intercourse by the anus. When I speak of his having rejected it, the first meaning of the phrase is that he would have nothing to do with it, in the sense of having repressed it. (*SE*, xvii: 84)

In this first passage, and despite the use of the term *rejection* (*Verwerfung*), Freud could be thought to refer to the operation of primal repression or after-repression. But he continues: 'This really involved no judgement upon this question of its existence, but it was the same as if it did not exist.' The second part of the passage shows clearly that it is not here a question of repression, for repression presupposes an affirmation, and here there is none. It was as if castration did not exist. Serge Leclaire, in one of his commentaries on the Wolf Man case-study, posits a primal sentence that, by means of its different parts, represents the significance of the primal scene (1968:86). But the sentence, much like a transversal section in an archaeological site, is stratified, and the different parts of the sentence bespeak different epochs. The primal sentence postulated is 'Shit! it isn't she' and may be divided into two parts, an exclamation and a negated proposition. The latter represents an affirmation of the existence of a feminine category (through the perception of the 'wound' in the primal scene) and the denegation that raises that affirmation to the level of the Symbolic. The exclamation, however, represents the *dislocation* effected by the primal scene, a dislocation that has the force of a repudiation and whose effects will still be in evidence in the adult's discourse. For, beyond the two currents in his psychic life that, to one degree or another, had 'recognised' castration, there was a third and deeper one:

> But beyond any doubt a third current, the oldest and deepest, which did not as yet even raise the question of the reality of castration (*which had purely and simply repudiated—verwerfen— castration*) was still capable of coming into activity. I have elsewhere reported an hallucination that this same patient had at the age of five . . . (*SE* xvii: 85, my additional gloss)

The child's hallucination therefore represents not the return of the repressed (which is the mechanism appropriate to the series primal repression-after repression) but the appearance in an hallucinatory form of the repudiated, the non-affirmed. How does Lacan explain this non-affirmation, this *Verwerfung?*

In the 1954 commentary Lacan proposes to translate *Verwerfung* as *rejet* or *refus* (*Le Séminaire* 1: 54), in the 1956 version he renders it as *retranchement* (*E* 381–401), and subsequently it is set as *forclusion*, i.e., foreclosure. Each of these different renderings imply a Symbolic abolition and therefore make clear the distinction between *Verwerfung* and repression, the distinction upon which the neurosis/ psychosis distinction turns. It is, however, of interest to note that the earlier commentaries (in particular, the two 'answers' that Lacan prints to Hippolyte's commentary on 'Die Verneinung') suggest a less critical separation between the two mechanisms than is subsequently asserted:

> at the origin, for repression to occur, there must exist a beyond of repression, something final, already constituted in a primitive way, a first knot of the repressed, which not only does not declare itself, but since it is not formulated, it is literally *as if it did not exist*—I am following what Freud says here. And yet, in a certain sense, it is somewhere, since, as Freud never stops telling us, it is the centre of attraction that calls all subsequent repressions towards it.
>
> I take this to be the very essence of Freud's discovery. (*Le Séminaire* 1: 54)

In this passage, Lacan's terminological distinctions are decidedly loose. He uses the term *refoulé*, 'repressed', where one expects him to say *rejeté* or *retranché*. In discussing the existence of the knot of primally repressed material that has to be in place for after-repression to occur at all, Lacan goes on, and in the same breath, to talk about foreclosure, *Verwerfung*. Therefore, there is, for all human beings, a primordial knot that is formed (in Freud's terms, a trauma) and the exact form that this knot takes determines the form that a neurosis and a psychosis will subsequently take. Yet this determination is complex and temporally dispersed, and in this 1954 commentary the historicisation backwards of the traumatic scene is a little obscured. The above passage could almost be read as asserting the identity of every element that is included within the dialecticising impetus of a judgement of existence. Whereas there is certainly a fundamental distinction between that which has been thrown out, that which has not been affirmed and therefore can never be judged to exist, and that which is caught up in the play of the primary pleasure go, inscribed as memory-trace, and, subsequently, with repression, dialecticised as human speech. This fundamental distinction rests on the function of time in the Freudian discovery, for the time of neurosis and psychosis are differently ordered. I will approach this problem of time through a reading of a paper of Freud's written in 1924, the year before 'Die Verneinung', and this reading will work as a preparation for a renewed discussion of the Wolf Man's hallucination.

NEUROSIS, PSYCHOSIS, THE LOSS OF REALITY

In the 1924 article, entitled 'The Loss of Reality in Neurosis and Psychosis' (*SE* XIX: 183–7), Freud discusses the distinction between the two conditions in terms of the temporality of the processes concerned. He divides both neurosis and psychosis into two different stages, the 'beginning' of the condition and the condition itself, and in this way is able to articulate more precisely their point of disjunction. He starts by summarising the argument that he had presented in a paper written on the same subject and in the same year:

> in a neurosis the ego, in its dependence on reality, suppresses a piece of the id (of instinctual life), whereas in a psychosis, this same ego, in the service of the id, withdraws from a piece of reality. Thus for a neurosis the decisive factor would be the

predominance of the influence of reality, whereas for a psychosis it would be the predominance of the id. (*SE* XIX: 183)

Despite the terminological differences (the presence of the ego/id terminology distinguishes it from 'Die Verneinung') one can recognise, in bare outline, the mechanisms with which we are here concerned. In neurosis, a representative of the drive stands in for the drive, which is therefore both suppressed and conserved. In psychosis, however, there is a withdrawal from a piece of reality, a foreclosure of it. Freud, however, soon admits that neurosis itself involves a withdrawal from reality, a flight. One has only to consider here the extent to which an obsessional's life can become punctuated by obscure ceremonies, aimed at warding off unseen dangers by meticulous repetition, in order to agree that a neurotic's behaviour does not fully participate in his or her society's contractual relation to the real. Yet even this assertion is problematic and begs many questions. The term 'reality' is better understood as a kind of sliding scale against which other dimensions of human experience are brought up short, rather than as an empirical ground. Desire is intimately connected to hallucination, as Freud had established as early as 1895, and if it is an hallucinated memory-trace that stands attendance on human desire we can hardly argue for the existence of any empirical real separate from the Symbolic order in which sociality is encoded. It is clear, therefore, that the myth of a neurosis is constructed out of the same cloth as myth in general.

To resolve this paradox, a paradox that threatens to place the boundary between neurosis and psychosis in doubt, Freud emphasises that the beginning of the neurosis and the neurosis itself are two very different things. The beginning of the neurosis is, of course, the moment of fixation of the drive to its ideational representative, the moment in which the 'primordial knot' is constituted. The neurosis itself represents a second stage and

consists rather in the processes which provide a compensation for the portion of the id that has been damaged—that is to say, in the reaction against the repression and in the failure of the repression. The loosening of the relation to reality is a consequence of this second step in the formation of a neurosis, and it ought not to surprise us if a detailed examination shows that the loss of reality affects precisely that piece of reality as a result of whose demands the instinctual repression ensued. (*SE* XIX: 183)

If we impose this sort of interpretation on to the materials given in the Wolf Man case-study, we can distinguish between the beginning of the neurosis, dated by Freud as $n+\frac{1}{2}$ year, and the infantile neurosis that emerges with the anxiety dream at the age of four. There is thus a sort of primitive real in which the child is immersed at the time of the primal scene, and indeed up to the time of the anxiety dream (when a separation with reality occurs, repressed material returns, and infantile neurosis proper commences). The break with reality, in the case of neurosis, therefore takes place later than it does in psychosis, and the sort of reality that is in question is fundamentally different. For the infantile neurosis represents an entrance into the mythological domains of European culture (animal symbolism in the child's animal phobia, obsessional Christianity in his religious period), and it is the identification with the paternal signifier that permits the child's entrance into an ark then so rocked by the waves of repressed material that return to beat against its sides.

The break with reality that occurs in the case of psychosis is held to take place at a prior stage, and this break with reality is defined in the Wolf Man case-study as *Verwerfung*, foreclosure, a break with the forms of identification that an affirmation of the paternal signifier permits. To say that psychosis breaks with reality at the first stage means that psychosis represents a fault in the stitching together of the imaginary and symbolic dimensions in order to ensure predication. The second stage in a psychosis therefore represents 'an active stage of remodelling' in which the psyche tries to patch things up. If a neurosis and a psychosis have in common the fact of raiding, in regression, from the same storehouse of phantasies, there is nevertheless this difference between the two, a difference that Freud defines temporally.[6] In psychosis the loss of reality is primordial and psychotic discourse therefore works to replace the lost universe in its entirety—relations between part and whole are not hierarchised, for lack of any stability in the 'shifters' that organise relations between code and message. The symbolicity of neurosis presupposes a capacity to play—hence the ludic quality of the 'formations' of the unconscious and their divinatory status in most human cultures— whereas in psychosis one cannot take a joke, for a joke is a gift that 'stands out' against something, and for lack of that relief there is no relief to be had.

But the difference that Freud defines as temporal, Lacan defines as symbolic. There is an abolition of something that is called real in a psychotic structure, and a preservation—by means of 'a secret meaning which we (not always quite appropriately) call a symbolic one' (Freud)—in neurosis of that same reality. One cannot, as I hope my argument has shown, claim that a neurosis has some empirical notion to a real order, and the loss from which a psychotic is said to suffer can only be *defined* in terms of the language from which he or she suffers, a language whose very style bears the marks of that original *Verwerfung*.

CONCLUSION

My exegesis of Freud's paper 'Negation' has turned on one crucial observation. I noted that there was a critical discrepancy between the terms *Verwerfung* and *Ausstossung*, and that '*Verwerfung* is linked to the signifier it does not affirm, and this non-affirmation is its most critical feature, whereas *Ausstossung* does not bear on the signifier at all.' This distinction may seem slight and the terminological debate a little arid, a little scriptural, and yet definitions of neurosis and psychosis turn on it. Julia Kristeva, in her work on poetic language, has turned back again and again to this same terminological problem .[7] In creating a new concept, *le rejet*, that englobes the two Freudian terms, she has clearly shown by this transgression just how critical the original debate is. Put another way, definitions of the 'real'—in the Lacanian sense—turn on it.

Psychosis in Lacanian theory is a foreclosure of the paternal signifier, and in the previous section of this paper I attempted to show that if one was to give any useful sense to the notion of 'a loss of reality', that loss had to be defined in terms of the Symbolic order rather than in terms of an empirical ground. Almost all the work of interest that was produced on the nature of psychosis in the late 1950s (from Lacan and Leclaire to Bateson and to Laing) did, after all, stress the problems of understanding a language that appeared to veer towards idiolect. But once the empirical ground is removed, it would seem to be true to say that, inasmuch as we desire, we all hallucinate, but that some hallucinate more than others. This somewhat startling observation suggests that the Lacanian theory of the 'real' is actually the pivot of the system, and that work there, in relation to earlier writing on the phenomenology of hallucination, is now one of the most critical tasks. It is clear that the very term 'hallucination' tends to smuggle in unfounded assumptions as to the manner in which the visual field is appropriated by different persons, and that we ought to concentrate on what can and cannot be said about what impinges on us as 'seen'.

The Wolf Man, for his part, hallucinates a severed finger, and is unable to speak of it to his nurse, who is sitting close by. This hallucination is interpreted by Lacan, following Freud, as a return in the real of what the child had refused to symbolise. But what relation does this foreclosure, this *Verwerfung*, have to the operation of expulsion, *Ausstossung*, of the primary pleasure ego? A glance at Freud's commentary on the primal scene will provide some answers to this.

Freud argues that the primal scene took place at $n + \frac{1}{2}$ a year. Suppose, and there are good reasons for supposing this, that n is zero and that the primal scene therefore took place when the child was six months old. The scene therefore represents an intrusion into a barely consolidated Imaginary domain (the specular ego only begins to be constructed in the sixth month). The child's sense of its own image, as loaned from that of its mother, is therefore shattered by the primary pleasure ego, whose dual operations of introjection and expulsion represent the human musculature's original operations.

But what event is it, within the primal scene, that provides the basis for the child's hallucination, aged $5\frac{1}{2}$, and for the subsequent confusions in its libidinal organisation? There is a moment that Freud omits from his narrative, and this is the moment at which the child actually responds to what it sees. It interrupts the primal scene by shitting, and Freud, in narrating this, stresses that 'here it is not a question of an impression from outside, which must be expected to re-emerge in a number of later indications, but of a reaction on the part of the child himself' (*SE* xvii: 80).

Freud analyses this event as follows. It represents both sexual excitement (as later in the scene with Grusha when the child urinates) and gift-giving. The child, it is argued, is willing to part with this bit of himself 'for the sake of someone he loves'. It is therefore interpreted as an (imaginary) prototype for (symbolic) castration, in that the child is parting with a narcissistically invested part of himself. This gift, because of certain linguistic connections that Freud had found in operation time and time again in the unconscious, is symbolically equivalent to a baby,[8] and Freud thus argues that the child had wanted, through identifying with the mother in the primal scene, to have a baby by his father. Yet the passages in which this is postulated are those that immediately precede the account that Freud gives of the child's foreclosure of castration and of its return in the 'real' in the form of an hallucination of a severed finger. This foreclosure thus facilitates the child's adherence to his theory of intercourse by the anus in order to disavow the perception of the wound (in the mother) that tells of the actuality of castration. This theory, known as the cloacal theory, depends on the analogy between the faecal mass and the penis, on the one hand, and between the mucous membrane of the rectum and that of the vagina, on the other, and in the primal scene the child therefore supposed that it was the rectum that received the penis in intercourse. Since there was, according to this theory, no vagina, there was therefore no castration.

This interpretation does, however, raise certain problems. To interpret the child shitting in the primal scene as a symbolic action, as a gift, is to attribute to the scene a meaning that derives from a set of symbolic equations that are only operative later. An attribution of this sort therefore makes it impossible to explain the very link in the Wolf Man case that is apparently being posited in these pages. For the foreclosure of castration results in its later appearance in the real as an hallucination, yet if the child's expulsion of the faeces in the primal scene has a *symbolic* meaning, how can it at the same time be the origin of a rent in the fabric of the Symbolic order?

In an essay written in 1957, and entitled 'A propos de l'épisode psychotique que présenta l'homme-aux-loups', Serge Leclaire emphasises that this expulsion has nothing to do with symbolicity or with gifts, and he goes on to assert that it represents a kind of imaginary bipartition, an auto-erotic giving birth. It therefore signifies a dual narcissistic relation. This modification would seem to me to be correct inasmuch as it lays the emphasis on the Imaginary order, but it also seems to under-estimate the element of invasion and disturbance implicit in the primal scene. The dual, specular, field is invaded by a thirdness that appears over and above the point at which one's own, one's self-same mother's face should be, and the effect is truly catastrophic (cf. Safouan 1979, esp. 66–82). The catastrophe is attributable to the fact that the specular order is, at that age, not yet cut across by the signifier and by human play. Unlike the $1\frac{1}{2}$ year old child who played the *Fort Da* game, who could play at making himself disappear, and was on the way to a human love in which death and absence also are, the six month old child is faced with an intrusion into a barely mastered narcissistic domain. Thus the stillness of the wolf in the anxiety dream represents not merely (through reversal into its opposite) the agitation of the child's parents making love, it also represents in masked form the phantasy of *le corps morcelé* that a memory of that multiplication of head and limbs would be likely to have constructed. If the child at that moment expelled faeces from its body it was in order to drive out from the primary pleasure ego an unassimilable entity. This expulsion therefore represented the sadistic aspect of the death drive, of the anal drive, rather than the passive and erotic aspect of the mucous membrane that later comes to be linked up, by means of the agency of the ego ideal, to the crucial symbolic equations. In so far as the catastrophe is affirmed, and therefore dialecticised, it returns in speech or in symptom, but in so far as the primary pleasure ego drives out the element uncaptured by symbolicity, it will return in the real as hallucination.

It thus appears that the distinction between *Ausstossung* and *Verwerfung* does, properly understood, hold the key to understanding the different ways in which neurosis and psychosis are structured in different social formations. For, in a social formation in which the ego ideal is not sufficiently operative to install anal demand[9]—and there is, after all, no shortage of monographs that assert the absence of the 'anal-sadistic' stage in the unconscious of persons in lineage societies[10]—one could argue that the operations of the pleasure ego are less completely captured by denegation, and that the domain subsisting outside of symbolisation is therefore more extensive. This less complete capture of what, in the 'Die Verneinung' paper, is called *Ausstossung*, by denegation, is more easily thought if the paper is properly translated and the discrepancy between *Ersatz* and *Nachfolge* registered. But this less complete capture suggests that in such social formations hallucination is more possible, and that when there is hallucination in a temporary psychotic state,[11] it is hard to map it back on to the notion of *Verwerfung*. For the nonaffirmation of the paternal signifier presupposes that the operation of the symbolic equations that capture the *Ausstossung* of the primary pleasure ego would be less operative and would therefore link the body less completely to the circuits of language. To provide an account of the formation of those equations would be to provide a theory of the origin of the transference situation itself, for they are its necessary precondition. Once the origin of the transference situation is understood one can also account for the appearance and then the disappearance of psychoanalysis.

The Platonic notion of love's poverty has been especially stressed by Lacan, and though we are all considered poor in that lack grounds us in a desire that cannot be satisfied, the mother's demand for love is posited as origin of this poverty. Linguistics, or a structural linguistic conception of *la langue*, may account for the link between love and death that Lacanian psychoanalysis posits, but it is also clear that a demolition of the equivalences postulated between parts of the body, as 'unconscious concepts', and children, would disrupt that link in a way that would at least place in question the negative marking of feminine sexuality so central to Freudian and Lacanian psychoanalysis and posited as universal. What then of the concept of the Name of the Father?

Lacan has continually stressed that the concept of the Name of the Father is to be distinguished from any actual father who might bear the name of father. He suggests, at one point, that a spirit of a water-hole—the reference is to indigenous Australian theories of conception—could as easily fulfil this function of mediating between the child and the mother's demand (*E* 555–66/199). The point of this example is that it emphasises the fact that in human culture there is an infinite variety of ways of attributing paternity. There are, however, dangers implicit in ethnographic citation. It is always possible to cite a contrary example. In the realm of what one might call 'folk genetics', it is all too easy to find mothers to whom maternity is, in a certain sense, not attributed. I mean by this that, just as one can find societies in which the father's part in contributing to the child's genetic make-up is explicitly denied, so too can one find societies in which the mother, although she bears the child, and everyone knows that this is so, is held to play no part in determining its biological inheritance. What is one to make of this? The example which I cited comes from E. R. Leach's 1961 Malinowski lecture, and in that lecture Leach is in fact concerned to wrench 'kinship' theory free from the sort of bio-psychological reductionism that had haunted it since Malinowski, in order to give it a purely logical basis, and to show that one cannot really impute psychological states to persons who simply make statements about what their societies' theories of genetic inheritance are (Leach 1961: 1–27). Does this vitiate Lacan's argument?

At first glance one might be tempted to argue that it does, and that the whole force of Lacan's concept of the Name of the Father rests on an almost Victorian notion of the way in which a social system builds up its descent categories after the fact of maternity, which is—according to Bachofen, and so many others—the one certainty about their descent that human beings can have. It is well known that evolutionary theories of kinship deduced from this that, after the original stage of 'primitive promiscuity', matrilineal descent must have been the subsequent form of reckoning consanguineal ties, for motherhood is empirically observable but fatherhood necessarily putative. However, my sense of Lacan's concept leads me to believe that he links it closely to the point in Freud's writing, in *Moses and Monotheism* (*SE* XXIII: 3–141), at which this same debate figures. The concept of the Name of the Father thus derives from the psychoanalytic domain, and any ethnographic qualifications to it are secondary. This is less of a retreat, in theoretical terms, than it might at first seem. Just as Marx had made the epistemological proviso that 'the anatomy of man is the key to the anatomy of the ape', and that it was therefore through attending to the structure of the capitalist mode of production that one could perceive the structure of other modes of production, so too, with psychoanalysis, we have no choice but to attend to the unconscious at the point at which we know it.[12] Rather than invoking the truth and beauty of ritual forms that preceded psychoanalysis, an enterprise in which phantasy will inevitably play its part, it seems to me more important to investigate the fissures apparent in its own organisation of concepts. One of these fissures is apparent in Freud's writings on the origins of human culture and on the origin of monotheism, and it is from these writings—considered dialectically in relation to the case-studies—that Lacan's concept of the Name of the Father emerges. It evokes the Pentateuch and the ferocity with which our own religious traditions set the metaphorical function to work, and demand that we sacrifice sensible image to absent law.[13] The concept is therefore itself ethnographic inasmuch as it includes reference to the symbolic conditions out of which psychoanalysis emerged. By examining the critical difference between the Symbolic, Imaginary and real fathers in Lacanian theory one is able to formulate an account of the emergence of the transference situation and of the symbolic equations that draw us inexorably towards the possibility of a talking-cure. It is therefore the fissures within psychoanalytic theory that permit a materialist account, first, of the historical conditions that prepared the way for the transference situation, and second, of the historical conditions that produce other sorts of ritual and therapeutic practice.

NOTES

1. The original German text is to be found in the *Gesammelte Werke* xiv: 11–15. It appears in two English translations, one by Joan Rivière in *Collected Papers* v: 181–5 and the other by James Strachey (*SE* xix: 233–9).

2. Thus, This and Thèves, in their long commentary on the use of the particle *ver*—in German, argue that it signifies both an action pushed right to the end (they give the examples of *bluten*, to bleed; *verbluten*, to lose all one's blood; *scheiden*, to separate; *verscheiden*, to die; *urteilen*, to judge; *verurteilen*, to condemn) and that, in certain cases, it can topple over into its negative form (thus, if *bieten* means to offer, *verbieten* means to forbid; and if *kaufen* means to buy, *verkaufen* means to sell). Freud was deeply interested in this sort of phenomenon and would certainly have been well aware of the resonances of the particle *ver-*. But one cannot help but be a little wary of This and Thèves's philological enthusiasm: do these same remarks hold good with respect to the deployment of the same particle in *Verwerfung* and *Verleugnung?*

3. One of the clearest and most convincing accounts of this aspect of Lacanian psychoanalysis is presented in M. Safouan's *Etudes sur l'Oedipe* (1974), ch. i–ix, which should be read in sequence. Cf. also ch. i of S. Leclaire's *Psychanalyser* (1968).

4. Strachey also gives, on different occasions, 'original pleasure ego' and 'initial pleasure ego'.

5. Cf. J. Dubois *et al.*, 'Transformations negatives et organisation des classes lexicales' (1965). In this essay on negative lexical transformations, Dubois, Irigaray and Macie note that such transformations do not require the obliteration of the original positive sentence, but a 'negative re-writing', a re-writing in which 'the fundamental signified of the original sentence is preserved intact'. The phrasing of this article is Chomskyan and therefore concerns 're-write' rules, but its basic statements are nevertheless still relevant here.

6. Much of my argument in this section derives from an essay by M. Safouan, 'De la forclusion' (Safouan 1974: 98–114).

7. The relevant passages in *La Révolution du langage poétique* (1974) are to be found at pages 43–50 and also at pages 134–50, but these passages make little sense outside of the book's entire argument. Many of the same points are made again, sometimes in an identical wording, in 'Le sujet en procès' (1977:55–106).

8. *SE* xvii: 81–4; see also, 'On Transformations of Instinct as Exemplified in Anal Erotism', *SE* xvii: 130.

9. Cf. E. and M.-C. Ortigues, *Oedipe Africain* (1973).

10. Cf. Ortigues 1973; also, A. Zempleni, *L'Interprétation du désordre mental et la thérapie traditionelle chez les Wolof et les Lébou* (1968).

11. Cf. E. and M.-C. Ortigues, 'Les bouffées délirantes en psychiatrie africaine' in *Oedipe Africain* (1973): 297–305. Also Collomb (1965).

12. Marx's remark comes from his *Introduction to a Critique of Political Economy*, and in citing it here I had in mind the gloss that Althusser gives it in *Reading Capital*:

Marx . . . says in so many words that we must elucidate the knowledge of the *'Gliederung'* (the articulated, hierarchised, systematic combination) of *contemporary* society if we are to reach an understanding of earlier forms and therefore of the most primitive forms. His famous remark that 'the anatomy of man is the key to the anatomy of the ape', of course, means nothing else; of course, it coincides with that other remark in the *Introduction* that it is not the historical genesis of categories nor their combination in earlier forms that enables us to understand them, but the system of their combination in contemporary society, which also opens the way to an understanding of past formations, by giving us the concept of the *variation* of this combination. Similarly, only the elucidation of the mechanism of the contemporary knowledge effect can cast light on to earlier effects. The rejection of any recourse to origins is therefore correlated with a very basic theoretical exigency which insists on the dependence of the explanation of more primitive forms on the contemporary mode of systematic combination of categories which are also found in part in earlier forms (1970:64).

13. Cf. Lacan 1938 an article published on the family in the very same year as Freud finally assembled the *Moses and Monotheism* papers. Kristeva develops the sort of argument that I have only hinted at here in *Des Chinoises* (1975b) and in 'A propos du discours biblique' and 'Pratique signifiante et mode de production', in *La Traversée des signes* (1975a).

9 On Discourse

COLIN MacCABE

Etymologically discourse finds its origin in the Latin verb *discurrere*, to run about, probably by way of the French form *discourir*. This particular genealogy is more indicative than it might first appear because discourse, as the term is used in classical rhetoric, emphasises language as motion, as action. If the rhetorician was concerned with arresting language so that he could specify the various relations into which words could enter, to classify the figures and the topics, discourse constituted both the object and the aim of the study. Rhetoric started from and ended with the running together of the forms and the subjects in a continuous utterance—in, exactly, a discourse. It is within this perspective that we can consider discourse as indicating the articulation of language over units greater than the sentence. The major divisions of rhetoric accomplish just such supra-sentential divisions: *exordium, narratio, argumentatio, refutatio, peroratio* (Curtius 1953: 70). A particular set of articulations will produce a field of discursivity—the site of the possibility of proof and disproof (it can be recalled that the study of rhetoric found its early rationale in relation to forms of popular law (cf. Barthes 1970: 175)). It is to such a notion of discourse that *Cahiers pour l'Analyse* made reference when, in the *avertissement* to the first number, Jacques-Alain Miller defined the magazine's task as the constitution of a theory of discourse, specifying that by discourse 'we understand a process of language that truth constrains' (1966: 5). And, in a reference to the content of that first number, Miller made clear that the constraint of truth has as its inevitable corollary the production of a subject, a subject divided by the very process of language that calls it into being.

   It is this division of the subject in language, a division figured in the Lacanian concept of the signifier, which is essential to the elaboration of any theory of discourse. Without it, and whatever its lexical possibilities, the term 'discourse' no longer indicates the site(s) of the articulations of language and sociality but simply functions as a cover for a linguistic formalism or a sociological subjectivism. The linguists Zellig Harris (1952) and Emile Benveniste (1971) will serve as important examples of these alternative hazards. If the Lacanian concept of the signifier articulates the initial support for the argument, the considerations advanced will necessitate further questions, ones that will lead, by way of the consideration of the work of Michel Pêcheux, to the problem of the politics of the signifier.[1]

EMILE BENVENISTE AND THE STATUS OF THE SUBJECT

Benveniste's use of discourse emphasises the lexical reference to the intersubjective use of language. In his famous article on the relation of tenses in the French verb he emphasises that 'Discourse must be understood in its widest sense: every utterance assuming a speaker and a hearer, and in the speaker, the intention of influencing the other in some way.' (1971: 208–9) Such a personal use of language must be differential from the unpersonal mode of *histoire*. Benveniste uses this distinction to give an account of the tenses of the French verb. His starting-point is the apparent redundancy of forms of the past tense which change according to whether one is speaking or writing. That used in the spoken language is a compound past tense formed by the verb *avoir* (to have) and the past participle (and hereafter called the perfect), that in the written is a distinct inflection of the verb (and hereafter called the aorist). It is a commonplace amongst both native speakers and linguists that the aorist, which is the older form, is disappearing and that it will be replaced, in time, by the perfect. It is this commonplace that Benveniste is concerned to dispute. Benveniste wishes to demonstrate that, despite its long disappearance from the spoken language, there is no question that it is similarly menaced in the written language, and this because despite appearances, it serves a different function from the perfect. What is needed to determine the future of the aorist is not statistical studies but an understanding of the tense system of the French verb. The double entry for the past tense is not a redundancy which the language has been slow to remedy but the visible evidence of the fact that there are two separate tense systems which are differentiated by the relation of the speaker/writer (hereafter called *the subject of the enunciation*) to the statement (hereafter called *the enounced*). In that relation which Benveniste terms *histoire*[2] 'events that took place at a certain moment of time are presented without any intervention of the speaker in the narration' (1971: 206). The tenses of this relation are the imperfect (with which Benveniste includes the conditional), the aorist and the pluperfect together with the atemporal present of definition and a compound tense which Benveniste suggests should be called the prospective. Benveniste notes that these three basic tenses articulate perfectly the world of *histoire* and demonstrates this with quotations from a history text and a Balzac novel (examples which, as we shall see, have a great deal more significance than Benveniste would assign to them):

> There is no reason for them to change as long as the historical narration is being pursued, and, furthermore, there is no reason for the narration to come to a standstill since we can imagine the whole past of the world as being a continuous narration, entirely constructed according to this triple correlation of tenses: aorist, imperfect and pluperfect. It is sufficient and necessary that the author remain faithful to his historical purpose and that he proscribe everything that is alien to the narration of events (discourse, reflections, comparisons). As a matter of fact, there is no longer even a narrator. The events are set forth chronologically, as they occurred. No one speaks here; the events seem to narrate themselves. The fundamental tense is the aorist, which is the tense of the event outside the person of a narrator. (1971: 208)

This is the impersonal relation that is opposed to *discours*. *Histoire* produces no involvement of the subject of the enunciation in the enounced while it is the very definition of *discours*. In speech the tenses are always related to the present instance and must thus give way to a tense which defines its pastness in terms of the present: 'Like the present, the perfect belongs to the linguistic system of discourse, for the temporal location of the perfect is the moment of the discourse, while the location of the aorist is the moment of the event' (1971: 210). By thus distinguishing the two forms of the past in French, Benveniste can also explain further features of the tense system. In particular, he demonstrates how the secondary compound tenses are produced in response to the pressure created around the first person forms of the two past tenses.[3]

It is not accidental that it is the first person which Benveniste isolates as the crucial articulation in the historical development of the language, for it is the category of person which provides the field within which Benveniste's tense distinctions are articulated. On the one hand there is the world of *discours*, the world of *je/tu* (I/you). On the other is the world without person, the world of *histoire*, the world of *il* (he/it). It is the emphasis on person which links this article to the others collected in Section 5 of the *Problems in General Linguistics*. The constant theme of this section is that the apparently regular structure of the three persons in many Indo-European languages is grossly misleading for the analysis of person. There are not, in fact, three persons but two *je/tu* which find themselves in opposition to a realm of 'non-person' *il*. Benveniste finds an awareness of this in the Arab grammarian's analysis of person which distinguishes the first and second person, 'he who speaks' and 'he who is spoken to' from the third 'he who is absent'. This division marks the asymmetry between the persons, an asymmetry which finds further support in the fact that in many languages the third person is unmarked in relation to the first and second and that the third person pronoun is not a universal phenomenon.

The argument so far outlined would seem to rest its analyses on a distinction between subjective and objective functions in language. Language is the combination of two autonomous but intersecting systems: the world of the first and second person, which define a subjective realm of *discours* with a tense system related to the moment of speech, and the world of the third person, which defines an objective realm of *histoire* with a tense system related to the moment of the event. It should be noted that, even granted Benveniste's assumptions, the distinction suffers from certain crucial weaknesses. Firstly there is the occurrence of the third person within the realm of *discours*, an embarrassment which provokes some of Benveniste's weakest arguments: even if it is not explicit, the relationship of person is everywhere present in *discours*; it is only with *histoire* that we reach the 'true' realm of the non-person (1971: 209). Secondly, and just as serious, is the fact that the anchor-tense of *discours*, the present, occurs within *histoire*; which occurrence Benveniste terms 'an atemporal present like the present of definition' (1971: 207).

Apart from such internal inconsistencies, however, there are more serious criticisms to be levelled at the whole project. Benveniste fails to give any account of the relation between the two systems which does not fall back into the subjective/objective couple. Objective, as always on this account, becomes the paring away of the *contingent* effects of subjectivity to arrive at the necessary relations beneath. Language, with an equal familiarity, is defined as a simple mirror to reflect reality, which becomes opaque once the realm of reason is disturbed by the illogicalities of passion. This caricature is designed to highlight the similarity of this position to the traditional denigration of the order of language in relation to the speaker (rhetoric) as opposed to the order of language in relation to the facts (logic). That this caricature captures at least some of the elements of Benveniste's position is evident in sections of the article on the use of pronouns:

> If each speaker, in order to express the feeling he has of his irreducible subjectivity, made use of a distinct identifying signal (in the sense in which each radio transmitting station has its own call letters), there would be as many languages as individuals and communication would become absolutely impossible. Language wards off this danger by instituting a unique but mobile sign, I, which can be assumed by each speaker on the condition that he refers each time only to the instance of his own discourse. (1971: 220)

This formulation approaches dangerously close to the Port-Royal conception of pronouns which holds that pronouns are simply used to avoid unnecessary repetition but are granted no effectivity of their own (cf. Arnauld and Lancelot 1969: 43–4), a conception which informs the whole of Port-Royal's theory of discourse. But that Benveniste's position is more ambiguous is indicated by the fact that he considers pronouns to be 'absolutely' essential to language function although he offers no theoretical justification of this absoluteness. It is when he approaches the question of subjectivity in language directly that these contradictions manifest themselves most clearly. For while the distinction *discours/histoire* would ultimately seem to rest on a clear distinction between the subject using the language and the language, Benveniste explicitly refuses such a position in a paper written practically simultaneously:

> We are always inclined to that naive concept of a primordial

period in which a complete man discovered another one, equally complete, and between the two of them language was worked out little by little. This is pure fiction. We can never get back to man separated from language and we shall never see him inventing it. . . . It is a speaking man whom we find in the world, a man speaking to another man, and language provides the very definition of man. (1971: 224)

It is clear that Benveniste considers that language is constituted in relation to the other. But he fails to investigate the linguistic basis of this other, and in what amounts to a tacit acceptance of a personalist other, he is left, however reluctantly, with an account which though it interrogates its own foundations at certain moments, is finally dependent if it is to be retained in its totality, on a classic account of subjectivity. The miscognition on which Benveniste's theory rests is the failure to grasp two elements as participating in the same structure. To distinguish them as elements is his major contribution; the task that remains is to provide the structure that articulates them and such an articulation will depend on cutting back across some of the original distinctions. To oppose *je/tu* to *il* is to shatter the assumptions that make the passage from 'I' to 'you' to 'he' to 'it' an inevitable and obvious progression but to ignore their interrelation is to ignore that I/you can only function as the deictic categories for the subject of the enunciation after the passage through the third person; a passage which allows this pronoun to assume both personal and impersonal forms. Similarly *discours* is determined in its forms by *histoire* for it is the involvement of the subject of the enunciation in *histoire* that determines its appearance in the enounced of *discours*.

The interrelation is analysed in Luce Irigaray's 'Communications linguistique et spéculaire' (1966). In my summary of this argument it is important to recognise that what is in question is a diachronic fable of a synchronic functioning. In the development of the child there is a moment when the infant (*infans*: unable to speak) enters language. In this process of entry, he/she becomes aware of certain places which he/she as subject can occupy—these are the points of insertion into language. Crucially this involves the learning of pronouns: the realisation that the 'you' with which the child is addressed by the father or mother can be permutated with an 'I' in a situation from which it is excluded—when the parents speak to each other. This realisation is the understanding that the 'you' with which he or she is addressed can be permutated with a 'he' or 'she', which is the possibility that the proper name is articulated in a set of differences—and that the child is only a signifier constantly defined and redefined by a set of substitution relations. The binary I/you is transformed from two terms into a relational structure by the passage through the empty place of the 'he' or 'she' and it is through the experience of this empty place that the child enters language. The passage through this empty place is the exclusion necessary to the proper control of language and the experience of this exclusion is the first taste of annihilation—the constitutive moment at which the entry into human life is preceded by a voyage through death. It is this which gives language its fearsome quality because the experience of the sign involves a castration at the linguistic level; a castration acknowledged in medieval depictions of grammar. The crucial text for the medieval description of the liberal arts was Martianus Capella's *De nuptiis Philologiae et Mercurii* (The wedding of Philology and Mercury). Curtius gives a thorough summary: Lacking a bride, Mercury is counselled to marry the learned maid Philologia. The major part of the poem is taken up with Philologia's admittance to the rank of the Gods: 'Philologia is adorned by her mother Phronesis and greeted by the four Cardinal Virtues and the three graces. At the bidding of Athanasia, she is forced to vomit up a number of books in order to become worthy of immortality. She then ascends to heaven in a litter born by the youths Labor and Amor and the maidens Epimelia (application) and Agrypnia (the intellectual worker's night labours and curtailed sleep).' More crucial for a metaphorical understanding of the process I have just traced is the appearance of Grammar: 'Grammar appears as a gray-haired woman of advanced age, who boasts that she descends from the Egyptian king Osiris. Later she lived for a long time in Attica, but now she appears in Roman dress. She carries an ebony casket, containing a knife and a file with which to operate surgically on childrens' grammatical errors' (Curtius 1953: 38–9).

To accede to the world of absence—to the world of the sign where one thing can stand for another—we must wound perpetually, if not destroy, a narcissism which would render the world dependent on our presence. This process is also the engenderment of the 'one' of identity in a contradictory movement by which this absence is taken up and named; this naming thus conferring a unity and an identity, a presence. The proper name is transformed from a set of physical qualities into the enumerable mark of an absence. The name is that which marks the exclusion of the subject from the realm in which he/she is thus constituted. And this exclusion is constantly relived in the progress through language. When the substitution rules have been mastered, the child finds itself divided between two worlds— the world of the enunciation, where he or she is constantly in play as signifier and the world of the enounced, where he or she is constantly in place as signified.

Benveniste's great contribution is to have distinguished two different axes of language, the enunciation and the enounced, but his exposition of their relation is vitiated by his uncritical accept- ance of the notion of the subject. The consequence of this acceptance is that the relationship between the subject of the enunciation and the subject of the enounced remains obscure. *Histoire* and *discours* are distinguished by the presence of the subject of the enunciation in *discours* and its absence from *histoire*. But the considerations just advanced demonstrate:

(1) that the subject of the enunciation does occur in the realm of the third person because even if there is no direct appearance in the pronouns of the enounced the subject is constituted in the signifier, and thus
(2) that *discours* is dependent on *histoire*, most evidently in that the predicates that can be attached to proper names will determine the place of pronouns in *discours*.

The interrelation between *discours* and *histoire* and the crucial role of proper names in this interrelation is evident in what I have termed elsewhere the classic realist text (MacCabe 1974, 1979). It is through the determination of the possibilities of predication that the novelist can produce the moral judgements of *discours*. What can and cannot be said in *discours* is determined by the articulations of *histoire*. A consideration of Benveniste's example from Balzac will enable us to understand this functioning:

Après un tour de galerie, le jeune homme *regarda* tour à tour le ciel et sa montre, *fit* un geste d' impatience, *entra* dans un bureau de tabac, *y alluma* un cigare, se *posa* devant une glace, et *jeta* un regard sur son costume, un peu plus riche que ne le permettent en France les lois du goût (1). Il *rajusta* son col et son gilet de velours noir sur lequel *se croisait* plusieurs fois une de ces grosses chaînes d'or fabriquées à Gênes; puis, après avoir jeté par un seul mouvement sur son épaule gauche son manteau doublé de velours en le drapant avec élégance, il *reprit* sa promenade sans se laisser distraire par les œillades bourgeoises qu'il *recevait*. Quand les boutiques *commencèrent* à s'illuminer et que la nuit lui *parut* assez noire, il se *dirigea* vers la place du Palais-Royal en homme qui *craignait* d'être reconnu, car il *côtoya* la place jusqu'à la fontaine, pour gagner à l'abri des fiacres l'entrée de la rue Froidmanteau.(1971: 208)

When the young man had gone round the gallery, he looked up at the sky and then at his watch, made an impatient gesture, went into a tobacconist and once inside lit up a cigar. He stood in front of a mirror and glanced at his clothes which were rather more dressy than is allowed by good taste in France. (1) He straightened his collar and his black velvet waistcoat on which one of those heavy gold chains made in Genoa was crossed and recrossed several times; then after throwing over his shoulder in one smooth movement his double cloak of velvet so that it draped him in elegant folds, he resumed his walk without allowing himself to be distracted by the stares of the bourgeoisie that were directed towards him. When the shops began to light up and the evening had become dark, he made his way towards the square of Palais Royal like a man who was frightened of being recognised for he hugged the walls of the square up to the fountain so that he could reach the entry to the rue Froidmanteau under cover of the carriages.

Benveniste underlines all the occurrences of the tenses of *histoire* and for the one occurrence of a present tense he adds as a footnote (1) 'Réflexion de l'auteur qui échappe au plan du récit' (Reflection of the author which falls outside the scope of the narrative).

The crucial moment in this passage is the moment which Benveniste recognises as escaping his division, the moment at which Balzac intervenes in order to inform us that the young man's clothes are a little too overdone. Benveniste argues that this present tense relates directly to the author independently of the narrative. But this is to ignore the extent to which the figure of the author is a function of the narrative. The introduction of a present tense locates the author as omniscient in the present but this position does not find its authority in the present tense nor in the historical figure Honoré de Balzac but rather in the wealth of detailed aorists which guarantee the truth of the narrative and, by metonymy, of its writer. The relation between the tenses in this type of novel, or better this practice of writing, is not one of separation or division but of solidarity. If the aorist becomes excluded from speech, this absence becomes the guarantee of the truth of the written form. And it is this truth which justifies the present tenses that occur within a novel.[4] Benveniste's distinction between the tenses finds its basis not in some grammatical features of the verb but in a certain practice of writing which has pulled in its wake certain grammatical features.[5] A practice is defined as a transformation of material through time and a practice of writing is a constant transformation, work on the signifying material of language. It is within this perspective that one might venture certain historical explanations of the tense system in French. In particular one might be able to situate the aorist's exclusion from speech and the rise of the novel as contemporary events. As to the contemporary situation: although Benveniste provides a perfectly satisfactory synchronic account of a stable system, it does not follow that the aorist is not menaced by extinction. If Benveniste is quite right to criticise the received notion that the aorist is succumbing to some inexorable natural process, it is important to recognise that in the last forty years (and particularly in the last ten) there have arisen various practices of writing which aim at the disruption of the stable system that Benveniste describes. In his first novel *L'Etranger* Albert Camus wrote a narrative which systematically avoided the aorist and in the wake of Camus's book a variety of anti-aorist ideologies have been articulated. The refusal to use the aorist has been theorised in terms of existential authenticity (it is the tense that burdens you with a past that exhausts your definition) or of a more structural sensibility (it is the tense of the novel in which one refuses to be written) or of a political refusal of the social and educational divisions inscribed within the French language (the aorist is an 'élitist' tense). *Histoire* and *discours* depend on a distinction between a language use from which the speaking subject is excluded and a language use in which the subject can identify his/her place. The detour through psychoanalysis demonstrates that the identifying of the place by the subject is the experience of exclusion and its modalities. We cannot find a language independent of subjectivity, nor a subjectivity independent of language but must attempt to understand their joint constitution. Beneveniste's analysis is a vital and important step in the attempt to understand the linguistic mechanisms across which the 'I' and the 'it' form and re-form: the process by which a subjectivity is produced, along with its constant subversion. But if Benveniste's distinction is of such crucial importance, it is necessary to recognise that because his own attempts to develop it are caught within the terms of classical philosophy, he is often forced to return, against his explicit theses, to a conception of language as transparent mirror between subject and object, a mere reflection for worlds constituted outside its operations.

ZELLIG HARRIS AND THE CONSTITUTION OF THE CORPUS

It is now so evident that for linguistics to constitute itself as a science it was necessary to drop normative concerns that one can all too hastily recuperate such a decision within a spontaneous 'objectivist' theory of science and ignore the complex play of theories and practices that were re-aligned by the Saussurean revolution. If, until then, the grammarian had been concerned with laying down the rules and means of expression in reference to an optimum then inevitably his concern was with *texts* of considerable length in which this optimum could be demonstrated with reference to specific effectivities. Once, however, the notion of *langue* as system has been introduced, language is studied in terms of the operations which allow the possibility of the specific production of sense and *no longer* in terms of a sense which it is language's function to produce. At this point the text ceases to be an object for the linguist because the set of systems which allow combination and regular substitution are smaller than the text. Over and above the sentence we leave the domain of *langue* to enter into the world of a full subjectivity where *langue* is simply at the service of *parole*. Jakobson, in a famous passage, states the position thus:

There is an ascending scale of liberty in the combination of linguistic units. In the combination of distinctive traits into phonemes the user's liberty is nil; the code has already established all the possibilities that can be used in the language in question. In the combination of phonemes into words his liberty is heavily circumscribed; it is limited to the marginal situation of the creation of new words. The constraints upon the speaker are less when it comes to the combination of words into sentences. But finally in the combination of sentences into statements the action of the constraining rules of syntax stops and the liberty of each speaker grows substantially, although one should still not underestimate the number of stereotyped statements. (Jakobson 1963: 47)

This belief in the creative freedom of the individual at the supra-sentential level (freedom limited only by what guarantees its reality—the risk of stereotype) has effectively vitiated the majority of work done by linguists on discourse analysis, or, as it is also described, text-linguistics.[6] If the lexical ambiguity of the term discourse indicates that the articulatory and inter-subjective functions of language are *one and the same*, that it is the major articulations of language which provide the field for the appearance of subjectivity, the example of Benveniste proves that as long as the problem of the subject is left unresolved then the analysis will collapse back into the presuppositions of the Saussurean concept of *parole*. To analyse discourse we must start from Lacan's insight that language operates on a continuous misconstruction of its constitution; which misconstruction is the appearance of the subject.

In this perspective the work of Zellig Harris provides a much more promising start in its resolute refusal of any problematic of subjectivity although we shall also see how this refusal blocks Harris's own development of his procedures of analysis. For Harris the failure of linguistics to pass beyond the threshold of the sentence can be ascribed to the fact that effective grammars can be constituted without so doing. In his concern to propose an analysis which does move beyond the sentence, Harris's starting-point is a definition of discourse as 'connected speech or writing', a definition which starts from the very opposite emphasis to Benveniste's intersubjectivity. Harris believes that there are regularities and constraints to be discovered at the level of discourse and, further, that these discoveries will relate language to its cultural situation: to the problem of subjectivity. However, the problem of subjectivity is left to a further stage of the analysis which must start from the formal investigation of particular texts. The choice of particular texts as the corpus is determined for Harris by two considerations. First, we can discover no general supra-sentential rules because of the heterogeneity of language-use, it is only within individual texts that we can discern regularities. Second, in relation to the problem of subjectivity and language, Harris holds that the relation of discourse to its cultural situation must be investigated in individual instances because the relation *changes in each instance*. Thus discourse analysis, by concentrating on one continuous text, allows both the construction of regularities that go beyond the sentence and, at the same time, the possibility of studying the relations between these regularities and the conditions of the production of the text. The method pre-supposes no knowledge except that of morpheme boundaries but, in fact, Harris uses grammatical knowledge in order to construct larger equivalence classes, a concept we shall come to in a moment. Harris summarises his position at the end of the introduction to the article 'Discourse Analysis' thus: 'We have raised two problems: that of distributional relations among sentences, and that of the correlation between language and social situation. We have proposed that information relevant to both of these problems can be obtained by a formal analysis of one stretch of discourse at a time' (Harris 1952a: 4–5). We shall return to these arguments after considering Harris's procedures.

The distributional methods that Harris proposes for the analysis of discourse are derived from those set out in Harris's *Methods in Structural Linguistics* which had been published the year before although composed some time earlier (it has since been reissued as *Structural Linguistics*). Lyons describes the methodology as follows:

> it was assumed that the proper task of 'structural linguistics' was to formulate a technique, or procedure, which could be applied to a corpus of attested utterances and, with the minimum use of the informant's judgements of sameness' and 'difference', could be guaranteed to derive the rules of the grammar from the corpus itself. (1968: 157).

Starting, that is, from a *corpus*, the result of the collection of statements produced by members of the same speech community at the same time, the distributional analyst, rejecting all explanations in terms of function or meaning, attempts to subdivide the corpus in terms of contexts or *environments*. To describe an environment is to describe what precedes and follows a particular unit. The problem then becomes one of ordering the occurrences of units within similar environments with the aim of producing an account of the distribution of a unit. If we imagine a language close to English but in which, for simplicity's sake, the adjective always preceded the noun and never appeared without the noun, a distributional grammar would describe it simply as a unit A which always precedes another unit N, this second unit having the possibility of appearing without unit A and in combination with other units. This is exactly the method that Harris follows, with the proviso that the corpus is constituted by one text because of the necessity of avoiding any criteria from outside language (including meaning) in specifying the corpus.

Given the simple aim of constituting classes with the same environment and considering their appearance within a specific text so that certain patterns and regularities can be analysed, Harris's paper on structural linguistics is devoted to sketching the difficulties involved in the analysis. Taken strictly the methods of distributionalism would prevent the analysis of any but the most simple kind of text because there are just not that many identical repetitions in any normal use of language. Harris is concerned to specify criteria of equivalence which are not dependent on meaning. The construction of equivalences is a question of paraphrasing the original phrase until the element under investigation can be isolated in the same position as the one with which an equivalence is to be established. This may seem rather a circular procedure. Harris comments:

> The criterion is not some external consideration like getting the longest possible chain, but rather the intrinsic consideration of finding some patterned distribution of these classes. In other words we try to set up such classes as will have an interesting distribution in our particular text. This may seem a rather circular safeguard for constructing equivalence chains. But it simply means that whenever we have to decide whether to carry an equivalence chain one step further, we exercise the foresight of considering how the new interval will fit into our analysed text as it appears when represented in terms of the new class. This kind of consideration occurs in descriptive linguistics when we have to decide, for example, how far to subdivide a phonemic sequence into morphemes. (Harris, 1952a: 12)

In rearranging the position of phrases we take the horizontal order of the segments of the sentence as immaterial. Our aim, however, is to construct a vertical order which will reveal in the regular distribution of the equivalence classes certain systematicities in discourse which were not evidently available.

In determining the equivalence classes it is the division of the sentences into segments that is crucial for 'we want not simply the same distributional classes but the same relationship between these classes'. Grammatical criteria will normally provide the necessary divisions but certain cases remain problematic. Harris's example of such a difficulty is the sentence 'Casals who is self-exiled from Spain stopped performing after the Fascist victory.' The problem for Harris is whether 'who' continues or repeats Casals: 'If *who* continues *Casals*, we have one interval, the first section (C) being *Casals who*, while the second section (S) is *self-exiled . . . stopped. . . .* If *who* repeats Casals instead of continuing it, we have two intervals, one embedded in the other: the first consists of *Casals* (again C) plus *stopped performing* (marked S_1), the second of *who* (taken as an equivalent of Casals) plus is *self-exiled* (S_2).' For Harris the choice simply depends on whether we can find elements of the second half of the sentence occurring separately. And this matter is considered relatively unimportant by Harris: 'The only difference between taking a dependent element as a continuation and taking it as a repetition is the number of intervals one or two into which one can analyse the total' (Harris 1952a: 16–17).

Harris's comments ignore the importance of the choice of analysis. In order to analyse the regularities of occurrence we must know what can count as an equivalence class for a predicate which contains two verbs might not be equivalent to a predicate with one. Indeed in this particular case we are dealing with a sentence for which it is extremely unlikely that one can set up any equivalence classes given Harris's original definition of the corpus. For in this passage Harris glides over the problem of relatives; a problem which is crucial to an understanding of discourse. Traditionally relatives are analysed into restrictive and non-restrictive. The restrictive relative cannot be removed from the sentence in which it occurs without a change in meaning because it determines one of the terms within the main clause. Transformational grammars tend to analyse restrictive relatives in terms of an embedded structure whereby the relative clause is found as a sentence attached to a noun phrase in the deep structure (cf. Huddleston 1976: 101–9). Thus an analysis of the sentence 'Mary believed the rumour that John had started' produces the sentence 'John started the rumour' as dependent on 'the rumour' in the deep structure. On the other hand, the non-restrictive relative can, in principle, be abstracted from the sentence without a consequent change in meaning; thus

'Moses, who was a prophet, led the Jews out of Egypt'. Here the relative does not identify a constituent part of the main sentence. Traditionally generative grammars analyse such sentences in terms of co-ordination instead of subordination with two separate sentences in the deep structure. But this grammatical distinction is not at all clear if we consider the discursive functioning of the relative. For in the sentence 'Casals, who is self-exiled from Spain, stopped performing after the Fascist victory' *who is self-exiled* does not identify the subject of the sentence because a proper name cannot be further identified. A proper name is precisely an identification and nothing more, the enumerable mark of a specific absence. But if we consider the sentence about Casals, we can recognise that the main and subordinate clause enter into a relation which produces something over and above their separate assertions. What is asserted is a relation of consequence which escapes our grammatical analysis. Casal's exile and his refusal to perform are bound together.

In fact it is relatives which provide a key fulcrum in the functioning of discourses and this precisely because relatives produce some of the crucial subjective effects of the discourse, effects which Harris's examples demonstrate clearly although Harris never explicitly concerns himself with them.[7] In brief, and following the arguments advanced by Michel Pêcheux in *Les Vérités de la Palice* (1975), we can describe the non-restrictive relative in terms of a discourse turning back on itself and constantly providing a series of equivalences for the terms it is using. The non-restrictive relative produces evidence of an alternative which would say the same thing only differently and it is this possibility of an alternative, of a set of alternatives, which constitutes the effect of sense and subjectivity and their necessary certainty. Sense does not arrive with each word but is produced across a set of alternatives within a discourse. It is this possibility which produces the effect that 'I' am in control of my discourses, that I say what I *say* because I can always go back and offer a set of explanatory alternatives: Moses—a prophet—the leader of the Jews out of Egypt, etc.

The restrictive relative, on the other hand, is the site of two discourses intersecting and being homogenised by the action of the relative. If we examine the example that Harris uses we can see that the operation in question is a binding together of the discourses of politics and music around the name of Casals. It is this 'binding' that the traditional analysis of proper names and relatives obscures by considering that the relation between Casals and the relative is one of non-restriction and, therefore, of simple co-ordination. For the elements of the sentence are held together because of the implied consequence between exile and the refusal to perform, a consequence which supports a conditional of the form 'If one is a musician (if one is Casals) then one would exile oneself from Spain and stop performing.' The proof that this relation of implication is contained in the indicative is that if one refuses the conditional then one is inclined to contest the indicative sentence. The text produces a complicity with its reader which provides the mechanism for understanding the movement from *histoire* to *discours* (in Benveniste's terms) that I have already discussed. Around the proper name is produced a general statement which then permits of substitution with 'you' or 'I'. Indeed if we think of the refusal of complicitiy it is obvious what is at stake. 'He doesn't care about Spain' 'He's just trying to make more money' 'He's just an artist.' Another discourse rescues us from an identification we reject.

Harris would object violently to the argument that I have just sketched. For I have assumed that I can specify discourses independently of the analysis. But we touch here at the arguments about the constitution of the corpus. By limiting himself to a single text, Harris cannot proceed very far with his explicit aim of relating the supra-sentential regularities to the cultural situation. It is extremely doubtful that the selection of the single text as a corpus can be given any justification other than there is no obvious alternative which would constitute the corpus independently of considerations of meaning. But to take this position is to ignore the reality of social institutions, however analysed, and to so ignore institutions is to run the risk of re-introducing meaning back into the field of linguistics (under the form of some logicist universal semantics). De Saussure's inauguration of linguistics takes the form of a double separation. On the one hand he separates *langue* from any problem of subjectivity (this subjectivity is not interrogated but simply re-placed in the realm of *parole*). On the other hand he separates *langue* from any other social institution because of the determinate and evident relation between means and ends in all social institutions except *langue* (cf. de Saussure 1972: 110/1974: 76).

The error about institutions is the reverse side of the mistake which constitutes *parole* as the realm of a pure subjectivity in control of language. To presume that means are directly related to ends in institutions and find their base in some 'nature' is a naivety which is no longer tenable sixty years after de Saussure's death. Both Marxist and sociological analyses refuse such transparency to the other institutions. The functioning of an institution is not reducible to its ends and its ends are not so easily specifiable as de Saussure seems to have imagined. One of the most important of 'means' within any institution is language and if we concede that the operations of language cannot be reduced to the institutions' ends, explicit or otherwise, then it is possible to see how one can specify a discourse institutionally while still being unable to answer any of the questions about the specific functioning and effectivity of that discourse. It is this functioning and effectivity which Harris's method of analysis offers the possibility of investigating. Obviously the discursive structure thus analysed will feed back into the original social analysis in certain ways. What the discursive analysis should reveal are the different linguistic methods of identification within a specific discourse. That is to say where it can turn back on itself and propose alternatives (the working of the conscious in retrieving material from the preconscious) and there where constitutive moments of fusion do not allow of investigation without the breaking of that very identity (the unconscious of the discourse).

The arguments of this section are taken directly from, or are simple elaborations of, the work of the French philosopher and linguist Michel Pêcheux (1969, 1975).[8] Pêcheux has argued consistently that linguistics constitutes itself by separating itself from any notion of 'subject' or 'institution' and that the refusal to theorise these notions at the level of language entails a return of the subject which haunts linguistics in the form of a universal semantics. He argues further that the only way to remove semantics as a threat to linguistics is to give an account of the effectivity of discourse which will be concerned to demonstrate how specific discursive processes work on a linguistic base to produce specific discursive effects. Discursive formations can be specified in terms of a social and ideological analysis but this specification will not demonstrate their modes of functioning. These modes of functioning may, in turn, reveal weaknesses in the original specification (Pêcheux 1978). Harris's method provides the first step towards the possibility of analysing the specific discursive processes but without a theory of ideology he cannot specify a corpus. And further, and this constitutes the second major argument against the original method, he is blind to the problem of determining those new sequences can be generated within a discourse and those which cannot.[9]

MICHEL PÊCHEUX AND THE
POLITICS OF THE SIGNIFIER

The argument of the paper so far has been as follows. If one examines Benveniste's distinction between *discours* and *histoire*, one discovers that, despite the appearance of a basis in grammar and particularly in the tenses of the French verb, this distinction rests on an unexamined notion of the subject which transforms a specific set of linguistic practices (largely practices of writing) into a set of eternal relations between subject and language which reproduce the rhetoric/logic distinction traditional to Western thought since the seventeenth century. However, in the course of his investigation Benveniste distinguished two different relations to language—the subject of the enunciation and the subject of the enounced—which are indeed central to an understanding of the functioning of language. Benveniste thought that one could specify language uses in which the subject of the enunciation was not involved (this indeed is the very definition of *histoire*) but a reflection on the psychoanalytic account of the subject contradicted this position. The crucial nexus in the acquisition of language (an acquisition which, on this account, must be understood as constant, as interminable) is the moment at which the child grasps the systematic substitutability of pronouns. This moment introduces, to use Lacan's terminology, the big Other, an introduction understood *not* as the encounter with the parents on the level of demand but as the encounter with the parent as the site of language and desire which outruns any particular statement of demand. This encounter turns on the parents' speech with each other about the child. It is this experience of articulation which produces the divided subject of psychoanalysis, for on the one hand the speaker is caught up in the play of signifiers, of the differential oppositions which produce meaning independently of the activity of the individual, and, on the other, the child takes its place as the 'I' of experience and language, the unified subject of classical philosophy and modern linguistics. (The field and modalities of this division can be understood as congruent with the division which locates the child both in the movement along the play of the parents' desire, a multiplicity of positions, and in its appropriate place, its signified sexuality.)

Before proceeding further, it might be useful to consider, if only to reject, an argument to the effect that this account is merely another version of the genesis of the subject and, like all such accounts, it presupposes what it proves, having need of a subject already in place who then recognises him/her self as subject. For, the argument continues, in order to ensure recognition there must already be a subject ready to recognise its own essence but, if this is so, it implies that this essence must be autonomous of its appearance in language. A feature of man (viz. the unconscious) is made the determining principle of language. The reply to this is that the recognition in question is not the recognition of an essence but rather the recognition of the possibility of another signifier. As such it is not a question of defining man with an unconscious and then discussing language but rather a question of defining language in such a way that there is unconsciousness for he or she who wishes to speak.

It is the recognition of the division of the subject in language that enables one to pass beyond the rhetoric/logic distinction to discover the speaker at play in every function of language. Harris's article offers a technique for attempting to grasp in more detail the relation between enunciation and enounced but if it has the immense merit of refusing the classical conception of the subject, it fails completely to render a more adequate account of the subject. This weakness affects Harris's analysis at the level of the constitution of the corpus where deprived of any theory of ideology or institutions, a banal empiricism ensures no real investigation of the 'correlation between language and social situation'. Pêcheux's work over the last ten years marks the most serious attempt to develop Harris's techniques in line with a theory of discourse which attempts to take account not only of the divided subject of psychoanalysis but also of language's place within the class struggle, where language is not only the instrument of communication, so beloved of linguistic theorists, but also the instrument of non-communication, so necessary to the divisions of modern capital. Pêcheux's work is itself marked, however, by a resurgence of the rhetoric/logic model, a resurgence which corresponds to an unresolved political difficulty with Lacanian theory. In this final section I want to sketch the arguments that Pêcheux develops in *Les Vérités de la Palice* and to indicate their weaknesses.[10]

Pêcheux's starting-point is the feebleness of those Marxist positions which, garnishing themselves with one or two comments from *The German Ideology*, accept unreservedly the whole structure of communications theory complete with autonomous senders and receivers using codes to convey messages. Pêcheux, on the other hand, stresses that language functions both as communication and non-communication, that when one moves from morphology and syntax to meaning, one must leave behind the notion of *langue*, to which each speaker bears a similar relation, and consider discursive formations, specific areas of communicability that set in place both sender and receiver and which determine the appropriateness of messages. Centrally Pêcheux is concerned to establish the moments at which a scientific theory of the social formation, namely Marxism, is intimately concerned with the discursive functioning of language and he proceeds about this task by a long discussion of the analyses of relative clauses since the time of Port-Royal, a discussion that ends, as we have seen above, with a demonstration that the distinctions between relative clauses can only be understood in terms of discursive rather than grammatical function.

Port-Royal's analysis of sentences start from the premise that one can understand the functioning of language, its grammar, in terms of the operations of the mind, operations which essentially consist of but one: predication. This position subordinates the order of grammar and rhetoric to the order of thought (a refurbished Aristotelian logic) and enables Arnauld and Lancelot to make a precise distinction between relatives in terms of the determination of the subject of the main clause. If the subject is determined by the relative then the relative simply functions as an aid in the identification of the subject and as such it can be understood as part of a rhetoric which, for Port-Royal, is now wholly defined in terms of a pedagogy. If, on the other hand, the subject can be identified independently (if it is a proper name for example) then the relative clause represents an autonomous act of judgement which must be understood in terms of the general logic of judgement.

Within Port-Royal's terms there is no problem of the subject of the enunciation. The world and its representation exist independently of the enunciation of language and thus, for example, pronouns can be explained on the grounds of economy and politeness (it would be rude to endlessly repeat one's own name— the pronoun 'I' thus saves one social embarrassment). But by the time we reach Leibniz and the British empiricists in the next century the relation between world and representation becomes less certain and the problem of the subject's place as the movement between the two becomes dominant. Leibniz solves this problem by creating an infinity of possible worlds in which the seeming alternatives offered by language find resolution if one occupies the position of God.

Significantly Leibniz's position leads him to analyse all relative clauses attached to names as restrictive. The effect of this is to multiply the population considerably as there are as many persons as there are names followed by relative clauses. The John Smith in 'John Smith who left his house this morning . . .' becomes different from the John Smith in 'John Smith who ate lunch in McDonald's at one o'clock . . . ' To understand this multiplicity of possible worlds in which representation is once again transparent we would have to be God. If Leibniz solves the problem by expanding reality to occupy the space allocated to it by language, the British empiricists undertake to reduce reality to the perspective of the subject. It is the subject who becomes the source of a language charged with no more than representing his needs or sense impressions. Thus instead of finding ourselves in a world of Leibnizian necessity, if only we were God, we occupy a world in which everything is merely a useful fiction or construction. What we can see at work in the consideration of Leibniz and the British empiricists is a movement from the problem of necessary and contingent towards the problem of subjective and objective, a problem which haunts philosophies of language up to the present day. What Pêcheux is concerned to demonstrate across a series of historical readings is that the traditional philosophical questions about language are produced within epistemological problematics and that both the rationalist and empiricist versions of language take their starting-point in a refusal to understanding the historical development of science as a set of theoretical struggles which have definite conditions of existence. Pêcheux's thesis is that the link between philosophy of language and epistemology is crucial and that as long as one does not have an adequate account of the development of science one will be stuck with a philosophy of language which will endlessly reproduce the idealist categories of subject and object instead of addressing itself to the problem of discourse and discursive formations. For Pêcheux this constitutive misunderstanding of science can essentially be resumed under two headings: that of metaphysical realism or logical empiricism:

> *empiricist theories of knowledge, just as much as realist theories, seem to have a stake in forgetting the existence of historically constituted scientific disciplines to the profit of a universal theory of ideas, whether this takes the realist form of an a priori and universal network of notions or the empiricist form of an administrative procedure applicable to the universe considered as*

a collection of facts, objects, events or acts. (Pêcheux 1975: 68, author's emphasis)

For Pêcheux the exemplary modern discussion of the problem of language in relation to science is Frege's and, in particular, the criticisms that Frege addressed to Husserl over the status of arithmetic. For Husserl the subject is the source and unifying principle of representations whereas for Frege the subject is the bearer of representations which it neither creates nor unifies. But if Frege succeeds in displacing the subject in his discussion of science, he fails, on the other hand, to understand the necessity of theorising the production of the subject in language. In the place of such a theory we find the dream of the production of a language from which all 'imperfections' have been removed, a dream to which one can have no objection in so far as it embodies a wish to liberate mathematics from the effects of language but which does, however, fall back into traditional concerns, if it is interpreted as the wish to liberate language from its own imperfections.[11] Once again the functioning of the relative provides a focal point for philosophical debate. Frege was worried by sentences like 'He who discovered the elliptical order of the planets died in poverty.' The problem for Frege is that one cannot logically disentangle the main and subordinate clauses because the main clause depends for its truth or falsity on the fact that the subordinate clause has a reference. For Frege the functioning of language produces an illusion: a pre-supposed statement of existence. What, for Frege, is a regrettable imperfection of the language is, for Pêcheux, the evidence of the functioning of language as discourse. Indeed such sentences provide the quintessential example whereby discourse produces within one domain of thought another domain of thought *as if* this other domain had already been introduced. In discourse there is no beginning for the subject who always already finds itself and its discourses in place. It is this particular functioning of the relative that Pêcheux uses as a justification for the thesis advanced by Althusser in his essay on Ideological State Apparatuses (1971) that the subject is always already interpellated in ideology. For Pêcheux it is the fact that the complex whole of the discursive formations, which he terms the *interdiscourse*, constantly provides already available positions, which he terms the *preconstructed*, within any specific discursive formation that provides the material basis for Althusser's theory of interpellation. It follows from this that the interdiscourse is identified with the Subject (with a big S) which Althusser had used in a reformulation (whose problems we shall shortly investigate) of Lacan's big Other. Pêcheux makes clear this equation between Subject and Other, identified materially with the interdiscourse, and attempts to distinguish this effect of the introduction of the preconstructed from another discursive function of the relative, which he terms the *support effect*, in which the relative signals a discourse turning back on itself (as in the example of Moses) rather than the introduction of the interdiscourse. This discursive function, as we saw above, is identified with the preconscious. So, on the one hand, we can identify the support effect, the doubling back, as the construction of the effects of sense and certainty; construction along and across the possible paraphrases that constitute a discourse. It is in these alternatives (often purely grammatical) that one can locate the effect of sense and an imaginarily full subjectivity—constituted by the very possibility of doubling back and restating. In the operations of the preconstructed, on the other hand, such paraphrase is not possible because so to do would be to step outside the discourse and locate its unconscious constitution.

If this account might seem to provide an account of the division of the subject in language and relate it to the problems of ideological analysis and struggle, it must be recognised that the division here proposed has little to do with Lacan's concept of the subject but rather involves the construction of an ego completely dominated by a super ego. An investigation of the problems of the Althusser-Pêcheux conception will, however, enable us to pose the political problem of Lacan's concept of the signifier and the divided subject which there finds its constitution. At a simple level one could accuse Pêcheux of failing to grasp the force of the Freudian unconscious, a failure which has its effects in the description of both discursive functions. If we consider the support effect, where paraphrastic relations produce both subject and sense, we can note that even if the subject is produced as effect rather than invoked as cause, it is a subject in full control of language. But the situation of paraphrase in which Pêcheux locates both subject and sense bears witness in itself to the functioning of a desire which is absent from Pêcheux's formulations. For the request for a remark to be paraphrased is always more than a demand for clarification which allows the production of inter-subjective sense, it always entails the desire for knowledge of the other which disrupts the sense by drawing attention to the surplus of signifiers. Even in the realm of the support effect, a parapraxis can bear witness to the divided nature of the subject. Pêcheux's production of the subject in relation to sense without any possibility that the truth of language can explode on to the scene of subjectivity finds its complement in an account of the production of the unconscious which, following Althusser, provides it with all the imaginary power of an omnipotent super ego. If we recall the central scenario of Althusser's essay, it describes the action of a policeman who calls out 'Hey You!', a shout to which our inevitable response is an index of the fact that we are always already there in the position of 'you', that we are always already interpellated in ideology. If we compare this scenario to that sketched by Irigaray—the child listening to the parents talk about it—we can notice that Irigaray's account emphasises that the child is only present as signifier in the parents' speech in so far as it is excluded from that very speech (conscious and unconscious are produced in the same turn of phrase). Althusser's account, from which nothing is excluded, leaves nothing unconscious: the subject is reduced by the terrorised presence of the ego to an imaginary super ego. (Houdebine makes this point in telling fashion when he insists that the Althusserian drama should be told from the point of view of the policeman). With this difference: as the interpellated subject turns the policeman sees that he has hailed the wrong person and thus experiences, even from the position of authority, the dominance of the signifier (Houdebine 1976: 91).[12]

To content oneself, like Houdebine with a superior condemnation of Althusser's ignorance of Lacan—'he hasn't read the *Ecrits* properly'—misses the importance of a mistake which requires, exactly, analysis. Althusser's re-articulation of Lacan is political and it comprises both a positive and negative aspect, aspects which are necessarily linked. Negatively, the identification of the Other and the Subject represses the Other as the heterogenous site of language and desire. Instead of Lacan's insistence on the impossibility of a consciousness transparent to itself, Althusser produces an omnipotent subject who is master of both language and desire. The consequence of this mastery is that there is no *theoretical* perspective for ideological struggle in the face of dominant ideologies for there is nothing which escapes or is left over from the original production of the subject by the Subject (this political pessimism coincides with the functionalism of the concept of the Ideological State Apparatus). If Althusser had simply transported Lacan's concept of the Other into the analysis of the social formation then it would have been possible for him to give an account of the construction of subversive ideologies. A Marxist reading of the division of the subject in the place of the Other would theorise the individual's assumption of the place produced for him or her by the complex of discursive formations and would insist that these places would be constantly threatened and undermined by their constitutive instability in the field of language and desire. Such a reading of Lacan's Other would immediately, and in its very account of dominant ideologies, offer a material basis for the construction of subversive ideologies. But, and here we come to the positive aspect of Althusser's transposition, such a Marxist reformulation of Lacan, deprived of its articulation within the drama of the Oedipus, would leave the formation of subversive ideologies and discourses to the chance play of the signifier. Althusser's positioning of the drama of the subject in the policeman's call for identity can be read as an effort to call in question the Lacanian concept of the signifier in so far as Lacan deduces the divided subject from the very fact of language itself and where the actual sites of language use (the family, the school, the workplace) are merely unimportant variations with no effectivity inscribed in the theory (this difficulty appears within Lacanian theory itself in the status to be accorded to the terms Father and Mother in relation to biological and social identities). To shift attention to the site of enunciation is to insist that it is not simply the formation of the unconscious that must be theorised but the formation of specific unconsciousnesses, a formation which cannot be divided into social and individual components but which dramatises in each individual case that which is generally unconscious.

If we now return to Pêcheux's division of discursive functions into the pre-constructed and the support-effect, we can indicate how this division, rectified in the light of our criticisms of the Althusser-Pêcheux conception of the unconscious, may well provide one of the starting-points for an investigation of the articulation of the general and specific in the unconscious. It should be noted that Pêcheux's division, as he himself formulates it, resurrects a logic/rhetoric distinction with the support effect understood as the simple substitution of grammatical equivalents (the logical) opposed to the preconstructed which introduces the interferences of the ideological (rhetoric). Thus even from a purely linguistic view there is every reason to be suspicious of the division as it stands. The problem with

Pêcheux's interdiscourse is that, like Althusser's policeman, it re-introduces the philosophical subject, coherent and homogenous, into a Lacanian schema which has as its explicit aim the subversion of that subject. The cost of the re-introduction is clear: the disappearance of the body and desire from the schema. The failure to grasp the radical heterogeneity of the Lacanian Other means that there is nothing left over in that place to function as the object of desire. A first step in the rectification of Pêcheux's position would necessitate a greater emphasis on the other practices imbricated with the interdiscourse and, in particular, the positioning and representation of the body. It is through an emphasis on the body and the impossibility of its exhaustion in its representations that one can understand the material basis with which the unconscious of a discursive formation disrupts the smooth functioning of the domi-nant ideologies and that this disruption is not simply the chance movement of the signifier but the specific positioning of the body in the economic, political and ideological practices.[13] The analysis of the operations of the preconstructed will thus involve a far more concrete attention to specific ideological and political struggles in which the discursive formations are articulated. If the emphasis in the analysis on the preconstructed is on its particular configuration within the social formation, the concept of the support effect must be reworked to take account of those moments where the unrolling of grammatical equivalences is interrupted by the irruption of a desire which can only be read in the specific form which resists any relation of paraphrase.[14]

NOTES

1. The first version of this paper was given in November 1976 at the seminar on Social Relations and Discourse organised by Paul Q. Hirst and Sami Zubaida at Birkbeck College, London. I am grateful to those who participated in the discussion there and to Michel Pêcheux for the conversations we had when I was writing the final draft.

2. The standard English translation of Benveniste's term *histoire* is *narrative*. Such a translation loses the force of the French term which combines the sense of history and story. I have therefore retained the French *histoire* and *discours* in my discussion of Benveniste.

3. Accounts of the relations between compound and simple tenses have run into difficulties because they have failed to analyse the two functions of the compound tenses and the way that these distinct functions intersect with the division between *histoire* and *discours*. On the one hand the compound tenses are all

'perfects', that is to say that they all denote an action as 'accomplished' with regard to the 'actual' situation which results from this accomplishment. As perfects, the compound tenses can occur outside any relations of subordination. But the compound tenses serve a second function which is to indicate anteriority and this anteriority is posed in relation to the corresponding simple form of the verb. This means that in their anterior function the compound tenses can only occur in a subordinate clause for which the main clause uses the corresponding simple form. But the compound tenses find themselves articulated within a double system of relations. While as the tenses denoting 'accomplishment' they find themselves in opposition to the other compound tenses, in expressing 'anteriority' they are simply defined in relation to their corresponding simple form. With this distinction in mind we can understand how the replacement of the aorist by the perfect in speech created certain strains within the tense system. The point of pressure between the aorist and the perfect occurred in the rival first person forms, e.g. *je fis* and *j'ai fait*.

In so far as the realm of *histoire* excludes person then *je fis* is inadmissible in that realm but in so far as it is the aorist it is excluded from the realm of *discours*. There is a slide from the accomplished of the present—*j'ai fait*—to a simple past. But if *discours* thereby gains a temporal distinction it loses a functional distinction.

In itself, *j'ai fait* is a perfect that furnishes either the form of the perfective or the form of anteriority to the present *je fais*. But when *j'ai fait*, the compound form, becomes the 'aorist of discourse', it takes on the function of the simple form, with the result that *j'ai fait* is sometimes perfect, a compound tense, and sometimes aorist, a simple tense. The system has remedied this difficulty by recreating the missing form. Alongside the simple tense *je fais* is the compound tense *j'ai fait* for the notion of the perfective. Now, since *j'ai fait* slips into the rank of a simple tense, there is a need for a new compound tense that in its turn will express the perfective, this will be the secondary compound *j'ai eu fait*. Functionally *j'ai eu fait* is the new perfect of a *j'ai fait* which has become the aorist. Such is the point of departure for the secondary compound tenses. (Benveniste 1971: 214–15)

4. The particular process by which the authority of the written is linked specifically to the aorist is peculiar to France and would have to find further explanation in terms of the ideological and political investment in language during the seventeenth century. In England there is no such evident index of the written although the contemporary growth of the periphrastic tenses and the rise of the novel suggest more complicated links between the grammar of the language and practices of writing.

5. The writing of history is as much a specific practice as that of the novel. The assumption that the past has its own order independently of its present enunciation finds itself challenged in the famous thesis of Walter Benjamin: 'To articulate the past historically does not mean to recognize it "the way it really was" (Ranke). It means to seize hold of a memory as it flashes up at a moment of danger. Historical materialism wishes to retain that image of the past which unexpectedly appears to man singled out by history at a moment of danger' (1973: 257). Such a conception of history will have an evident effect on the distribution of tenses within a particular text.

6. This freedom will often be theorised in terms of its limitations in a variety of sociological perspectives but it is never radically questioned in the posing of

subjectivity as an effect of discursivity. Gadet and Pêcheux (1977) offer a comprehensive over-view of the contemporary situation in linguistics.

7. This political thrust of discourse analysis is even more evident (although still not explicit) in the detailed analysis of an article from *Commentary* that Harris published in the same year (1952b: 474–94).

8. For the sake of clarity I have not emphasised the changes in Pêcheux's position. In fact there is a considerable difference between the *Analyse automatique du discours* (1969) and the two texts of 1975: *les Verités de la Palice* and 'Mises au point et perspectives de l'analyse automatique du discours' (a text written with the linguist Catherine Fuchs). In particular this involves a shift from the analysis of discourses defined through a sociology of institutions to the analysis of discursive formations defined through the contemporary political and ideological struggles (cf. Pêcheux 1978).

9. Pêcheux's formal method superposes sub-sequences with similar contexts rather than setting up the chain of equivalences. One has then to consider the relation within those sub-sequences which have been grouped together (Haroche, Henry, Pêcheux 1971: 104–105).

10. These criticisms owe much to Jean-Louis Houdebine's review of Pêcheux in *Tel Quel* (1976) and to Pêcheux's own self-criticism which is to appear as an appendix to the English version of *Les Vérités de la Palice* (1981).

11. 'It is not contestable that logic as the theory of artificial languages in effect developed by taking "natural" language as its original material but one must immediately add that this work always and exclusively aimed to free *mathematics* from the effects of "natural" language (in the way that logic has progressively come to be a part of the domain of mathematics), and not in any way to free *generally* "natural" language itself from its illusions. If not logic would contain within itself all the sciences to turn a remark of Frege, concerning psychology, against himself,' (Pêcheux 1975: 86–7)

12. What Houdebine does not, however, add is that the policeman who has made the mistake is *all the more likely* to give his interpellation a retrospective justification. But to offer this analysis would risk contradicting the major (and indeed only) political thesis of his article, namely that the only agent of repression in France is the French Communist Party.

13. It is through a greater attention to the positioning and representation of the body that Pêcheux would be able to give more political weight to what is politically the most interesting, if theoretically the weakest, section of the book: the discussion of identification. Pêcheux distinguishes three forms of relation to a discursive formation. First, identification (the 'good subject') who assumes without problem, the positions offered; then, in direct opposition, counter-identification (the 'bad subject') who identifies him or herself through the refusal of a certain discourse, a refusal which finds itself marked by a variety of grammatical and discursive functions, notably an increased presence of 'shifters': '*Your* social sciences', 'What *you* call liberty', and the deliberate negation in the main clause of an existence that is asserted in the preconstructed of the subordinate clause: 'He who died on the cross to redeem the world never existed.' This position, which could be politically qualified as that of revolt, is essentially defensive but can open onto a third possibility: *disidentification*. It is this concept which is the most vital and least developed part of Pêcheux's work. In it he attempts to describe those practices which displace the agent from that position of subjective centrality which is the

result of both identification and counter-identification. These practices are defined as those of science and proletarian politics. Pêcheux's difficulty is that he, quite rightly, finds it impossible to accept a classic science/ideology or proletarian politics/bourgeois politics distinction in which universal and formal features define the divisions. On the other hand Pêcheux remains committed to a *general* description of ideology and bourgeois politics with the result that ideology and bourgeois politics become the eternal hell to which we are subjected and their alternatives are only momentary displacements into a better world. Ideological subjection thus becomes a feature in language while science and proletarian politics are transformed into ephemeral agents of grace which fleetingly rescue us from the sin of the subject position into which we inevitably relapse. The strengths and weaknesses of Pêcheux's position resemble Althusser's. The weakness is the identification of subject and ego, a formulation of the grounds of political and ideological struggle such that defeat is inevitable, the strength is the posing of the problems of identification as politically and ideologically crucial. To rectify the schema offered by Pêcheux it is necessary to stress the incoherence of the interdiscourse, an incoherence grounded in the contradictory positioning and representations of the body. It is in terms of these contradictions that one can provide a material base for an account of the elaboration of specific sciences (there is no need of a general theory of science, simply the specification of the particular developments, which displace and break with the experiential-perceptual centrality of the body). Politically the effect of the emphasis on the body is to stress the importance of a politics of sexuality as the crucial moment in the subversion of the policeman's demand for identification.

14. What is in question here is perhaps the most important of the disidentificatory practices of language which Pêcheux fails to mention: those practices of writing which are generally named as 'literature'. If much literature is devoted to a re-articulation of crucial social identifications, there are certain practices of writing which break definitively with the very possibility of identification. 'Literature' may be limited to certain élites in our class society but its disidentificatory practices on language find wider social currency in certain forms of jokes.

Bibliography

All works except those with a standard system of reference, e.g. Aristotle, are given with a date and place of publication. If a work has been translated into English then the date of the translation is indicated at the end of the entry and a further entry can be found under the new date, i.e. Benveniste, Emile (1966), *Problèmes de linguistique générale*, tr. Benveniste (1971).

Althusser, Louis (1970), *Reading Capital* (London).

—— (1971), 'Ideology and Ideological State Apparatuses: Notes towards an Investigation' in *Lenin and Philosophy and Other Essays* (London) pp. 121–73.

Anscombe, G. E. M. and P. T. Geach (1967), *Three Philosophers* (Oxford).

Aristotle, *Posterior Analytics*.

Arnauld, A. and Lancelot, C. (1969), *Grammaire générale et raisonée* (Paris).

Aubenque, Pierre (1972), *Le Problème de l'être chez Aristote* (Paris).

Barthes, Roland (1967), *Elements of Semiology* (London).

—— (1970), 'L'Ancienne Rhétorique: Aide-Memoire', *Communications*, no. 16: 172–223.

Benveniste, Emile (1966), *Problèmes de linguistique générale* (Paris), tr. Benveniste (1971).

—— (1971), *Problems in General Linguistics* (Miami).

Besançon, Pierre (1971), *Histoire et expérience du moi* (Paris).

Bourdieu, Pierre (1972), *Esquisse d'une théorie de la pratique* (Geneva), tr. Bourdieu (1977).

—— (1977), *Outline of a Theory of Practice* (Cambridge).

Brentano, Franz (1944), *Psychologie du point de vue empirique* (Paris), tr. Brentano (1973).

—— (1973), *Psychology from an Empirical Standpoint* (London).

Collomb, H., (1965), 'Les bouffées délirantes en psychiatrie africaine', *Psychopathologie Africaine*, 1, 167–239.

Curtius, Ernst (1953), *European Literature and the Latin Middle Ages* (London).

Cutler, Antony, Barry Hindess, Paul Q. Hirst and Athar Hussain

(1978), *Marx's 'Capital' and Capitalism Today*, 2 vols. (London).

Derrida, Jacques (1967), *L'Ecriture et la différence* (Paris).

Dubois, J., L. Irigaray and P. Macie (1965), 'Transformations négatives et organisation des classes lexicales', *Cahiers de lexicologie*, VII.

Erikson, Eric (1968), *Identity: Youth and Crisis* (New York).

Felman, Shoshana (1974), 'La méprise et sa chance', *L'Arc*, LVIII, 40–9.

Ferenczi, Sandor (1933–4), *Thalassa: towards a Theory of Genitality*, in *Psycho-analytic Quarterly*, II, 361–403, III, 1–29, 200–22.

—— (1955), *Final Contribution to the Problems and Methods of Psycho-analysis* (London).

Findlay, J. N. (1963), *Meinong's Theory of Objects and Values* (Oxford).

Forrester, John (1980), *Language and the Origins of Psychoanalysis* (London).

Freud, Anna (1936), *Das Ich und die Abwehrmechanismen* (Vienna), revised tr. Anna Freud (1968).

—— (1968), *The Ego and the Mechanisms of Defence* (London).

Freud, Sigmund (1940–68), *Gesammelte Werke*, 18 vols. (vols. I–XVII, London; vol. XVIII, Frankfurt am Main, 1968).

—— (1924–50), *Collected Papers*, 5 vols. (London, 1924–50).

—— (1953–74), *The Standard Edition of the Complete Psychological Works of Sigmund Freud*, 24 vols. (London).

—— (1974), *The Freud/Jung Letters* (London).

Fuchs, Catherine and Michel Pêcheux (1975), 'Mises au point et perspectives de l'analyse automatique du discours', *Langages*, XXXVII, 7–81.

Gadet, Françoise and Michel Pêcheux (1977), 'Y a-t-il une voie pour la linguistique hors du logicisme et du sociologisme?', *Equivalences*, nos. 2–3: 133–46.

Gilson, Lucien (1955), *La Psychologie descriptive selon Franz Brentano* (Paris).

Green, André (1967), 'La diachronie dans le freudisme', *Critique*, no. 238: 359–85.

Grice, H. P. (1969), 'Utterer's Meaning and Intentions', *Philosophical Review*, LXXVIII, 147–77.

Grossman, Reinhardt (1974), *Meinong* (London).

Haroche, Claudine, Paul Henry and Michel Pêcheux (1971), 'La semantique et la coupure saussurienne: langue, langage, discours', *Langages*, XXIV, 93–106.

Harris, Zellig (1951), *Structural Linguistics* (Chicago).

——(1952a), 'Discourse Analysis', *Language*, no. 28: 1–30.

——(1952b), 'Discourse Analysis: A Sample Text', *Language*, no. 28: 474–94.

Heath, Stephen (1978), 'Difference', *Screen* XIX, no. 3: 50–112.

Hegel, G. W. F. (1977), *The Phenomenology of Spirit* (London).

Heidegger, Martin (1949), *Uber den Humanismus* (Frankfurt), tr. in Heidegger (1978).

—— (1957), *Identität und Differenz* (Pfullingen), tr. Heidegger (1969a).

—— (1962), *Being and Time* (New York).

—— (1967), *Sein und Zeit* (Tübingen), tr. Heidegger (1962).

—— (1969a), *Identity and Difference* (New York).

—— (1969b), *The Essence of Reasons.* A bilingual edition, incorporating the German text of *Vom Wesen des Grunds* (Evanston).

—— (1975), *Die Grundprobleme der Phänomenologie*, in *Gesamtausgabe*, XXIV (Frankfurt).

—— (1978), *Martin Heidegger: Basic Writings* (London).

Henry, Paul (1977), *Le Mauvais Outil* (Paris).

Houdebine, Jean-Louis (1976), 'Les Vérités de la Palice ou les erreurs de la police? (D'une question obstinément forclose)', *Tel Quel*, no. 67: 87–97.

Huddleston, Rodney (1976), *Introduction to English Transformational Syntax* (London).

Hume, David, *Treatise of Human Nature*.

Irigaray, Luce (1966) 'Communications linguistique et spéculaire', *Cahiers pour l'Analyse*, no. 3: 39–55.

Jakobson, Roman (1963), *Essais de linguistique générale* (Paris).

—— (1971a), 'Quest for the Essence of Language', in *Selected Writings* vol. XI (The Hague) pp. 345–360.

—— (1971b), 'Two Aspects of Language and Two Types of Aphasic Disturbances', in Roman Jakobson and Morris Halle, *Fundamentals of Language*, 2nd edn (The Hague) pp. 69–96.

Jones, Ernest (1918), 'The Theory of Symbolism', in *Psycho-analysis*, 2nd edn (London).

—— (1935), *Psycho-analysis*, 3rd edn (London).

Kant, Immanuel (1970), *Kant's Political Writings*, ed. H. Reiss (Cambridge).

Klein, Melanie (1964), 'The Importance of Symbol Formation in the Development of the Ego', in *Contributions to Psychoanalysis, 1921–1945* (New York) pp. 236–250.

Kristeva, Julia (1974), *La Révolution du langage poétique* (Paris).
—— (1975a), *La Traversée des signes* (Paris).
—— (1975b), *Des Chinoises* (Paris), tr. Kristeva (1977b).
—— (1977a), *Polylogue* (Paris).
—— (1977b), *On Chinese Women* (London).
Lacan, Jacques (1938), 'La Famille', in *Encylopédie Française*, ed A. de Monzie, vol. VIII.
—— (1956), 'Le séminaire sur *La Lettre volée*', *La Psychanalyse*, II, 1–14.
—— (1956–7), 'La relation d'objet et les structures freudiennes', Compte-rendu du séminaire, *Bulletin de Psychologie*, no. 10.
—— (1959–60), 'Le désir et son interprétation', Compte-rendu du séminaire, *Bulletin de Psychologie*, no. 13.
—— (1966a), *Ecrits* (Paris).
—— (1966b), 'Réponses à des étudiants en philosophie sur l'objet de la psychanalyse', *Cahiers pour l'Analyse*, no. 3: 5–13.
—— (1973), *Le Séminaire. Livre* XI. *Les quatre concepts fondamentaux de la psychanalyse* (Paris).
—— (1975a), *Le Séminaire. Livre* I. *Les écrits techniques de Freud* (Paris).
—— (1975b), *Le Séminaire. Livre* XX. *Encore* (Paris).
—— (1978), *Le Séminaire. Livre* II. *Le moi dans la théorie de Freud et dans la technique de la psychanalyse* (Paris).
Laplanche, J. and S. Leclaire (1961), 'L'Inconscient: une étude psychanalytique', *Les Temps Modernes*, no. 183: 81–129, tr. Laplanche and Leclaire (1972).
—— (1972), 'The Unconscious: A Psychoanalytic Study', *Yale French Studies*, no. 48: 118–75.
—— and J.-B. Pontalis (1968), 'Fantasy and the Origins of Sexuality', *International Journal of Psycho-analysis*, XLIX, 1–26.
—— (1973), *The Language of Psychoanalysis* (London).
Leach, Edmund (1961), *Rethinking Anthropology* (London).
Leclaire, S. (1957), 'A propos de l'épisode psychotique que présenta l'homme-aux-loups', *La Psychanalyse*, IV, 88–111.
—— (1958), 'A la recherche des principes d'une psychothérapie des psychoses', *Evolution Psychiatrique*.
—— (1966), 'Compter avec la psychanalyse', *Cahiers pour l'Analyse*, no. 1: 55–70.
—— (1968), *Psychanalyser* (Paris).
Leibniz, G. W. von *Nouveaux Essais sur l'entendement humain*.
Lemaire, Anika (1970), *Jacques Lacan* (Brussels), tr. Lemaire (1977).

—— (1977), *Jacques Lacan* (London).

Lévi-Strauss, Claude (1950), 'Introduction à l'œuvre de Marcel Mauss', in Marcel Mauss, *Sociologie et anthropologie* (Paris) pp. ix–lii.

—— (1969), *Totemism* (London).

—— (1970), 'A Confrontation', *New Left Review*, no. 62.

—— (1972), *Structural Anthropology* (London).

Locke, John, *Essay on Human Understanding.*

Lyons, John, (1968), *Introduction to Theoretical Linguistics* (Cambridge).

MacCabe, Colin (1974), 'Realism and the Cinema: Notes on Some Brechtian Theses', *Screen* xv, no. 2: 7–27.

—— (1979), *James Joyce and the Revolution of the Word* (London).

Major, R. (1977), *Rêver l'Autre* (Paris).

Mally, E. (1912), *Gegenstands theoretische Grundlagen der Logik und Logistik* (Leipzig).

Mannoni, Maud (1970), *The Child, Its 'Illness' and the Others* (London).

—— (1979), *La Théorie comme fiction* (Paris).

Martinet, André (1970), *Eléments de linguistique générale* (Paris).

Mead, George Herbert (1934), *Mind, Self and Society* (Chicago).

Meinong, A. (1899), *Uber Gegenstande höherer Ordnung* (Leipzig).

Merleau-Ponty, Maurice (1945) *Phénoménologie de la perception* (Paris).

Metz, Christian (1975a), 'Le Signifiant imaginaire', *Communications*, no. 23, tr. Metz (1975b).

—— (1975b), 'The Imaginary Signifier', *Screen*, xvi, no. 2.

Miller, Jacques-Alain (1966), 'Avertissement', *Cahiers pour l'Analyse*, no. 1: 4.

Milner, Jean-Claude (1978), *L'Amour de la langue* (Paris).

Moreau, J. (1958), *La Conscience de l'être* (Paris).

Ortigues, E. and M.-C. (1973), *Oedipe Africaine* (Paris).

Pêcheux, Michel (1969), *Analyse automatique du discours* (Paris).

—— (1975), *Les Vérités de la Palice* (Paris), tr. Pêcheux (1981).

—— (1978),'Are the Masses an Animate Object' in David Sankoff (ed.), *Linguistic Variation* (New York).

—— (1981), *Stating the Obvious: Language, Semantics and Ideology* (London).

Plato (1975), *Philebus* (Oxford).

Pontalis, J.-B. (1965), *Après Freud* (Paris).

Rank, Otto (1959), *The Myth of the Birth of the Hero and Other Writings* (New York).

Ricoeur, P. (1970), *Freud and Philosophy* (London).

Rifflet-Lemaire *see* Lemaire.

Russell, Bertrand (1937), *Principles of Mathematics* (London).

Safouan, Moustapha (1968), 'De la structure en psychanalyse', in François Wahl (ed.), *Qu'est-ce que le structuralisme?* (Paris) pp. 239–98.

—— (1974), *Etudes sur l'Oedipe* (Paris).

—— (1979), *L'Echec du principe du plaisir* (Paris), tr. Safouan (1980).

—— (1981), *Pleasure and Being: Hedonism—a Psychoanalytic View* (London).

Sartre, Jean-Paul (1943), *L'Etre et le néant* (Paris), tr. Sartre (1966).

—— (1966), *Being and Nothingness* (New York).

Saussure, Ferdinand de (1971), *Les Mots sous les mots; les anagrammes de F. de Saussure*, ed. J. Starobinski (Paris).

—— (1972), *Cours de linguistique générale* (Paris), tr. Saussure (1974).

—— (1974), *Course in General Linguistics* (London).

Tausk, V. (1933), 'On the Origin of the Influencing Machine in Schizophrenia', *Psychoanalytical Quarterly*, II, 519–56.

This, B. and P. Thèves (1975), '*Die Verneinung*, S. Freud (1925–1975), Nouvelle traduction, étude comparée de quelques traductions et commentaires sur la traduction en générale', *Le Coq-Heron*, no. 52 (Bulletin d'un groupe d'étude du Centre Etienne Marcel).

Timpanaro, S. (1976), *The Freudian Slip* (London).

Tort, M. (1974), 'The Freudian Concept of Representative (*Repräsentanz*)', *Economy and Society*, no. 3: 18–40.

Twardowski, K. (1894), *Zur Lehre vom Inhalt und Gegenstand der Vorstellungen* (Vienna).

Wittgenstein, Ludwig, *Philosophical Investigations*.

Zempleni, A. (1968), *L'Interprétation du désordre mental et la thérapie traditionelle chez les Wolof et les Lébou*, thèse du 3ᵉ cycle, Université de Paris–X.

Index

NOTE: Because there are references to Freud and to Lacan on virtually every page of the present book, their names have not been included in the index.